First World War
and Army of Occupation
War Diary
France, Belgium and Germany

51 DIVISION
Divisional Troops
Royal Army Medical Corps
2/1 Highland Field Ambulance
2 May 1915 - 10 April 1919

WO95/2858/2

The Naval & Military Press Ltd
www.nmarchive.com
Published in association with The National Archives

Published by

The Naval & Military Press Ltd

Unit 10 Ridgewood Industrial Park,

Uckfield, East Sussex,

TN22 5QE England

Tel: +44 (0) 1825 749494

www.naval-military-press.com

www.nmarchive.com

This diary has been reprinted in facsimile from the original. Any imperfections are inevitably reproduced and the quality may fall short of modern type and cartographic standards.

© **Crown Copyright**
Images reproduced by permission of The National Archives, London, England, 2015.

Contents

Document type	Place/Title	Date From	Date To
Heading	WO95/2858 51 Div 2/1 Highland F.A. May 15-Apr 19		
Heading	51st Division 2-1st Highland Fld Ambulance May 1915-1919 Apl		
Heading	51st Division 2/1 Highland Field Ambulance Vol I June 15 July 15		
Heading	2/1 Highland Fld Ambce May 1915		
War Diary	Bedford	02/05/1915	02/05/1915
War Diary	Southampton	02/05/1915	02/05/1915
War Diary	Havre	03/05/1915	04/05/1915
War Diary	Bourgette	05/05/1915	05/05/1915
War Diary	Norrent Fontes	05/05/1915	06/05/1915
War Diary	Colonne Sur La Lys	07/05/1915	07/05/1915
Heading	2/1 H F Amb		
War Diary	Colonne	08/05/1915	14/05/1915
War Diary	Merris	15/05/1915	18/05/1915
War Diary	Lagorgue	19/05/1915	20/05/1915
War Diary	Locon	20/05/1915	11/06/1915
War Diary	Pierre Au Beure	12/06/1915	16/06/1915
War Diary	Locon	17/06/1915	25/06/1915
War Diary	Estaires	26/06/1917	26/07/1917
War Diary	Merville	28/07/1915	29/07/1915
Heading	51st Division 1/1st Highland Field Amb Aug Sept Oct 15		
War Diary	Puor Neyelle	30/07/1915	06/08/1915
War Diary	Baulincourt	08/08/1915	08/08/1915
War Diary	Behencourt	09/08/1915	13/08/1915
War Diary	Ebart Farm	31/08/1915	16/09/1915
War Diary	Ebart	12/09/1915	31/10/1915
Heading	51st Division 2/1 Fd. Amb. 51st (Highland) Div. Nov 1915 Vol III		
War Diary	Ebart	01/11/1915	30/11/1915
Heading	2/1 Fd. Amb.51st. Div Dec 1915 Vol IV		
War Diary	Ebart	01/12/1915	23/12/1915
War Diary	Montonvillers	27/12/1915	27/12/1915
Heading	2/1 High Fd. Amb. Jan 1916 Vol. V		
War Diary	Montonvillers	04/01/1916	04/01/1916
War Diary	Villers Bocage	04/01/1916	31/01/1916
Heading	51st Division 2/1 Highland Field Ambulance Feb March 1916		
Heading	2/1 High. Fd. Amb. Feb Vol VI		
War Diary	Villers Bocage	07/02/1916	07/02/1916
War Diary	Daours	09/02/1916	29/02/1916
Heading	2/1 High. Fd. Amb. Vol VII		
War Diary	Mirvaux	01/03/1916	05/03/1916
War Diary	Doullens	06/03/1916	09/03/1916
War Diary	Ivergny	09/03/1916	09/03/1916
War Diary	Maroeuil	10/03/1916	17/03/1916
War Diary	Haute Avesnes	18/03/1916	31/03/1916
Heading	51st Div 2/1st Highland F.A. April 1916		
Heading	2/1 Highland Fd. Amb Vol VIII		

War Diary	Haute Avesnes	01/04/1916	30/04/1916
Heading	2/1st Highland F.A. May 1916		
War Diary	Haute Avesnes	09/05/1916	31/05/1916
Heading	51st Division 2/1 Highland Field Ambulance June 1916		
War Diary	Haute Avesnes	07/06/1916	30/06/1916
Heading	51st Division 2/1 Highland F. Ambulance July 1916		
Miscellaneous	A.D.M.S. 51st (High) Div.	01/08/1916	01/08/1916
War Diary	Haute Avesnes	07/07/1916	10/07/1916
War Diary	Mingoval	13/07/1916	14/07/1916
War Diary	Doullens	15/07/1916	16/07/1916
War Diary	Bernaville	16/07/1916	19/07/1916
War Diary	En Route for Flesselles	20/07/1916	20/07/1916
War Diary	Meaulte	21/07/1916	21/07/1916
War Diary	Becordel	21/07/1916	31/07/1916
Heading	2/1st Highland F.A. Aug 1916.		
War Diary	Becordel	03/08/1916	06/08/1916
War Diary	D.18.b	06/08/1916	08/08/1916
War Diary	Liercourt	10/08/1916	10/08/1916
War Diary	Ebblingham	12/08/1916	13/08/1916
War Diary	Blaringham	14/08/1916	17/08/1916
War Diary	L'Estrade	18/08/1916	28/08/1916
War Diary	Steenwerk	30/08/1916	30/08/1916
Heading	51st Div 2/1st Highland Field Ambulance Sept. 1916		
War Diary	Steenwerk	07/09/1916	24/09/1916
War Diary	Estaires	25/09/1916	30/09/1916
Heading	51st Division 2/1 Highland Field Ambulance Oct 1916		
War Diary	Fienvillers	01/10/1916	03/10/1916
War Diary	Sarton	03/10/1916	03/10/1916
War Diary	Couin	04/10/1916	06/10/1916
War Diary	Bus	07/10/1916	14/10/1916
War Diary	Couin	16/10/1916	17/10/1916
War Diary	Vauchelles Les Authie	18/10/1916	31/10/1916
Heading	51st Div 2/1st Highland Field Ambulance Nov 1916		
War Diary	Vauchelles	04/11/1916	23/11/1916
War Diary	Puchevillers	24/11/1916	25/11/1916
War Diary	Albert	26/11/1916	27/11/1916
Heading	51st Div 2/1st Highland Field Ambulance Dec 1916		
Miscellaneous	ADMS 51 H Div	31/12/1916	31/12/1916
War Diary	Albert	01/12/1916	12/12/1916
War Diary	Aveluy	15/12/1916	26/12/1916
War Diary	Ovillers Huts	27/12/1916	27/12/1916
Heading	51st Div 2/1st Highland Field Ambulance Jan 1917		
War Diary	Ovillers Huts	05/01/1917	13/01/1917
War Diary	Puchvillers	13/01/1917	14/01/1917
War Diary	Longvillers	14/01/1917	15/01/1917
War Diary	Cramont	15/01/1917	15/01/1917
War Diary	Les Masures De Cramont	15/01/1917	16/01/1917
War Diary	Nouvion	16/01/1917	31/01/1917
Heading	2/1st Highland Field Ambulance Feb 1917		
War Diary	Nouvion En Ponthieu	02/11/1917	05/11/1917
War Diary	Cueschart	06/11/1917	07/11/1917
War Diary	Buire Au Bois	07/11/1917	08/11/1917
War Diary	Framecourt	09/11/1917	09/11/1917
War Diary	Ostroville	10/11/1917	10/11/1917
War Diary	Frevillers	11/11/1917	27/11/1917
Heading	2/1st Highland Field Ambulance March 1917		

War Diary	Frevillers	07/11/1917	30/11/1917
Heading	51st Div 2/1st Highland F.A. April 1917		
War Diary	Frevillers	03/04/1917	04/04/1917
War Diary	Caucourt	05/04/1917	28/04/1917
Miscellaneous	Summary Of Medical War Diaries Of 2/1st Highland Field Ambulance		
Miscellaneous	B.E.F. 2/1st H.F.A., 51st Division	01/04/1917	01/04/1917
Heading	51st Div 2/1st Highland F.A. May 1917		
War Diary	Caucourt	07/05/1917	09/05/1917
War Diary	Arras	10/05/1917	13/05/1917
War Diary	St Nicholas	14/05/1917	30/05/1917
War Diary	Chelers	31/05/1917	31/05/1917
Miscellaneous	Summary Of Medical War Diaries		
Miscellaneous	2/1st H.F.A., 51st Division.	01/05/1917	01/05/1917
Diagram etc	Diagram		
Heading	2/1st Highland F.A. June 1917		
War Diary	Chelers	01/06/1917	03/06/1917
War Diary	Huclier	04/06/1917	04/06/1917
War Diary	Lugy	05/06/1917	06/06/1917
War Diary	Guemy	07/06/1917	21/06/1917
War Diary	Les Cinq Rues	22/06/1917	29/06/1917
Miscellaneous	Summary Of Medical War Diaries Of 2/1st Highland F.A.	22/06/1917	22/06/1917
Miscellaneous	2/1st Highland F.A. 51st Div. 8th Corps. 5th Army. Western Front	22/06/1917	22/06/1917
Miscellaneous	Summary Of Medical War Diaries Of 2/1st Highland F.A.	22/06/1917	22/06/1917
Miscellaneous	2/1st Highland F.A. 51st Div. 8th Corps. 5th Army. Western Front. June 1917.	22/06/1917	22/06/1917
Heading	2/1st Highland F.A. July 1917		
War Diary	Les Cinq Rues	05/07/1917	22/07/1917
War Diary	St Janster Biezen	23/07/1917	26/07/1917
War Diary	Poperinghe	27/07/1917	31/07/1917
Miscellaneous	Summary Of Medical War Diaries Of 2/1st Highland F.A.		
Miscellaneous	2/1st Highland F.A. 51st Div. 8th Corps. 5th Army. Western Front. July 1917	01/07/1917	01/07/1917
Miscellaneous	Summary Of Medical War Diaries Of 2/1st Highland F.A		
Miscellaneous	2/1st Highland F.A. 51st Div. 8th Corps. 5th Army. Western Front July 1917	01/07/1917	01/07/1917
Heading	2/1st Highland F.A. Aug 1917		
War Diary	Poperinghe	01/07/1917	07/07/1917
War Diary	St Janster Biezen	08/07/1917	24/07/1917
War Diary	Poperinghe	27/07/1917	28/07/1917
War Diary	Essex Farm	29/07/1917	30/07/1917
Map	Map		
Heading	2/1st Highland F.A. Sept 1917		
War Diary	Essex Farm	07/09/1917	24/09/1917
War Diary	X Camp	25/09/1917	30/09/1917
Miscellaneous	Appendix A	21/09/1917	21/09/1917
Heading	2/1st Highland F.A. Oct 1917		
War Diary	Courcelles	01/10/1917	03/10/1917
War Diary	S.2.b.	04/10/1917	31/10/1917
Heading	2/1st Highland F.A. Nov. 1917		
War Diary	Avesnes Le Comte	02/11/1917	17/11/1917

War Diary	Bapaume	17/11/1917	18/11/1917
War Diary	Le Chelle	18/11/1917	21/11/1917
War Diary	Q.14.d.18 (Campbells INN)	22/11/1917	23/11/1917
War Diary	Q.14.d.1.8.	23/11/1917	27/11/1917
War Diary	Dernancourt	24/11/1917	30/11/1917
Heading	2/1st Highland F.A. Dec 1917		
War Diary	Rocquigny	01/12/1917	01/12/1917
War Diary	Bertincourt	02/12/1917	02/12/1917
War Diary	N.11 Central	02/12/1917	16/12/1917
War Diary	Bihucourt	17/12/1917	31/12/1917
Heading	2/1st Highland F.A.Jan 1917		
War Diary	Bihucourt	02/01/1918	19/01/1918
War Diary	Courcelles Le Comte	20/01/1918	20/01/1918
War Diary	Bailleulmont	20/01/1918	23/01/1918
Heading	2/1st Highland F.A. Feb 1918		
War Diary	Bailleulmont	01/02/1918	01/02/1918
War Diary	Logeast Wood Ablainzevelle	02/02/1918	12/02/1918
War Diary	Beugny	13/02/1918	24/02/1918
War Diary	Gropi Camp	25/02/1918	28/02/1918
Heading	2/1st Highland F.A. March 1918.		
War Diary	Gropi	01/03/1918	09/03/1918
War Diary	Gropi Camp	09/03/1918	17/03/1918
War Diary	Lebucquiere (I 30 C 2.4 Sheet 57c)	17/03/1918	21/03/1918
War Diary	Loch Camp Near Fremicourt	21/03/1918	23/03/1918
War Diary	Grevillers	24/03/1918	24/03/1918
War Diary	Auchonvillers	25/03/1918	25/03/1918
War Diary	Beaussart	25/03/1918	25/03/1918
War Diary	Henu	26/03/1918	26/03/1918
War Diary	Barly	27/03/1918	29/03/1918
War Diary	Frevent	30/03/1918	30/03/1918
War Diary	Cense-Le-Vallee	31/03/1918	31/03/1918
Heading	2/1st Highland F.A. Apr. 1918		
War Diary	Cense La Vallee	02/04/1918	04/04/1918
War Diary	Auchel	06/04/1918	08/04/1918
War Diary	Cense La Vallee	08/04/1918	12/04/1918
War Diary	Ham-En-Artois	12/04/1918	24/04/1918
War Diary	Lambres	24/04/1918	30/04/1918
Heading	51st Div 2/1st Highland F.A. May 1918.		
War Diary	Lambres (near Aire)	01/05/1918	05/05/1918
War Diary	Mont St Eloi	06/05/1918	07/05/1918
War Diary	Ecoivres	08/05/1918	08/05/1918
War Diary	Ecoivres (Near Mont St Eloi)	09/05/1918	31/05/1918
Heading	2/1st High F.A. June 1918		
War Diary	Ecoivres (Mont St Eloi)	04/06/1918	30/06/1918
Heading	2/1st Highland F.A. July 1918.		
War Diary	Ecoivres (Mont St Eloi)	03/07/1918	13/07/1918
War Diary	Houvelin	14/07/1918	15/07/1918
War Diary	Herme (Seine & Marne)	16/07/1918	17/07/1918
War Diary	Le-Mesnil-Sur-Oger	18/07/1918	19/07/1918
War Diary	Champillon	19/07/1918	19/07/1918
War Diary	St Imoges (Rheims)	20/07/1918	27/07/1918
War Diary	Nanteuil La Fosse	28/07/1918	31/07/1918
War Diary	Auban-Moet Epernay	20/07/1918	25/07/1918
Heading	2/1st High. F.A. Aug. 1918		
War Diary	Nanteuil-La-Fosse (Marne)	01/08/1918	01/08/1918
War Diary	Champillon (Marne) Near Epernay	02/08/1918	02/08/1918

War Diary	Moslins (Marne)	03/08/1918	03/08/1918
War Diary	Aubigny (Pas De Calais)	04/08/1918	19/08/1918
War Diary	Agnez-Les Duisans	21/08/1918	29/08/1918
Heading	2/1st High. F.A. Sept. 1918.		
War Diary	Ecoivres	02/09/1918	13/09/1918
War Diary	Brant Camp (Mont St Eloi)	14/09/1918	22/09/1918
War Diary	Ecoivres	23/09/1918	28/09/1918
Heading	2/1st Highland Fld. A. Oct 1918		
War Diary	Ecoivres	29/09/1918	06/10/1918
War Diary	Queant Riencourt	07/10/1918	07/10/1918
War Diary	Riencourt	08/10/1918	10/10/1918
War Diary	Fontaine Notre Dame	11/10/1918	11/10/1918
War Diary	Point De Tour	11/10/1918	11/10/1918
War Diary	Escaudoeuvres	12/10/1918	12/10/1918
War Diary	Thun St Martin (T 10 C 1.8)	12/10/1918	13/10/1918
War Diary	Thun St Martin	13/10/1918	20/10/1918
War Diary	Pave De Valenciennes	21/10/1918	25/10/1918
War Diary	La Pyaramide De Denain	25/10/1918	28/10/1918
War Diary	Douchy	29/10/1918	31/10/1918
War Diary	Fbg St Roch Near Cambrai	31/10/1918	31/10/1918
Heading	2/1st High F.A. Nov.1918.		
War Diary	St Roch Cambrai	03/11/1918	30/11/1918
Heading	2/1st Highland F.A. Dec 1918		
War Diary	Fd. St Roch Cambrai	01/12/1918	31/12/1918
Heading	51 Div. 2/1st Highland F.A. Jan 1919		
War Diary	St Roch (Cambrai)	01/01/1919	01/01/1919
War Diary	Houdeng Goegnies (Belgium)	11/01/1919	31/01/1919
Heading	2/1st Highland F.A. Feb 1919		
War Diary	Houdeng Goegnies Belgium	01/02/1919	28/02/1919
Heading	2/1st High. F.A. Mar.1919		
War Diary	Houdeng Goegnies	01/03/1919	21/03/1919
War Diary	Bellecourt	22/03/1919	27/03/1919
Heading	2/1st. High. F.A. Apr 1919		
War Diary	Bellicourt Belgium	01/04/1919	10/04/1919

WO95/2858

51 Div

2/1 Highland F.A
May '15 - Apr '19

(2)

51ST DIVISION

2-1ST HIGHLAND FLD AMBULANCE

MAY 1915 - ~~DEC 1918~~
1919 APL

121/6390

51st Division

2/1.

1st Highland Field Ambulance = 1st Highland

Vol I

121/6390

May '15
June "
July "

2/1. Highland Flat Aurbree.

WAR DIARY
or
INTELLIGENCE SUMMARY.
(Erase heading not required.)

2/1 Highland F.A.

Place	Date	Hour	Summary of Events and Information	Remarks and references to Appendices
	1915			
Bedford	2/5/15	2 A.M.	Unit entrained in two portions & Major R. & Lt Brand for 1st portion & Major Matheson, Golden Eagle (Major R. & Lt Evans reported) Roate (Lt Arp)	
Southampton	2/5/15	11 a.m.	Embarked in three Ships Matheson, Golden Eagle (Major R., Lt Evans reported) Roate (Lt Arp)	
Havre	3/5/15	11 a.m.	Disembarked and concentrated in Camp 4. Horses watered by 5 P.M. Camp' advance articles obtained from O.C. there as first issues on half table & other' lost in transit. Three horses have been exchanged with Remounts for colds. Birthplace lost in transit.	I thought poles lost + hand + Badgia
Havre	4/5/15	9 a.m.	Entrained in 1 train with Brig Signal Section & Arg. Train. Left Havre at 8.19	
Bouzetta	5-V-15	10 A.M.	Detrained and marched by road to Nonant Pontin – 8 miles. Dinner served at 7 P.M.	
Nonant Pontin	5.v.15	2 amphres	Section C on Hospital. Spare available in the Palais de Justice for about 20 – 25 cars. On way to Nonant Pontin picked up a trooper (Middleton) of Horse belongings in our crown by 10os Field.	
Nonant F.	6.v.15	1 P.M.	Received 6 horse collars to Same Driver Bridle.	
do	do	7 P.M.	Read, Brains, orders not received till 4.30, orders filed. Roate Dr Nicholas, Letters Browns Dr Vernant, Patorme sent to hyp. Nicholas found Nicholas (lumps) had travels the horses Ambulance Wagon forward to 2.54 Cleany troop Killens with 12 cases received earlier in the day.	
Calmpy Im	7 do	4 a.m.	Arrived, no casualties, no Ambulance, no stables & Rooms to Billets	

INTELLIGENCE SUMMARY.

War Diary

H. F. And.

INTELLIGENCE SUMMARY.

(Erase heading not required.)

Place	Date	Hour	Summary of Events and Information	Remarks and references to Appendices
Calonne	1915 8th	11 a.m.	Rosters, cleaning up, inventory. Sunday. Conference with Adj. re tobacco.	
"	9th	11 a.m.	Adm. instr to R.Surg & Confce with A.D.M.S. General instruction.	
"	"	6 p.m.	Wrote home notes to room.	
"	"	9 p.m.	Hosp. San. Oper. orders. Chch parade at 10.30.	
"	10th	11 a.m.	Shed on hour notice. Drive. Wrote...	
"	11th	11 a.m.	B. Sector wards & relieve [spoke] 1/2 day of hospital visit of DDMS 3rd Rough	
"	"		(+ Colonel) with a Colonial attached (6 hrs) Motorcycle hospital books & duty orders	
"	12th	1 1/2 p.m.	Staff Meeting. Relieved by Thepe. Jom Brig HQ.	
"	13	6 p.m.	B. Sector Assumes duty at hospital.	
"	14	11 a.m.	Applied to Bourlon Hôtel for premium. Road toss & Saxon as a hospital.	
"	"	11 a.m.	No permission received auto Brigadier sim to reposition the place.	
"	"	6 p.m.	on hospital. Ambulance arrives from hospital. Clear up hospital	
Miris	15th	9 a.m.	Brigade to move. Bowl moved at 9.35 this morning.	
"	15	3 p.m.	Arrived at Miris. See Field... Motored in to Albert, Secretary de Mairie (B. Julian)	
"	16	11 a.m.	Ch. Parade 10.30 set re Spooks. 5 pm Ambulances departs 2 hrs later	
"	17	11 a.m.	Start on 2 hr wain. 2.20. Arrived with wounded 2.30. 3.20 fresh 9 am - 2 hr Arrive - no more.	

(Erase heading not required.)

Place	Date 1915 (May)	Hour	Summary of Events and Information	Remarks and references to Appendices
Merris	18	7.20	Relief received from at 9.30. Bus [illegible] as Rue Bertels, 2 m[?] Rue [illegible] Battalion Hdqrs not moved - Lt. Argo moved to La Sogne where from shelter opens. No hills of Rue Bertels.	
Lapogne	19	5.20	Quartermaster started at 6.30 a.m.	
do	20	8 a.m.	Brown to form up brigade at 9.30	
		9.30	Proceeded to Steen by front Reynolds Bruno Road	
Steen	21	2 pm	Opened Divisional — tea at La Caron near Steen	
do	22	10 am	Had interview with 2nd Canadian who had been [illegible] the 6th Canadian — [illegible] neighbourhood	
do	22/23	9 pm	A note arrived out at Hdqtrs KOC orders Rations.	
do	23rd	2.30	Orders to open K.O.C. [illegible] for receipt & [illegible] of the [illegible] to [illegible] hold the town [illegible] & [illegible] Brigade of [illegible] from [illegible] the line [illegible] by adjacent homes.	
	23rd	12 night	Night staff to about 12 midn'ght. Would have alwh/y hours from Syck — Headquarter office garrisoned at Strathcona, bivouacked & [illegible] by 20? & h.a.c.	

WAR DIARY
or
INTELLIGENCE SUMMARY.
(Erase heading not required.)

Army Form C. 2118.

Place	Date	Hour	Summary of Events and Information	Remarks and references to Appendices
Locon. 8th Janv.	19.15	11 a.m.	Lieutenant Blériot field promoted 9th Division 7th [Bn?] to [?]o left to 9th [?] moves after this [?] have received orders to proceed to Winnezeele & Rebecque [?] till further orders.	
Wyppe 11th Janv.		11 am.	Capt. Cam St Pierre [?] patrol party given orders to his [?] at [?] Winnou Farm and to take over duties of Trench Command Drinny Fabre. B Section is due to [?] duty & to [?] take L Tourret on 12th inst.	
Proper qua 12th Janv.		10.30	[?] and Rebecque Farm with Cush & 3 heavy [?] & 3 More [?] Pomps [?] to 9 Belgian Waggon proceeds to L Tourret & take our duty for S.P. 10 & 7 Aout. [?] Mer. attends fort — is 6 heaves on duty for [?] for [?] a load at Reyf and fort — Rue de Cailloux. O Ruyssit (Dandane) & 3 heaves at [?] Rue d'Ypres the whose [?] 1 foot with two officers attended [?] wounded [?] & hypnoses A fort & Eyelet [?], has gone to bring up 8 Cars from L Tourret. Reg [?] the Hon [?] with him between am. evening part thus d'[?]th.) Another 50 yards Reg. and Lieut. [?] gone first in [?] from S.B. and [?] both attendees with [?] and accompany at colhorty first and advances Dressy Station. Thence Ry en route & Locan.	

WAR DIARY
or
INTELLIGENCE SUMMARY.
(Erase heading not required.)

Army Form C. 2118.

Place	Date	Hour	Summary of Events and Information	Remarks and references to Appendices
Gurkha Ravine	1915 14th April	10.0pm	Mr Reed, Mr Kinninger & Mr Scott (Workshop Unit) from abroad to enquire into injuries sustained by M.A. Coy 2017 which had hit a ditch at 11.5 mst — feeling strongly to justice. Saw British advancement train.	
			Arrived Tenret. Found Algo wound. Infantile agitation ripe. Found Algo Arabs + had the member with evening. Found Mr tejenter as arthur had to Purva Seera Argo & met letter by night. Accompanied Mr Nelmacke + I to Azames Dress Station II & Remote Aid posts of left half Advanced Front. Arrived Dress Sta. includes. Just was at much Mac d'Epinette with Mr de Bers. Remotes Aid just was a point attacked on left half ad Station 1½ miles W.E. of Perkelstput at a place called India Village — Condition These a fine Aug. into entrenched huts. New few One horse ambulance trip pelico between Perkels post + India village.	
	15th		Returns to Tenret about 11.30 a.m. The 152nd Brigade attack tonight. Casualties are events by 2nd + 3rd F. Amb. The 3rd Field Amb has been ordered to take over everything from & Tenret in conjunction with W. Arzo's Section (No Sect via Dhrand Side)	
	16th		Battle Continues	

WAR DIARY
or
INTELLIGENCE SUMMARY.
(Erase heading not required.)

Army Form C. 2118.

Place	Date	Hour	Summary of Events and Information	Remarks and references to Appendices
Hazim	17th June	6.30	Workers received to proceed from [?] an Bruce [?] and act as overflow recover of wounded. Intake camp in field between Marin Farm Th main road. Also despatched 20 horses & [?] [?] to Z. Memel - Kochelet. Buela to meet 720 horses & ducts to St Front. Interviews, Merrigan Rue Ana, & Const on [?] & Sa men overpowered with work. Started reports - Military stat. It Brown admitted to [?] troops. Suffering from what appears to be measles - very run am	
	18			
	19		rain - nights shown.	
	20			
	21-24		Lt. W. Brown employed by order of med. Board. Stated W. strength of Unit.	
	25th		Moved & Staines and 10th ar from WT [?] [?] Rding lies Aid [?] St Louis School. Divisions moving from Indian Rimer Chapelle to Estaires. (List - [?]	
Estaires	26th		Visits & Reports [?] ditto hostels an une Indiain, W.T. (Van Carteran) to visit our sick. Proceeded to Briac Scabies offices to this help.	
Estaires	2nd July		Established Advanced Crutching Post for Sick Wounded at [?] a later to [?] J.J.J. W[?] the Bazaar. Collecting Cars. Ambulance. have dealt 6.30 am to 8.30 pm [?] (existed of staff including input Collections	

WAR DIARY
or
INTELLIGENCE SUMMARY.

(Erase heading not required.)

Army Form C. 2118.

Place	Date	Hour	Summary of Events and Information	Remarks and references to Appendices
Belair	16th July 1915		Bgn HQ and take over duties at events also open for receipt & despatch	
Ochaen	25th July		35th Div having been relieved in the 3rd Army Intelligence the day moves to Brett. New Divisional HQ Rest march M.T. & Rns & Rents made to despatch Runners for movement by Armies at 6am	
"	29th		Army Runners same. March to junct north where Brakes are sent to Argue & the Sub. Commun the chains to Corbie & GS CCS. Spur pass. Rolls & be sent O.P. M Are. Instruments - tracy Calcium open for Armsion	

121/7381

51/1st Division

1st Highland

2/1
1/1st Highland field amb:

Vol II
Aug Sep, Oct 15

Aug
Sep. 1915
Oct

WAR DIARY or INTELLIGENCE SUMMARY

Army Form C. 2118.

2/1 N.F. Amb,
Sig 2 hyr Div
J. Whelan Lt Col. Ramc
Cmdg

Place	Date	Hour	Summary of Events and Information	Remarks and references to Appendices
Fort Rompu	30/7/15		Whelan was detailed both days	
do	1st Aug		at Ouchy & AUTUILLE rehearsing thus ordering the relief for the half of Brantary Division. Came to MELLINCOURT. AUTUILLE Stabes hands over to Indian Cavalry. Ordered to meet here today. No greater suitable found — reports sent to ADM S.	
Behoulintlaye	13th Aug		Moved to Behoulintlaye when B Section was sent to Inprevraaux temp near the Crucifix. A number of bricks required (about 3000) to make flooring. B Section relieves C Section in charge of Advanced Dressing Station. A section army duty at the Hospital here.	
Braxtons Farm	Aug 1st		Moved HQ & Ambulance to a farm nr Bavlincourt. Am in use which had been in preparation. Orders received to make quarters here. Am't 30,000 brick required to make floors. Also large amount of wood & water mud to repair the walls. (A section DAUELY 25th Augs)	
	Sept 11		Wilson Staples to U.K. C section DAUELY D.Whelan A section	
	Sept 16		Assumed Charge of AUTUILLE Collection path again replacing Indian Cavalry to Amli.	

Aug – Sept. 1915

WAR DIARY
or
INTELLIGENCE SUMMARY.
(Erase heading not required.)

Army Form C. 2118.

2/1 H.F. Amb.
57th North Div.
M[idlothian] F.T.C.R.
Comdy

Place	Date	Hour	Summary of Events and Information	Remarks and references to Appendices
			Aug – Sept – Oct	
Elant	Sept 19		Received leave to proceed to United Kingdom for seven days. Major RORIE of 1/2nd High Field Amb. attention was directed by DDMS x Corps by letter to the fact that State of Readiness for the Field Amb. in Reserve was 1/3 horse vehicles. Articles of equipment which Comdg personally looked without for three or four days were chosen and started forwards in triplicate being Ireland. Returned to duty from leave to U.K.	very urgent front theory
Grand Apres Ebert Oct 15			Unit continues to receive the more sick & to convalescents from Divisional front having three 8–3rd High Field Amb. to talk the Field Amb. in Reserve of the 57th High Div.	
Vlant Oct 23			By orders to Division through A.D.M.S. THREE G.S. wagon outfits will divide whatever were attached for duty with 2/1 Res Coy RE from the Kitsband. Iyper [works?], Road making for Conveyance Ambulance wagons up to the Rear of AUTVILLE re-	
Elant Oct 31			Ambulance claims to tractors attack under Oct 15 date alone	

Nov 1915

51/9/Kurow

2/1 F. Amb.
5/8 (Argyles) Dn.
$\frac{2}{102}$
vol III

$\frac{121}{7721}$

1st Highland

WAR DIARY
or
INTELLIGENCE SUMMARY.
(Erase heading not required.)

Army Form C. 2118

Xxxx
2/1 N.F. and
5/3 D.D. Whitechapel
H.F.A. Essex B.

Place	Date	Hour	Summary of Events and Information	Remarks and references to Appendices
Shad.	Nov 1st		The Officers of this unit at present serving:—	

Malachi, Stoll (1st May) joined unit at its beginning on 7th April 1914 from 1/1 N.F. and
W.N. Edenbrand Capt. (4th Apl 15) joined on first Commission 4th Oct 1914. Proceeded
to France on 2nd May '15. Invalided home 26th June. Returns to unit
Sept 19th Lieut. '15.

Dr. N. Brunt Capt. (1 Feb 15) joined the unit on first Commission 5th Oct 14 serves above
noted.

M. McNamechi Capt. (8 Oct 15) Same as Capt. Brunt.

H.J. Burridge Capt. (21 May 15) joined 16th Dec 14   16th Dec 14 to
                                                         appointment appended abroad and went to France Capt.
                                                         29th April. Serving with the unit   27th Oct 15

Henry Begg Lieut. joined the unit from 1/1 N.F. and. Serving with have on
H.O. in. A.H.A. prior... of R.E. and came abroad with it.

Capt. Ganis Orys Pome, Supy. Commision must by orders of W.O. when
a private as part of the R.E.E. temporary Commission given June
(Supernumerary) having with us. Three Officers are required to free strength
                                                Any joined by W.O. order transfer to and to free strength
                                                of their. Three officers are reported as three had been
                                                struck off strength (1st time) to an employee. Consider. Having
                                                taken the 2nd time write of them.

#333 Wt. W3544/T434. 700,000 5/15 D D & L. A.D.S.S./Forms/C. 2118.

Army Form C. 2118

WAR DIARY
or
INTELLIGENCE SUMMARY.
(Erase heading not required.)

2/1 1st Ant. 51st Div. Whitenall Rd.

Instructions regarding War Diaries and Intelligence Summaries are contained in F.S. Regs., Part II. and the Staff Manual respectively. Title pages will be prepared in manuscript.

Place	Date	Hour	Summary of Events and Information	Remarks and references to Appendices
Shade	1st Nov. 1915		The names of the other two Temporary Maj. Lieut. Miller, Redmond were entered as Australian officers 2/1 1st Ant. Captain Geo. Dick joined from à la Suite: service at home as a Captain, date of joining 11 Oct 1915. Capt. J.B. Rawlins Barnet joined with Lieut. 15 from 3rd London Fin. Stores, being Capt. J. Andrew Titmas Selected from their unit for Service with 1st Div.	Capt. H. McC...
Shad.	13th Nov.		The following Officers & other ranks are doing duty as Regimental medical Officers while T.M.O. others unit are home on leave or sick. Lieut. Henry Boss? — 3rd Hrs. Quarts. Brigd. Capt. Geo. Dick — " " Capt. Bey. Hurnicks 1/6 Redor Rifles (Cameron) T.5th April Dollar Hts Capt. J.Sra Titmas 1/4 Royal Lane. Regt. (Kings own) Capt. Garnet? Oup 5th N.D. A.S.C. Capt. H. McCumaklie 1/6 KOS? Hosforths Halt Capt. J.m Stewart 1/5 " H. D. ammun. Colum.	
(Shad?)	27th Nov. 30th Nov.		Capt. J.B.Rawlins Barnet? returned to unit 1/6 Scott Rifles to Tr getsbourg Duke. The Field Ambulance Continued transport work. Islands in Mesap. Speraden Advance Dressing Station for Left half of the Div. Frontage	

#353 Wt W2544/1454 700,000 5/15 D. D. & L. A.D.S.S./Forms/C. 2118.

Highland
2/1 F². Amb. 51ˢᵗ D

See

Vol. IV

121/7930

1ot. Highland

Dec. 1915

Army Form C. 2118.

Original XII
2/1 W.F.Amb.
Mulwhs MLD. 12th Jan 16

WAR DIARY
or
INTELLIGENCE SUMMARY.
(Erase heading not required.)

Place	Date	Hour	Summary of Events and Information	Remarks and references to Appendices
Ebart	18/11/15		Lieut J.H.C. Gatehie R.A.M.C. (TC) attached this unit for instruction as from 30th Nov. 15, previous duty attached to Medical Charge of a Bn Fusiliers	
Ebart	18/12/15		Lieut J.H.C. Gatehie R.A.M.C. (TC) admits No. 40 1/1 Royal Scots Regt.	
Vinl	23/12/15		2/Lt H.F. Aub, leas a detachment under Cast and rendezvous Brand (Personnel advanced Dressing Station AUTUILLE), advance drove to new Billets at MONTONVILLERS about seven miles N of AMIENS, and open a Dressing Station there for care of the 153rd Brigade. This Brigade of the 51st High Div has been relieved by Infantry of the 32nd Division. This is the first move of the 51st Div into new Billets. The frontage previously held by 51st Div is being taken over by 32nd Div. Now 2 Ambulance secured without incident over by the 91st Red Ambulance.	
Ybart		1.0 pm	Quarters attached over by the 91st Irish Red Amb, having been vacated by the 91st Irish Red Amb.	
MONTON -VILLERS	23/12/15	4 pm	Capt Broms & party arrived at MONTONVILLERS having handed over charge of advanced Dressing Station to 90th Field Ambulance.	

51st. Div.

F1 223/1

2/1 High⁰ L⁰ Anne.
———————
Sam
———————
Vol V

1st. Highland

Jan 1916

Army Form C. 2118.

WAR DIARY
or
INTELLIGENCE SUMMARY.

(Erase heading not required.)

Place	Date	Hour	Summary of Events and Information	Remarks and references to Appendices
MONTON VILLERS	Jan 6/16	10 a.m.	Handed off 10 a.m. Drove the unit to new billets at VILLERS BOCAGE. Injuries informally of twenty-two men on a billet for the Divisional. The place allotted was not suitable for a hospital.	
VILLERS BOCAGE	6th Jan 16		He and Nurse and me Villers Bocage Hospital being opened by C Section under Captain Dick. On account receipt of our 50 sick certain accommodation has been found difficult with inhabitants was interviewed who were not hospitable, he eventually after reference to the 13th Corps Liaison Officer the ECOLE DE FILLES was handed over. The class being suspended for a time.	
	7th		I was granted leave to Aberdeen from today the 15th inst. v Travells by Boulogne. Captain W.H. EDEN BRAND of this unit assumes Command in my absence. I rejoins the unit on 16th Jan.	
	16th		A. ORS. intimated that Capt. D.M GRANT was permanently posted to 57/2 H.D. in Army Corps. from 15th Dec. 14.15 & he is therefore Struck off Strength of this unit from that date.	
	26th		Major G.F. WHYTE R.A.M.C. was hurt in attacks the further orders on his rejoining Expeditionary Force from sick leave.	
	31st		This unit while in VILLERS continued to attend sick Brandt of neighbouring units billeted with some fitting their billets into snubhy from standings - Kings out the month.	

51st Division

2/1 Highland Field Ambulance   1st. Highland

Feb.
March } 1916

51

2/1 High Ld Amb
Feb
Vol VI

WAR DIARY
INTELLIGENCE SUMMARY.

Sheet I Feb 1916
XIV / H.F.Amb.
9/1 Munster F.A.

Place	Date	Hour	Summary of Events and Information	Remarks and references to Appendices
VILLERS BOCAGE	7th Feb		Orders received for movement of this unit under 154th Bgd. Command to DAOURS 3 miles W. of CORBIE there to form Dressing Station & Rest Station for 51st High. Div. (see M.A.D. 1 in 100,000 AMIENS No. 17.)	
		9.15 a.m.	Unit marches off	
DAOURS	9th	1 p.m.	Arrived DAOURS and took over from 58th F. Amb. 18th Div. buildings & a disused mill immediately W. of Canal mainly north front to the E. end of DAOURS village. A Nissen-hut & several huts in course of erection; a Killingham billet the mess to appear was acquired as an Officers Hospital. W.M. Orders returned from lower D.V.R. - 9 days & Section opened as a Field Amb Dressing Station. 15 Sick admitted as Officers Hosp. and C out as Rest Station.	
	15th		Capt WN Edie Brand was granted leave to U.K. for 9 days. Major GF WHYPE having been posted to this unit assumed Command. W.B. Sackin. RAMC Brand was ordered to Command C Section on his return from leave. (Brand protested against any c'sh'p adventurement & refused his protest DMS heard Brand afterwards was ordered the service & proposed stat'n and further action.) Ref Correspondence File on S.F. 3.56	
	25th		While Major at DAOURS this unit Amb. admitted all sick of the DIVISION including Rabies cases. During this time the average number of cases in Hosp. was 150. Many cases of Venereal Disease were admitted - most arriving in AMIENS.	

Army Form C. 2118.

Part 2 Feb 1916

XV

WAR DIARY
or
INTELLIGENCE SUMMARY.
(Erase heading not required.)

2/1 N.F. Amb.
Mubutar H.Q.

Place	Date	Hour	Summary of Events and Information	Remarks and references to Appendices
DAOUDS	28th Feb		The bulk of the cases were admitted from of uncertain origin but corresponding with a type of Fever described as mild Trench Fever. Few cases of Trench Feet were admitted from the Div. Ammn. Column but one case — a man of a draft who had got Trench Feet in trains / 1914-15 at onset, part of the knee. Had there remained was to me of no at a very large amount. Had. Had Cases marked as to mens the Rest Station. It included 90 beds with bedding. This was main reason why my few cases required the tent and Div. Area — Average about 3 per day. The limit of time cases could be kept in hosp was ten days. A period A.D. Y.D booth was kept for the Rest Station. When all shown as an though of AD.S.Amb. aspirants during that time. All cases / Smoken were sent to Canvals Clearing Station. And are included with Army of 3 today. The field Ambulance also maintains the Fodau Trunk Disinfection during this month. Disinfecting the Blankets of units / the Division. A Dentist from No. 5 C.C.S. visits the Rest Station and days men cases of a Dental nature sent there from the various units. The O.O. Mule made a very useful Rest Station. There being big rooms and plenty of water. Every convenience was available in the Officers Hosp	

2333 Wt. W3544/1454 700,000 5/15 D. D. & L. A.D.S.S./Forms/C. 2118.

Army Form C. 2118.

Nov 3, Feb.
WAR DIARY
or
INTELLIGENCE SUMMARY.

XVI
2/1 W.F. Amb.
Lt Col Murphy

(Erase heading not required.)

Place	Date	Hour	Summary of Events and Information	Remarks and references to Appendices
DAOURS	28th Feb.		Orders received by Infantry Brigade on Tuesday 29th Feb. to billet Elsewhere. Unit to evacuate under orders of 154th Brigade. As several days had marching was anticipated all cases not likely fit absolutely for move were sent to C.C. Station CORBIE. 108 Cases were cleared in twenty minutes by 2.0.10. M.A.C.	
do	29th.		Unit started from DAOURS at 11.15 a.m. & joined the 154th Brigade at cross roads just South of PONT NOYELLES. and marched to MIRVAUX – 10 miles via North West steep hill had to be negotiated which was hard on the Transport. Horses, as the unit is short of 6 H.D. draught Horses. Casualties amongst the Horses have been preserved. 7 Late and reinforcements althou sufficient to Maintain 4 H.D. have been a demand for three weeks, & has now been announced. During Vet Sectionre an infit prior to the march. Unit had been had by Representative J.R.A.C.O. the fodder scheme developed now left to 13th Corps.
Arrived MIRVAUX at 3.30 p.m.
Captain Geo Dick Murphy died this morning was sent to O.C.S. from which he went to Base by Ambulance Train same day – Captain McConnachie ordered to assume Command VC Ambee, Captain Brand out having returned from leave	

51

2/1 高地 Fd Amb
―――――――
Vol VII

XVII

Unit 1/1st High Field Ambulance
WAR DIARY or INTELLIGENCE SUMMARY. Wilhelm A. Col.
Army Form C. 2118.

Place	Date	Hour	Summary of Events and Information	Remarks and references to Appendices
MIRVAUX	1/11/16		Moved two sections of the Field Ambulance to PIERREGOT including Headquarters. B. Section remained at MIRVAUX. Spared for receipt of sick of the Brigade.	
do	7/11/16		Operation order no 6. copy no 5 by Brig. Gen. Candy 154th Infantry Brig.	
DOULLENS	8/11/16	6 pm	This unit moved today in accordance with above order arriving at DOULLENS at 2 pm and being quartered in the town. Hospital was opened for sick in the Schools Building.	
do	8/11/16		In accordance with operation order no 7. by G.O.C. 154th Brigade copy no 9 of which was received hurriedly, this unit moved to IVERGNY where the night was spent. This is a village DNE of DOULLENS. about five miles.	
IVERGNY	9/11/16		In accordance with Operation order no 8. copy no 9 G.O.C. 154th Infantry Brigade. This unit moved independently to MAROEUIL 18 mile march. East of IVERGNY. Opened a Dressing Station. The A.D.M.S. No. 1891 orders this unit to form the Dressing Station of the road area of 51st High Division to take all such wounded of the Division also to provide advanced Dressing Stations and Carrying posts at available places on our Front. Clearing and Rest Station provided by another Field Ambulance of the Division and Casualty Clearing Station at HAUTE AVESNES and AUBIGNY respectively. An advance party was accordingly sent forward by motor car to examine the	

XVIII

Part 2 March

WAR DIARY
or
INTELLIGENCE SUMMARY

2/11th High[land] F[ield] Amb[ulance]

Wilhelm Lieut R A M C

Place	Date	Hour	Summary of Events and Information	Remarks and references to Appendices
IVERNY	9/11/16		The force at present used by the French Army (Hd. Qrs. Brigade of 93rd Division) from which 51st High[land] Div[ision] is taking over. Advance guard consisted of Major S[m]o Wyte and Captain J.S. Macnamara.	
MAROEUIL to	10/11/16	5 pm	Field Ambulance arrived MAROEUIL	
"			Dispatch party under Capt Argo & Capts Titins to ANZIN ST AUBIN to form advanced Dressing Station for Right Divisional Front was Chutiry post at MADASCAR in line of reserve trenches. Dispatch party under Capt McConachie and Captain ... Bess 9. Ls. for advanced Dressing Station at Aux Rietz with orderly post at LA MAISON BLANCHE for self half of Divisional Front. Additional Orderly posts for right half half J Div front formed at ABRI du MOUTON and Post Central respectively.	
	14/11/16		Twelve shells fired in MAROEUIL the afternoon so decided to close all patrols to Revt Molin V.C.S. (No 50, No BIGNY) as the Hospital was hit both in Department for Sick and Dept for wounded – Dispatches 170 cases under fire.	
	15/11/16		Shells again this forenoon. 6" shell went through front of wounded shelter wounding three. Renne men slightly. I ordered the removal of equipment to the Hospital for this as it's less conspicuous not trying to ms.	
	16/11/16			

WAR DIARY or INTELLIGENCE SUMMARY.

Army Form C. 2118.

XIX

2/1st High? Field Amb?
M.... Lieut. Col.

Place	Date	Hour	Summary of Events and Information	Remarks and references to Appendices
MAROEUIL	10/11/16	4pm	Dispatches following Telegram to A.D.M.S. "It is submitted that the existing method of collection of wounded on this front would be improved by the Dressing Station being moved to a safer place at by HAGNEZ or LARESSET AAA The working of the Dressing Station is seriously interfered with when enemy has and then it is necessary for all personnel & patients to take to Cellars. Serious Cases must be attended as they arrive AAA A line not every piece however the front of hospitals today fortunately it did not burst" Received instructions to proceed to HAUTE AVESNES evacuating from MAROEUIL except for a Medical Officer and three men who would form a Medical Aid Post there.	
M.IIII R HAUTE AVESNES		Noon	Arrived 10 a.m. and opened Dressing Station under canvas. The grounds allotted us are evacuated of the French private Field hospital under Professor Proust Ofsario. Obtained one Barraque from the French for patients. The French hospital moved today and we received other than Barrayues making accommodation for 150 patients.	
	18th-III 22-III		On the 51st High Division taking up new frontage just north of ARRAS, the 5th Div being on Right & 163rd Division on left of it, this Ambulance carries out the duties of Advanced FIELD Ambulance, Collecting & Distributing all sick & wounded of the Division	

51st Div

2/1st Highland F.A.

April 1916.

COMMITTEE FOR THE
MEDICAL HISTORY OF THE WAR
Date 9 - JUN. 1916

51

2/1 High Ja Amb

Vol VIII

April

XX High Field Amb Co
2/1. High Field Amb
Wilmington Company

WAR DIARY
or
INTELLIGENCE SUMMARY
(Erase heading not required.)

Army Form C. 2118.

Place	Date	Hour	Summary of Events and Information	Remarks and references to Appendices
HAUTE AVESNES	10th		The around dressing station for left half 1 Divisional Front at AUX RIETZ was handed over to the 1/½nd W Rid Field Ambulance personnel & all materials. 15th supplies by them Cars 6 the cleared to the Field Ambulance at HAUTE AVESNES.	
	15th		Many Arrangements for Collection wounded on 51st Div. front	

ARRAS

ST CATHERINE

ADVANCED DRESS. STN
ANZIN ST AUBIN

5 DIV

ROCLINCOURT
ROUTE de LILLE POST

COLLECTING POST MADAGASCAR

DRESSING STATION
HAUTE AVESNES

ARIANE

DRESSING MARŒUIL

MARŒUIL

51st DIV

COLLECTING POST St VAAST
LA MAISONNE BLANCHE

AUX RIETZ ADVANCED DR. STN 8TH

NEUVILLE St VAAST

ROADS
MED POSTS
NAMES OF POSTS
ROUTE

4th DIV

WAR DIARY or INTELLIGENCE SUMMARY

Army Form C. 2118.

Place	Date	Hour	Summary of Events and Information	Remarks and references to Appendices
HAUTE AVESNES	15th April		All three brigades of the Division hold sectors of the Div. Front. Casualties from the are extended either BAY RIETZ or ANZIN ST AUBIN. The Centre Brigade (152) had no suitable Dug out for an attacking fort so under direction of RE personnel of this unit are engaged in making a Field Officers Dug out at ARIANE estate of Lothuing & Sabattre caves with a Dressing Room & Officers Room attached.	
do.	30th April		During the month the Field Ambulances have continued to collect all wounded & sick of the Division & distributing all cases to Rest Station, Cas. Cl., S(Cotin or Convol. Cy. except those likely to be better in two days which are treated in the Ambulant. With a few exceptions medicine Stores have been issued to all units of the Div and attached units. - numbering in all between 56 and 60. The following Appendices units have continued to be medically attended by med Officers of this unit :— 1/6th Notts & Derby (Sherwood Foresters) 1/2 High F. Cy. RE 1/6th Notts & Derby (Sherwood Foresters) do 1/1 High T. Cy RE 9/2" R.G.A. 1/5" Royal Scotts (Detachment) 1/56" R.G.A. 4/2" T.M. Battery 1/6th Henry Hall (Howitzer) 6th Ammunit Details 6/2" Siege Battery 4th Gordon 10 do one Battery 91st Group RFA 1/1 Monmouth Regt 251st Div Supounce RE.	51st Div. Batt. Staff Scottish Cy. 5th Div 21st A.T. Cy R.E. 1/2 High Bng. R.F.A. (Heavy Battery) 1/1 Russian Body Armour Column

51st Do

2/1st Highland F.A.

May 1916.

COMMITTEE FOR THE
MEDICAL HISTORY OF THE WAR
Date 26 JUN 1916

WAR DIARY
INTELLIGENCE SUMMARY

2/1 N.F. Amb.
2/1 Northumbrian Div. Dist Col. 9

Place	Date	Hour	Summary of Events and Information	Remarks and references to Appendices
HAUTE AVESNES	9th May		Returned from leave to United Kingdom today. During my absence Major G.W. Miller 1/3 High. Field Amb. & Capt. Rm Fraser joined the unit.	
do	14th May		Captain R.M. Fraser RAMC is granted 8 days leave to U.K. on 15th inst.	
	15th May		Capt. King R/AMC returned from 8 days leave. He was now from one part of the advanced dressing station to another in the Highland Division A.N. 2117 to continue evacuation of certain Divs into wood by the Field Ambulance in Front of the 5th Division — an ambulance A. Dvs. No. 2624 received instructions in accordance with order by A.D.M.S. to report at War Office London on 30.9 forthwith with D.G.A.M.S. with a view to taking command of 2/2 High Fd Amb, Major G.W. Miller 1/3rd N.F. Amb to take our command from me 9/1. 2 N.F. Amb. In accordance with this order I proceeded today to England after handing over to Major Miller.	
		9pm		

Army Form C. 2118.

Sheet 2

X XIII

2/1. High F? Amb
(Robertson Lieut Colonel RAMC)
Molveston Camp

WAR DIARY
or
INTELLIGENCE SUMMARY.
(Erase heading not required.)

Place	Date	Hour	Summary of Events and Information	Remarks and references to Appendices
24.V.16 HAUTE HESDIN			Today I received command of the 2/1 H.F. Amb. Copies of Authority will be forwarded below and onwards in the files of the unit correspondence. WAR OFFICE letter begins " Lieut Colonel J. Robertson 2/1 High F. Ambulance "You are directed to return to France & rejoin on Monday next 22nd instant. Railway warrant to Folkestone attacks from Thames Charing Cross at 12.25 p.m. You should report to Folkestone Commandant for orders before." (signed) J McKinnon Major for Director General Army Medical Service letter infra. War Office 20/5/16 A.M.D.1. T.F. ADMS. 51st Hyl Div announces " Major G.W. Millen RAMC TF will hand over command of 2/1 High F. Amb to Lieut Colonel J ROBERTSON RAMCTF and upon 1/3rd H.F. Ambulance for duty. Lieut Colonel Robertson will take command at 9.am. 24 May 15/6." (signed) C.C. Fleming Colonel 51st Hyl Dis ADMS 51 Hyl Div letter inclo 23.V.16.	

WAR DIARY
or
INTELLIGENCE SUMMARY.

Army Form C. 2118.

May 1916
3rd 1/1st N Fd Amb
9/1 N Fd Amb
(Mobilization Crest)

Place	Date	Hour	Summary of Events and Information	Remarks and references to Appendices
HAUTE AVESNES	25th May 16		Captain Jarvis McAyo & eight men went forward with C.O. and one man was wounded on 21/5/16 while moving the personnel of the 131 Heavy Battery which was being shelled by gas shells and machinegun shells. The battery was about 200 yards East of ANZIN M & V B1 IV.	
	31/5/16		During the past week a standard relation of the Infantry Brigades has taken place so as to take over the front formerly held by the 152nd Infy Brigade which was between Stream with the exception that the unit and orderlies remains from the 154 Inf. Brigade Coy, no change in the duration of the unit has taken place. During the month the Ambulance has continued to admit all Sick & wounded "Hospital" patients of the Division + affiliated units.	

51st Division.

2/1. Highland Field Ambulance

June 1916.

COMMITTEE FOR THE
MEDICAL HISTORY OF THE WAR
Date 31 AUG 1916

Army Form C. 2118.

WAR DIARY
or
INTELLIGENCE SUMMARY.
(Erase heading not required.)

Sheet I

June
2/1 W.F.Amb.
Wheatin W.F. Amb

57

Hour, Date, Place	Summary of Events and Information	Remarks and references to Appendices
HAUTE AVESNES 7th June	This unit continues to work for 154th Staff Brigade and admits are not received sufficients cases during past week. Received orders from 2nd June that 1/2 W.F.Amb., Trucs opened at ECOIVRES on receiving (Variello) in the movements to nite of certain units (Variello) in the movements & neighbourhood, and that 1/3 W.F.Amb. admit all scratic cases in addition to finding the Durine Rest Station	Vol 10
do 9th June	The weekly returns of "Trench Feet" was discontinued from this week. Today a "Summary" of Medical arrangements in view of active operation was received. There are to be put in action on receipt of orders dated Lo. (Secret File.)	1st ms. orders H.Dnl. No. 25.6.5 (9.vi.16)
do 20th June	On Main (Colts Rm Frow) I New, & F Beaver details proceeded tomorrow to 30 C.C.S. to report for duty with OC of that unit. Special Returns of Wounds admitted between hours 6 am & 6 pm. required commencing on 25th inst. Also number remaining in F. Amb. in clearing stn at 6 am, Noon, & 9 pm.	H.Dnl. 25.6.5 (26.vi.16) S.D.M.3. 20 8/36 (21.vi.16) Mems 25.6.5 (26.vi.16)

Army Form C. 2118.

Sheet II

WAR DIARY
or
INTELLIGENCE SUMMARY.
(Erase heading not required.)

Instructions regarding War Diaries and Intelligence Summaries are contained in F.S. Regs., Part II. and the Staff Manual respectively. Title pages will be prepared in manuscript.

7 x VI
9/ I H.F. Amb.
Wiltshire Regt
Wiltshire cois

Hour, Date, Place	Summary of Events and Information	Remarks and references to Appendices
30th June HAUTE AVESNES	The inward activity of Trench mortars & artillery prevalent during past few days has in retaliation slightly risen. The wounded & wounded list this moving is partly caused by accidental bursts of bombs of which there have been as many as ten in one day. Movements Certain Officers attached with the unit are as follows:— Officers on Leave with sickness due to sickness Captain E.J. BLAIR previous Temporary attached Rejoined 14.VI.16 Officers Joining Capt. J. Mc A TITMAS from Hospital (No XII Stationary) 16.VI.16 LIEUT H.D. WRIGHT Rame. Confinement. attached Officers Quitting the unit Capt E.J. BLAIR Rejoined 1/7 R. Watch 14.VI.16. his original unit. lieut H.D. WRIGHT to 1/4 Durham for Duty. LIEUT. H.E. Fotrell Rame. Enjoined attached — per Latain & duty 24.VI.16 He last officer did duty for several days prior to previous Separation with 25th Brig, R.F.A. as RMO.	

51st Division

2/1 Highland. F. Ambulance.

July 1916

COMMITTEE FOR THE
MEDICAL HISTORY OF THE WAR
Date 13 SEP. 1915

2/1st HIGHLAND FIELD AMBULANCE
No. 2346
Date 1-8-16

A.D.M.S.
51st (High) Div.

Herewith please my War Diary for July 1916, tendered to you for necessary action under 51st Div. R.O. 567 of 13th July.

Robertson
Lt Col.
OC 2/1st (High) Div.

1-8-16.

WAR DIARY
or
INTELLIGENCE SUMMARY.
(Erase heading not required.)

Army Form C. 2118.

Sheet 1.
July.

XXVII
2/1 NZ Ambl

Hour, Date, Place	Summary of Events and Information	Remarks and references to Appendices
HAUTE AVESNES, 7 July 16	During the first week working parties from this unit have continued to improve the Dug out Breathing huts. Inspecting them against Drift Gas by Austin Screens and also attaching hose Dry out of Anamone Dressing Station with anti-gas machine – Vermorel Sprayers with sufficiency of Hyposulphite Thiosomine Solution Sprayers and the volume & wetting the Blanket Screens. Improvements for General character have also been continued. The Advanced Dressing Station equipment is now moved into a new bomb-proof shelter together with the Telephone wire for Ambulance with the shelter trains in ANZIN ST AUBIN have also been laid. Orders settings are also proceeded with. The Ingestion of sick & wounded passed through has been about normal. Ambulance trains carrying men of Bns. that the main Dressing Station "De kept clear for possibility of Salvonia number of Casualties have brought about a greater evacuation to C.C.S. & Casio firmans trains in	

Sheet II
July 1915

WAR DIARY
or
INTELLIGENCE SUMMARY.
(Erase heading not required.)

Army Form C. 2118.

XXVIII
9/1.1st Army
Wharton A.D.S.
Corny

Hour, Date, Place	Summary of Events and Information	Remarks and references to Appendices
HAUTE AVESNES July 9th	1st Field Ambulance and Rest Station has been therefore been struck as units furnish. Relieving of the Field Ambulances of the 60th Division have been attached to them and for training purposes. B Section 2/4th London 7th Ambulance joins 2nd Ame and on 2nd June and no Strength of The Strength (Ration) on 5th instant. Whereupon C Section of 2/5th London 7 Amb joins our ration strength. Under A.D.M.S. 51st H.Dis. N° 2719 received Operation order No. 13 by Colonel C.C. FLEMING, DSO. A.D.M.S. 51st H.D. Copy 4. This gives necessary orders for the relief of 51st Divisional Medical Units by 60th Div. The Ambulance will be relieved by the 2/6th London 7 Amb. An exchange of quarters was to effected this event moves to MINGOVAL on the 15th July at hour 5 grant. Subsequents 62 ratspies Today C Section 7 2/5 L.F. Amb rejoins its H.Q. and 1 platoon 7 2/4 London F. Amb joins.	Stock of units/rations
HAUTE AVESNES 10th July	Received from A.D.M.S. March Table dated 10th July.	

WAR DIARY or INTELLIGENCE SUMMARY

Army Form C. 2118.

Sheet III
July 1916

XIX & Corps / XIX Corps
J. Mulvahiri Cmdr

Hour, Date, Place	Summary of Events and Information	Remarks and references to Appendices
HAUTE AVESNES 10th July Contd	The Guards - marched. 9/6 Ludn. F. Amb. in conjunction with D.M. of this unit have arranged to exchange units & articles of Equipment - to save transport in accordance with D.D.M.S. instructions. Inventories & Receipts in duplicate are being prepared. Tents, Field Army Medical Panniers, Surgical Dressgs, and Wamco Serum reigns (a difference being retained by us) patients falls out Stores & Buckets. Red Cross Stores have been handed over to 9/6. Also practically the whole of unused Ordnance Station Equipment, people incl. Store Tent. The articles was handed over. Corresponding articles so far as were in possession of 9/6 London Sand. were left at MINGOVAL by that unit & taken over by us.	
MINGOVAL 13th July NOON	Intrale morning arm transferred to 9/6 London F. Amb. Corby. Orders instructions regarding defence & supplies Stores in event of an advance were handed to Captain Mathews as Adjutant. O.C 9/6 Ludn F. Amb. Receipt Vouchers for Stores Transports, recerus & Twen and this unit paraded at 8.30 A.M. in marching order, rendez...	

Army Form C. 2118.

Sheet 1
July
1916

91 N.F. Amb
Mindingen CS
Cmy

WAR DIARY
or
INTELLIGENCE SUMMARY.
(Erase heading not required.)

Instructions regarding War Diaries and Intelligence Summaries are contained in F.S. Regs., Part II and the Staff Manual respectively. Title pages will be prepared in manuscript.

Hour, Date, Place	Summary of Events and Information	Remarks and references to Appendices
MINGOVAL 13th July NOON	A Section Hy Section of Amb. having reported to H.Q. is struck off the ration strength. This Field Ambulance opened for receipt of sick at Noon today in Huts W. of MINGOVAL village. Instructions were received (A.D.M.S. no 22/9) that the 2/1 Hy. 3d Amb. would be responsible for evacuation sick in new Divisional Billeting area — and area T.T. & T. (Eastern) Also that all scabies cases would be admitted by them into.	
MINGOVAL 14th July 16 10 p.m.	Operation order no 14 by Colonel Fleming A.D.M.S. 51st N Dis received giving details of move of this unit to DOULLENS on 15th inst.	
DOULLENS 15th July 10 p.m.	Parading at 9.30 a.m. today the unit marches to DOULLENS in the rear of H.Q. Coy. Divisional Signals. A halt for an hour for feeding & watering was arranged in a field by the road side just north of GRAND RULLECOURT. Thence the unit marched by LUCHEUX arriving DOULLENS 7.15 p.m. The unit occupies billets at SOCIETE de PHOSPHATS	

(73989) W4141—463. 400,000. 9/14. H.&J.Ltd. Forms/C. 2118/10.

Army Form C. 2118.

XXXI
Sheet I Unit 1st Aust
July 2/1 W/Sqt 1st Aust
1916 M/Machine
       Corps

WAR DIARY
or
INTELLIGENCE SUMMARY.
(Erase heading not required.)

Hour, Date, Place	Summary of Events and Information	Remarks and references to Appendices
DOULLENS July 16th 3.30 a.m.	Orders recd from A.D.M.S. 31/2 D a form "Your unit will move today 16th from DOULLENS to BERNAVILLE AAA Starting point forked roads S.E. of CITADELLE at 7.10 am AAA Route GEZAINCOURT – FIENVILLERS AAA Report to Div H.Q. on arrival AAA Refilling point on 17th will be on road between BERNAVILLE and GORGES at 9 am. AAH Div H.Q. 6pm at RIBEAUCOURT at 11am AAA advbarty.	A.D.M.S. No 1488 Telegram
BERNAVILLE 16th July. 11.30	Arrived with whole unit at 11.30 am Today & were billetted in Billet No 93 & neighbourhood. Small number of sick of various units have been admitted. A dail total 1 Sick to be returned to A.D.M.S – non D – non abil. All sick have been transport to C.C.Stations unless treated case in A.P.D. Boster.	
BERNAVILLE 19th July. 6.30 p.m.	Received operation order No 37. 154 Infantry Brigade Copy no. 8. ordering movement of this unit to FLESSELLES Starting time 8 p.m. First Ambulance to move with Brigade transport of 154 Inf Brigade 78yd. M.G. Coy & with 1/2 High Fd Coy R.E.	

WAR DIARY or INTELLIGENCE SUMMARY

Army Form C. 2118.

Sheet VI XXII / 2/1 H'ghd Cas'ty Clg Stn
July 1916   of 51st (Highland) Division

Hour, Date, Place	Summary of Events and Information	Remarks and references to Appendices
BERNAVILLE. 19th July contd	6.30 G.P.M. Accordingly I proceeded to fit all available personnel & motor ambulances & filled the three M. Ambulances with men. The parts' marching with the Column were all mounted. Our journeys & the Motor Ambulances lifted the men. — Ambulance 11 miles	
EN ROUTE for PLESELLES 20th July 8 a.m.	Received High Div. Op. order no. 65 Army no. 26 which ordered the movement of the unit to RIBEMONT — the unit Rd at the starting point AMIENS — DOULLENS — DOUTHENS road, S. exit of VIGNIES GARAGE at 8:40 am today & march with 4thmcly Brampton Field Companies R.E. Route POISY, ALLONVILLE, QUERRIEU, LA HOUSSOYE, BONNAY and HEILLY.	
do. 6 p.m.	The unit transport, waited & passed before starting for PLESELLES personnel marched on foot. RIBEMONT reached by 1 P.M. Bde Gp. Guides waited in to point out Bivouacing ground which was from trakes further on at a Spot on Side of Road in North Side of River AMEE & midway between BERNANCOURT and MEAULTE — distance for the day 25 miles. I rode alone the men the A & M.T. journeyed in advance to Bivouac Ground.	
MEAULTE 12 midnight	indicated & returned to RIBEMONT for the men, also lifted men 1/2 FA Gy R.E. All personnel materials arrived satisfactorily. Other Communications from A.D.M.S. affecting the move but embraced by the Practice orders of 154 Bde and the Div. also numbered as follows:— M 1509, R1, W3, M1517 and M 1519	
do. 21st July 20. 11.10 a.m.	A.D.M.S. no. 1594 Intimate necessity of preparation for movement into the line at short notice	

WAR DIARY or INTELLIGENCE SUMMARY

Army Form C. 2118.

XXIII / 2/1 117th Field Ambulance / Autumn 1916 / Mametz–Guinchy(?)

Hour, Date, Place	Summary of Events and Information	Remarks and references to Appendices
MEAULTE. 21.VII.16	A.D.M.S. S.R. 2769. Cancels all previous appointed advanced Field Cards. A new list is issued. 51st Div. H.Q. SOME, Code Carbs S 1/2 - H-FAND STAG SF 1/3 " " STAR SI 2/1 " " STAY SJ	
do 6.20 pm	A.D.M.S. No. R.P. as follows received: "Your unit will take over the existing positions of the 19th Field Ambulance F.4, C.2.0. AAA advanced Dressing Station at Z. BLACK HUT. X.29.6.5.2. will also be taken over by you tonight AAA Bearer division from 1/3 proceeds to BLACK HUT to work with you 9 1/2 W.F. AMB where advanced Dressing Station is now FLATIRON COPSE AAA Div. H.Q. moves to FRICOURT tonight AAA Refilling Point nr- de VIVIER - ALBERT ROAD AAA Time unit to arrive later AAA A.D.M.S. Office will be near forked roads leading SE. J ALBERT. to Certs" General Arrangements Ohm of evacuation at present so far as possible north of BAZENTIN le GRAND wood. Advanced Bearer Post x road S.9.2.9.0. (2) QUARRY advanced Dressing Station S.14.C.3.4. (St. Blanes) (3) BLACK HUT, advanced Dressing Station X.29.6.5.2. (Bearer heart Entertainms) (4) "SUBWAY" BECORDEL F.7.a.9.4. (lying cases this is not a main Dressing Station and has no A.T.D Posts evacuate to MERICOURT	

WAR DIARY
or
INTELLIGENCE SUMMARY.
(Erase heading not required.)

Army Form C. 2118.

XXXIV Div Amb
9/1 Infy Bn
Mahacho? Comdt

Hour, Date, Place	Summary of Events and Information	Remarks and references to Appendices
MEAULTE. 6.30 pm. contd.	MEAULTE (5) FILE FACTORY Collecting Station for walking cases. Wounded Yorks to evacuated on main road alone BECORDEL F.7.c.20. The taken by horse transport to FILE FACTORY. A & D Sect men here Evacuate by Char-a-banc. (6) MERICOURT main Dressing Station for whole division. Evacuate by M.A.C. (stored to wires for).	
BECORDEL. 10 pm. 21. VII. 16	The unit arrives in accordance with above movement orders at F.7.C.20. and took over on from 19th Field Ambulance. The mess of B section & part of C were despatched forthwith to BLACK HUT. under Captn H. BEGG & Capt J. S[?] TITMAS. They were placed under orders of Commander of Bearer Div and were authorities heads to QUARRY (FLATIRON COPSE).	
BECORDEL 5 pm. 22nd July. de. 23 Jul.	ADMS No 2719 Containing new medical arrangements for new area received & filed after notice. The 2/1 High Fld Amb is in reserve. The 1/3 W. Amb is finding the principal advanced Dressing Station and the Divisional Collecting point. The latter is for walking cases. The 1/2 H.F. Amb provide the main Dressing Station. The Bearers of all three Ambulances are carrying wounded from Divisional Front - HIGH WOOD + neighbourhood.	

WAR DIARY
or
INTELLIGENCE SUMMARY.
(Erase heading not required.)

Army Form C. 2118.

Hour, Date, Place	Summary of Events and Information	Remarks and references to Appendices
BECORDEL 23rd July A.M.	To noon today 1 Corporal & 7 privates have been wounded by artillery fire.	
do 24th	Relief of Officers goes on. Four heavy Companies arrived. No Casualties today to noon.	
do 25th	To 12 noon today from noon yesterday 3 privates have been wounded by artillery fire. Subsequently 1 additional wounded was reported – 4 in all	
do 26th noon	By A.D.M.S. orders two tent Subdivisions complete were dispatched at 6 a.m. to Corps Dressing Station near DERNANCOURT, to co-operate with 13th Field Ambulance there. B + C Sections were dispatched. The position of the Dressing Station on map. Sheet 62 D.N.E is E.19.a.6.4. Casualties to personnel to noon today 1 N.C.O. & 12 men wounded. Artillery fire	
6.31st Noon	Total Casualties up to date for this unit are 1 killed and 47 wounded.	

2/11th Auckland F.A.

Aug. 1916.

WAR DIARY
or
INTELLIGENCE SUMMARY.

Army Form C. 2118.

Vol 12

Hour, Date, Place	Summary of Events and Information	Remarks and references to Appendices

BECORDEL.
3rd Aug.

In pursuance of orders from ADMS Captain D. McKELVEY MBBS has detailed to take temporary medical charge 1/8 Argyll and Sutherland's Pld in place of Capt. H. A. LUCAS who on relief reported to this unit for duty.

—do—
5th Aug

51st Division RAMC Overdrafts under 20/15. City No 7 was received today divesting the relief of medical units of protest under 9 53rd Division and this on relief their Ambulance Units move to another Area.
The area for the unit is Ref ALBERT Contour Sheet 1/40,000.

D. 15.6.

BECORDEL
6th August 9 am.

The HQ of 101st Field Ambulance arrived at tour our Ambulance's Stores from transport. That unit moves off at

D. 15.6
6th August.

9.30 leaves two tent subdivisions which are on duty at "Y" main Dressing Station, SENANCOURT.

2/1 Highland Field Amb, less 8TC under Capt. Sub-division arrived at our Billeting Areas.
During the morning with our 54 fm Rouse Bank
R.A.M.C. STABLES. Lieut W.P. was included in the 54

Sheet II

LXXVII 1st Canadian
2/1 1914/15 2nd Army
Manchester
(Cavalry)

WAR DIARY
or
INTELLIGENCE SUMMARY.
Army Form C. 2118.

(Erase heading not required.)

Hour, Date, Place	Summary of Events and Information	Remarks and references to Appendices
D.I.5.b. 11 A.m. 7th Aug.	A.D.M.S. to R.I. Menu on forms. Division moves on 7th 9th August to Area PONTREMY - LONGPRE as follows. (a) All horse Transport and Dismounted train by road on 7th & 8th Aug. (b) All infantry and Ammunition limbers by train under orders to entrain 5.A.M. & Q.M.G. AAA Refilling points 7th Aug. E14c 4.5. at 9:30am 8th - E14c A.5. at 7am. 9th - AMIENS - ALLONVILLE road West of ALLONVILLE at 5:30 a.m. 10th August SOREL at 9 a.m. AAA Divisional H.Q. opens at PONT REMY at 10 a.m. on 9th inst and closes at RIBEMONT at 7th same hour AAA Transport of Divn units move with their under orders of 154th Infantry Bde AAA 7th Aug to POULAINVILLE starting point X roads D30.a.9.4. 15/10 a.m. H.Q. group at ½ mile distance (H.Q. Group thence at 9 p.m.) Route HANGUEVILLE QUERRIEUX ALLONVILLE 9-August L'BERONDELLE LIERCOURT. DOUDEL- AINVILLE HUPPY HACHENNEVILLE Starting point X roads at E. of POULAINVILLE at 9:10 a.m. AAA ack	

Sheet *X*
XXXVIII
2/1. N.F. Amb.
August 1916
Major in Comd.

Army Form C. 2118.

WAR DIARY
or
INTELLIGENCE SUMMARY.
(Erase heading not required.)

Place	Date	Hour	Summary of Events and Information	Remarks and references to Appendices
D.19.b.	6/8/16	2 pm	Dispatched the whole of Horse Transport with all stores required under the command of Captain B.G. BEVERIDGE, & Captain H. BEGG, to join the Brigade Group Transport at starting point.	
do	do	10 pm	Received A.D.M.S. No. 2719 of this date being "Extracts from administrative instructions for Railway movement to No 5 Area." "The Brigadier General Commanding Supply Area will issue orders for the march & entraining station & all units in that area. The Senior Ambulance officer on each train will command & be responsible for the entrainment & detrainment of the troops. Troops will not arrive at the entraining station before the times laid down on the attached Time Table. Troops will be entrained with the utmost speed and will not wait the zero off in Supplies. Detrain at station for all trains is LONGPRÉ.	

Railway Time Table — 9th August.

Units	Time btw at station	Departure	Type of Train	Remarks
EDGE HILL	2/1 N.F. Amb.	16.15 horse	17 horse	2 Lieut Colman 152 2d Brigd. 2/2 attached to Command the trains
	1/2 do	do	Supply	
	1/3 do	do		

WAR DIARY
or
INTELLIGENCE SUMMARY

Army Form C. 2118.

XXXIX / 1st N.M.F.Amb. M.L.R.
Wilhelm
9/1 N.F.Amb. M.R.
August

Instructions regarding War Diaries and Intelligence Summaries are contained in F.S. Regs., Part II. and the Staff Manual respectively. Title pages will be prepared in manuscript.

(Erase heading not required.)

Place	Date	Hour	Summary of Events and Information	Remarks and references to Appendices
HERCOURT	10th Aug.		The personnel of this unit duly arrived at Bullshit Area in No 5 Ama, at 9am. today. 154 Brigade Operation order no 68 contain information to Instruction for move of Dismounted Troops into march Table reserves (Offre no ZZ/444) It was the same as Parking Time mounts of M.D.A.S. also noted. Delay was experienced in entraining the troops of our 6 horse due to fact that the train had just be unloaded of Ammunition which took over 4 hours and then there was no Engine to pull it back to LONG PRE. The 8t. Train Telegraphs to MERICOURT & MERICOURT about an engine and the train started about 1.30 a.m. on 10th inst. The men were distributed 40 to a truck & the trucks from hinge were kept for Officers. The railway journey took over 3 hours. Reported to A.D.M.S. & 154 Brigade on arrival. Unit is located in Chateau & Grounds HERCOURT. The Medical Arrangements in the area (Orders Offre no 2719) of Corps date (Apport dead) provides for evacuation of sick to No 2 Stationary Hospital ABBEVILLE. Supplies of Medical Stores from 2 Stationary Hosp. Base Depot Med. Stores ETAPLES or No 14 A.D.M.Stor CORBIE. Self inflicted Injuries to be sent to 39 C.C. Station ALLONVILLE. Arrangements for Entraining of the Division at PONT REMY as LONG PRÉ are contained in Opd no 26. 51st W. Div. 2d A.I. no 4. which was receive. A medical Officer for each Station (see details).	

Army Form C. 2118.

WAR DIARY
or
INTELLIGENCE SUMMARY.

(Erase heading not required.)

Sheet V
August

Instructions regarding War Diaries and Intelligence Summaries are contained in F. S. Regs., Part II. and the Staff Manual respectively. Title pages will be prepared in manuscript.

Place	Date	Hour	Summary of Events and Information	Remarks and references to Appendices
LIERCOURT	10/VIII/16		The march table accompanying Div. Op. order SKG (as above) Entrainment at PONTREMY	DETRAINMENT at Detrain STEENBECQUE
Cont'd			Train no.	Notific. no.	Unit	Arrive	Entrained	Departs		
			15¢	517¢ 5193	No 2 Coy Div Train 2/1 H.F. Amb	19.55	21.55	22.55	
			A billeting party consisting of Capt. J.H.A. TITMAS, interpret Lcombe, were despatched by train no.1 about 23.35 today to proceed to EBBLINGHAM and arrange billets for the unit.	
			In accordance with A.D.M.S. 20. 27/9. an ambulance car machine gun unit supply of drugs dressings was and stores entraining station to remain at station. The entrainment of the Division is complete & the train to Strackens are to proceed by road to EBBLINGHEM on 12th inst.	
FEBLINGHAM	12/VIII/16		The unit arrived here at 2 P.M. and formed hospital in Chalon & Granges 1000 yards East of EBBLINGHAM Station the medical personnel sent to Rolaine Station Farm. The evening being completed to establish	
do	13/VIII/16		A.D.M.S. states need for stores must be done on 14th inst before 12 noon to BLARINGHAM and file out the RASC accepts 5th & ½ Hqr Field Ambulance this was Div affiliated with the 152nd Infantry Brigade	

Army Form C. 2118

Sheet II XLI.
August N.Z.1 (N.Z. Cavalry) N.Z.

WAR DIARY
or
INTELLIGENCE SUMMARY. 9/1 (N.Z. Cavalry Bde) of Western Front

(Erase heading not required.)

Instructions regarding War Diaries and Intelligence Summaries are contained in F.S. Regs., Part II. and the Staff Manual respectively. Title pages will be prepared in manuscript.

Place	Date	Hour	Summary of Events and Information	Remarks and references to Appendices
ERRINGHAM	13/VIII/16		A.D.M.S. nos. 27/9, 9/12 P. content indicate that this unit will take over the Rest Station and present occupants by the 2nd NEW ZEALAND Fd Ambulance at L'ESTRADE. Advance party reported on 17th man body on 17th August. Transport by road. Dismounted personnel by train on 18th in 2 STEENWERCK thence by road.	
BLARINGHEM	14/VIII/16	noon	This unit duly arrived at BLARINGHAM and took over from 1/2 & H.F. and 1 army hounds over the Birmingham Rest Stn to 2nd New Zealand Field Ambulance. 51st H.D. Division A.R.A.M.C. Operation order 2016, copy 12) dated 13th August received, for moves for the relief of the Ambulances of New Zealand Division in the front line, by the H.Y. and 15 Divisions. Fd Ambs. Respectively. Duty taken by 4 Hrs Divs, 51st Div. 16-17th August of further gas anchor but in our area given.	
do	17/VIII/16		152nd Infantry Brigade Operation order No. 45, 59 Chs 12 appendices for the moves of the Brigade & appendices around ARMIENTIERS.	
L'ESTRADE	18/VIII/16		In accordance with orders received this unit and arrived at L'ESTRADE F. Stn on Rest Station taken from rear party of 2nd New Zealand Fd Ambulance. Receipt was given for a large amount of stores & treasuries.	
do	19/VIII/16		H.Q. Div. Rest. Station opened for receipt of patients at 2 p.m. today.	

#353 Wt W2544/1454 700,000 5/15 D.D. & L.   A.D.S.S./Forms/C. 2118.

Army Form C. 2118

Sheet XI
August

WAR DIARY
or
INTELLIGENCE SUMMARY.
(Erase heading not required.)

XLII
9/1 W.P. Anderson
[signature] Lieut Col. RAMC

Place	Date	Hour	Summary of Events and Information	Remarks and references to Appendices
L'ESTRADE	22/VIII/16		Information having been received that Sniping Stores that left behind at the Divisional Dump prior to going South to Somme area, were now available for them at ARMENTIERES, 2 G.S. Wagons were sent with the N.C.O. who handed over the Stores from the unit to the Dis Dump. The N.C.O. found the items of our Stores were at A.R.M.I.S. NT15 20s & that no handing of them in respect to the unit to 6th Brigade of Canadians Enquiry about when to start.	
L'ESTRADE	23/VIII/16		MEDICAL ARRANGEMENTS for burial of 51st Highland Div AREA, carefully gone into & settled with DO. RAMC 51st H. The Rendezvous for collecting stretcher wounded. Nominations position for all advanced units. Arrangements for Bearer Divn Bearers Regiments Subdivd.- BAILLEUL; (2) Arrangements in Event of Active Operations (3) Arrangements for Joint Retreat to Intermediary and Retreat Summary Line. (4) Arrangement for Retreat measure of Advice Conseille. 51st Highland Divisional RAMC Orchestra relief in 15 minutes. This provides for the movement of 51st DS Rest Station & STEENWERCK on 30th August by 12 horses, arriving there by 10 Divisional on 27th inst.	
STEENWERCK	30/VIII/16		REST STATION moved into new position & selected in STEENWERCK Town and villas of 71st Field Ambulance.	

2/1st Highland Field Ambulance.

51st Div.

Sept. 1916

COMMITTEE FOR THE
MEDICAL HISTORY OF THE WAR
Date 26 OCT. 1915

WAR DIARY
or
INTELLIGENCE SUMMARY.
(Erase heading not required.)

Army Form C. 2118.

2/1 Westriding Sanit
9/1 WF Front Mesopotamia Sept

Place	Date	Hour	Summary of Events and Information	Remarks and references to Appendices
STEENWERCK	1/9/16		On take of A.D.M.S. Capt J.S. McCormack of the village Sanitary offices of this village Question raised re refuse	
			27th Aug. Administrative Instructions on O.O. 79 Copy No 94	
			28 Aug. 51st H. Div RAMC O.O. No 15 Copy No 7 Provides for movement of D.R.S. to STEENWERCK	
			29 Aug. ADMS Table. No 1957. Officers GOCs mounts kitted up to STEENWERCK	
			2.IX.16 ADMS 2949. Med of Issue Book of the 153 Brigade Transport	
			2.IX.16 51st H. Div RAMC O.O. No 19 Copy No 6 Provides medical arrangements for an extra Brigade area to inundated North of Armt. Line Arrangements taken up by 1/2 H.F. Amb.	
			5.IX.16 51st H.D. RAMC OO No 20 Copy No 9 received providing for the relief of the Indian personnel doing duty with 154 Ind Bngde in this area. Relief by 57 Fd Amb	
			7.IX.16 ADMS No 2942. The IVth Div. Supply Column interfered with Field Ambulance lorry of this Division has fourth order.	
			On this date the 2nd ANZAC regis-tered their protests Thus reports from The Church Authorities of STEENWERCK. The Schools etc required by this Field Ambulance 51st H. Div r.g.O. No 21. Arrangements for attachment to Brigade - Fd Ballys - Artillery - 1/2 HF Amb. Captain D. McKELVEY was posted to Medical Charge 16th Gordon Highlanders 5 ads./ADMS	
	8/9/16			

WAR DIARY or INTELLIGENCE SUMMARY

Army Form C. 2118.

XLIII
3/1 West Rid Amb
Wdn Coy
Mthn

Place	Date	Hour	Summary of Events and Information	Remarks and references to Appendices
STEENWERK	19th Sept 16		Captain R.M. FRASER posted to Assistant Charge of 1/9 Royal Scots	
	20		Captain T. J.A. TITMAS posted to relieve Charge of 1/7 Gordon Highlanders	
			Capt. D. MCKELVEY evacuated to Base as a patient - Strained Ankle from 1/6 Gordons	
	20		Captain GEORGE DICK from England reinforcement arrives as 19 Z and taken on strength pro tem status	
			Aug. 51st H.D. RAMC OO No 22. Army M.S. provides for relief of the 1/3 & 1/2 H.F Amb's 4th Australian & 102nd Fd Amb. respectively. Relief of the 51st H. Div. commences 22-23rd Septr	
	21/IX/16		ADMS. No 30/27 must evacuate to Estaires Cy and advances to D.R.S. from Today. "D.R.S. evacuates all sick to C.O. Stn".	
	24/IX/16		51st H. Div RAMC OO. No 23 Cny ws I. reward providor for the move of this unit to ESTAIRES on 25th instant to form the 154th Inf Brigs troops marching by PONT MORTIER LANNOY STEENWERK at 2pm	
ESTAIRES	25/9/16		Arrived at H 30(pm), and Demed Hospital in PENSIONAT DEMOISELLES. Received Accommodation Arrangements 30.12 in new town area	

Attc: DRS, at STEENWERK and the 10/4 7th Fd Amb, Rue DAVIS of 8/1 West Rd arranged to take over sketch. Accompanying of furniture etc of Same It

Army Form C. 2118.

Sheet 3

WAR DIARY
or
INTELLIGENCE SUMMARY.

2/1 N.F. Amb.
Wakuhtu 2/Lt Pah
Coulp

XLIV

Instructions regarding War Diaries and Intelligence Summaries are contained in F. S. Regs., Part II. and the Staff Manual respectively. Title pages will be prepared in manuscript.

(Erase heading not required.)

Place	Date	Hour	Summary of Events and Information	Remarks and references to Appendices
ESTAIRES	26/9/16		Received 154 Inf Brigade No. S. 12/15 Secret instructing Brigade to form Bde to proceed to DOMART EN PONTHIEU. The 51st Division is moving to Rear Army area. Detailed Captain Dick as billeting officer. Received A.I. 51st N Div. No. 13. Cpl. No. 255 will take horses, Mrs. Inst transport by train. Motor Omnibus arrives 5 hours to CRAMONT. (by LENS) (11 hours) Debanny Siding CANDAS, From J departure 2.05 am. 12 October for MERVILLE. A.D.M.S. number 8027. Received orders by Medical Officer 65th detachment for embarkment & detrainment date at MERVILLE & CANDAS respectively. Commences at 9am on 30th Sept October.	
do	29/9/16		Since departure of the unit from STEENWERCK Captain G.E. ARGO has resumed return to records attend the Commandant Company of 51st Div A.I. as 14. Copy No 32. Amendments to administrative instruction on move received. Amendments to Brigade OO. N. 56 received (22.603) No attachys of men of this unit after decorations. Provincial time resumed at midnight tonight. Ambulance to move away at 10 pm to Sutherm at MERVILLE.	
do	30/9/16			

149/196

51st Division

1/1. Highland Field Ambulance

Oct 1915.

COMMITTEE FOR THE
MEDICAL HISTORY OF THE WAR
Date -2 DEC. 1916

Army Form C. 2118.

WAR DIARY
or
INTELLIGENCE SUMMARY

1/1 H.F. Amb.
Wheeler KCB Comdg

Vol 14

Place	Date	Hour	Summary of Events and Information	Remarks and references to Appendices
FIENVILLERS	1/7/16		After train journey by night the unit detrained at CANDAS & marched to FIENVILLERS where hospital was opened for Sick 154th Brigade. Captain GAEARGO performed the Bn [illegible] medical duties at MERVILLE. Capt. B.G. BEVERIDGE at CANDAS during retirement. 1st Divisional Hospl. Capt. Ross Reaves reported with his Coy to Hd Qtrs of 3rd Horse Feds. 154th Infantry Brigade operation order no 57 Cpy no 10 received	2nd rpt Capt Ross Capt Beck reported Capt Off att 29th B.G.S. for Duty 27/5 - 3/7 1953
	2/7/16		51st High Div. R.A.M.C. O.O. No 84. Copy No 28 received. Transport for the field Ambulances taking over from 100th Field Ambulance the Dressing Stn at COVIN (J.1.b.6.6.) and advanced Dressing Stn at HEBUTERNE (K.15.6.7.3.) and opening for reception of Sick. Transmitted from the Brigade in the line. (152 Inf Brigade.) Advance parties were now up ready on 3rd [illegible].	R.P.L.
			Motored from COVIN & HEBUTERNE in charge of the 154 Inf. Brigade ranks, main body of Ambulance to SARTON accompanying Major Wright, Officer of Scouts. Command.	
	3/7/16		154th Infantry Brigade O.O. No 58 Copy No 9 received. Brigade minor & Bush in ARTOIS Lieut. T.A. MATTHEWS ROME posted to unit for duty	
			Mar. 4 1/7/16. Lieut (A.) moved to COVIN & ambulances riding of 100th F. Amb.	
SARTON		11:30 a.m.	Hospital opened in the Ambulance buildings for Sick evacuated from El. Bois. Old Mill & [illegible] [illegible] relatives with Rank of 2 privates platoon at AID POST	
			BAILLY AU BOIS (J.16.a.7.7.)	

Army Form C. 2118.

WAR DIARY
or
INTELLIGENCE SUMMARY

(Erase heading not required.)

XLVI
1/1 H.F.Amb.
Major ?J.W.?
Oct 5

Place	Date	Hour	Summary of Events and Information	Remarks and references to Appendices
COVIN	5/7/16		51st H.Div. RAMC O.O. No 25, Cap. No 23, received. Transfer for move of H.F.Amb. not required. Advanced Dressing Station to BUS NO.MAISON. from 10 a.m. on 6th October. Evacuation from Corps via the line we held via Advanced Dressing Station HEBUTERNE to main Dressing Station 1/2 H.F.Amb. at COUIN to AMIS.	
	6/7/16		Handed over Dressing Station COUIN to 57th Field Ambulance 17th Div. and moved to huts at I.26.c.0.4.	
BUS	7/7/16		51st H.Div. RAMC O.O. No 26. Cap. No 26. received. Provides for relief of Advanced Dressing Station HEBUTERNE by 59th Field Amb. on 8th Oct. Personnel to regain H.Q. unit as relief. Two MCs Ambulances to be left for movement of 51st Div. Canadian(?)	
	8/7/16		Personnel returned H.Q. from Advanced Dressing Station together with equipment belonging to this unit - All other stores handed over and receipt obtained.	
BUS	9/7/16		RAMC O.O. No 27. Cap. No 28. refers Dressing Sta H.F.Amb. to Corps main D.S. Station. COUIN for duty in woods & Camps. A working party of 70 men and an officer detailed for duty with 1/2 908(?) R.E. on Michig(?) front for innumered(?) K.21.C.97. Making from Bus huts steel frag	XIII

WAR DIARY or INTELLIGENCE SUMMARY

Army Form C. 2118.

XLVII
2/1 N.F. Amb: Mobilisation LCol Crosby

Major [illegible] Sheet 3

Date	Hour	Summary of Events and Information	Remarks and references to Appendices
13/8/16		Act as relay post for trams carrying patients for BRIGGS – Reg. As/pt. and COLINCAMPS. adv. Dressing Statn.	
14/8/16	8AM 00 to 28	8h to 32. Received 1/2 N.F. Amb. with open car Drivers Station at COLIN CAMPS on 15th Oct. taking charge of the evacuating cases from 57th H. Div. up to the camion ad of 59th Field Amb 14th Div. The two cars supplies to the Amb. (½) began to on 15th 7.30 pm	
		ADM.S. No. 3027. 7 to-day act. receive ordering the Tent Division of the units to COVIN. VIIIth Corps Main Dressing Station Beauchamp etc. Units evacuate sick in BUS to ARTOIS and thence to COVIN. B Section of Majors of the XIIIth Corps Main Dressing Station set apart for that unit in which B-teen for receipt of wounded)	
	6 PM	1 Medicine accompanied VIIIth Corps aviation No. 2 becoming on 19th inst – 10.35. And on temp duty amendments to same. Draft notice arrangement 57th H[?] Division Received. Provides for dispatch of advice message in orders[?] [illegible] accompanies person referring advice of action. The Main Dress: 2/1 N.F. Amb. will accept wounded from Divisional Front 24 hours after Zero following up & taking orders of 1/3 N.F. Amb. relieves [illegible] for Main Division 12 hours later	

#353 Wt. W2544/1454 700,000 5/15 D.D.&L. A.D.S.S./Forms/C. 2118.

XL VIII

Army Form C. 2118.

WAR DIARY
or
INTELLIGENCE SUMMARY.
(Erase heading not required.)

Mc Fawlu
Midcolmon West
County

Place	Date	Hour	Summary of Events and Information	Remarks and references to Appendices
BUS	14/7/16		Tent Divisions of 31st MT and will work at COUIN Main Dressing Station along with the Tent Divisions of 51st H. Divisions. Print medical arrangements for 51st H. Div. received. (Mentioned hereon in draft)	
COUIN	16/7/16		51st H. Div. R.A.M.C. O.O. nos 28, 29 Chr. no 13. received. Orders for the handing over of Advanced Dressing Station & Main Dressing Station held by Tn at Chin Comps & BUS respectively to 1st and 2nd/1st and of 31st Division	
	17/7/16		Warning order A.D.M.S. no 3/115 received extending movement of 31st Div. to BEAUMONT HAMEL front. Action of return on Northern front being postponed.	
	18/7/16		R.A.M.C. O.O. no 30 Chr. no 26 of A.D.M.S. 31st Div. received. 2/1 H.F. amb will march on 18th October to PUCHEVILLERS and extract fresh from 154 Brigade.	
VAUCHELLES LES AUTHIE	19/7/16		PUCHEVILLERS changes to VAUCHELLES taking over from a Tn amb of 31st Div. (93 ")	(93)
	28/7/16		Medical arrangements V Corps. no 6. Chr. no 21 received 31st H. Div. Administrative Instructions for Operations (21/8/16) Chr. no 87 received 31st Div. Medical arrangements Operation 2, with Annexture 2, with Annexture to Operation Keens.	

Army Form C. 2118.

WAR DIARY
or
INTELLIGENCE SUMMARY.

(Erase heading not required.)

Army Form C. 2118.

XLIX

2/1 W.R[iding] Field Ambulance West County

Place	Date	Hour	Summary of Events and Information	Remarks and references to Appendices
AVEUELLES	24/6/16		For forth coming operation This unit will be divided into four portions for separate departments –	
			1. Field Ambulance NAVEHELLES – In V.Corps Stock 2 Coll. Prisoners in	
			2. Reserve Division with Officer Incharge MAILLY-MAILLET in Reserve during first 48 hours.	
			Litters and carrying between Fire trenches and Advanced front at AUCHONVILLERS for Subsequent	
			3. Unloading 2nd & 31st Div Walking wounded Collecting Station BEAUSART	
			1 Tent Subdivision (C Section) will do two hospitals transport	
			4. Divisional parked motor ambulance Cars met a Divisional Officer of this Unit Evacuating wounded between AUCHONVILLERS & FORCEVILLE	
			5. Distribution of this Unit to be made at 8p.m. on Y day which will be day previous to commencement of active operations known as Z day. Stretcher whole left	
do	25/6/16		Lieut T.A. MATTHEWS nominated from the army on posting to 11th Division Capt. McGraw Rowe returned from duty with 29th C.C.S.	
			The complete and not of this of the ambulance & relief registry of the walking wounded Collecting Station proceeds with these officers and are Surveying the trenches R.A.p.165 &c	
do	27/6/16		Capt. RM Ennis ordered to proceed forth with to 15 pm 39 Division.	
do	30/6/16		While Active operations are in abeyance this unit continues to admit sick, accidents from the Division & neighbouring Country.	

140/849.

2/1st Highland Field Ambulance.

51st Div.

Nov 1916

COMMITTEE FOR THE
MEDICAL HISTORY OF THE WAR
Date −3 JAN. 1917

WAR DIARY
or
INTELLIGENCE SUMMARY.

Army Form C. 2118.

Vol 15
L.
2/1 High: 9 Ambs YOA
(Yeomanry amb)

Place	Date	Hour	Summary of Events and Information	Remarks and references to Appendices
VAUCHELLES	6/11/16		2 day having performed from day to day since the mine & Operation orders were postponed indefinitely. Today rations were known would be given on W day if not first. Intimation received that 2 day was to be 9th November.	
	9/11/16		2 day was postponed D→O th Inst and today "Active Operation postponed indefinitely" was intimated. NOMS w. 311F	
	10/11/16		Intimation received 2 day to be 13th November.	
	11/11/16		NOMS. am. 311F of today intimate that 51st H.D. medical arrangements operation 2 of 22nd Oct. with amendments come into force from 6 p.m. Sunday 12th Nov. 1916.	
			Election 2nd Lieutenant and Capt J.S. McConnachie with Capt Tetlow took up new positions at BEAUSART. January 1/1f of the Combined 2nd & 51st Div. Walking Wounded Collecting Station. The officer i/c 2nd Div 2nd Subdivision to be in charge of the combined station. Capt J.S. McConnachie reports for duty with his party at 3 p.m. on 12th Nov. to Capt. Roberts 5th Field Ambulance.	
	12/11/16		Captain E.G. BEVERIDGE was placed in charge 2/1 W.Y. Amb. Reserve Division with Captain G.A.E. ARGO & Captain Henry BEGG, m/o of this unit. He reports to Lt. 1/c W.Y. Amb. at MAILLY-MAILLET (0% Welling Wounded, 5th Div) at 5 p.m. this day.	

Army Form C. 2118.

WAR DIARY
or
INTELLIGENCE SUMMARY
(Erase heading not required.)

2/1 H.C. amb.
1st Bn
Yorkshire
army

Place	Date	Hour	Summary of Events and Information	Remarks and references to Appendices
VAUCHELLES	12/11/16	4 p.m.	The Motor Ambulances will draw 7 days rations reported to O/C Convoy of Vaucelles, mounted.	
			The first dressing of A.T.S. units received at VAUCHELLES for reception of wounded if all sick & surplus moved.	
			ZERO HOUR intimated as 13th Nov. 5:45 am.	
	13/11/16		The Highland Division attacked "Y Ravine" "Beaucourt Ravine" to EAST of BEAUMONT HAMEL. Other Divisions to Right & Left also attacked. Objectives attained by 9 am. Snow and rain incurred.	
			Captain HENRY BEGG was killed in action this morning about 9 am. It was in the Company of LIEUT PETERS. No 16 Forsyth when at the front and Sgt.T.P.B. EMSLIE of the unit. Capt Emslie was appointed this day by the Commission of Reg. Body. Capt Begg was removed to N.R. I and home for burial which took place at 3 pm. Very light, rain and Maj P. SINCLAIR, Staff Officer, Minister, Hines. Burial was at with side of the Village to annexe of Civilian Cemetery extended for burial of Military & other Burials about 50-60 yards to E of a shrine seen from the South side of Civilian Cemetery between U and a road running S.W of village Evin. main MARIEUX Road	Vauchelles France Sheet 57D I 26 d. 9.8.
	20/11/16		Capt N.E. Macdonough RADTC.	
	24/11/16		154 Inf Brigade OO. no 79 copy no 60 received. Promoting Temp Lieut/Temp Lieut. Lieut. (paras 1, 2, 3, 19 & 21 '16) and under Bn. Gen. Com. 2/134 Brig. in 6 VARENNES. Marie Table attending Lecture on 23	
			Memo. OO. no 31 Copy no 17 transfer for name J 1/3 W. Ambl. to PUCHVILLERS with 153 Inf Brigade (2ch) and inventory form sent to 6 ANEPE with rigs on 23rd next.	

Army Form C. 2118.

Aout 2 1916

WAR DIARY
or
INTELLIGENCE SUMMARY.

(Erase heading not required.)

2/11st Amb.
Malvern Well
Army

Place	Date	Hour	Summary of Events and Information	Remarks and references to Appendices
VARENNES	23/7/16	9pm	Arrived here & parked in huts beside 11th C.C.S. & Varennes Asbury Road. ADMS. O.C. moves to No 44 C.C.S. Puchevillers stopping for Chi. Bronfarts	154 Bde. O.O. No 70.
PUCHE-VILLERS	24/7/16	2pm	Orders here from Varennes accompanying the 154 Inf Brigade.	
do	25/7/16		March O.O. no 372 M. Bde received. Orders to move this unit to ALBERT & take over from 11th Canadian Field Ambulance. Stated at the Schot W.28.c.2.5. Sheet 57 D. have to take place on 26th. No 372	
do	do		154 Inf. Bde. O.D. no 57. Copy to 10 & Recons parties for new 65 Brigade Area at x.4.d., x.8.d., x.13.b. Convoy under orders 92nd Corps, on 26th inst	
ALBERT	26/7/16		Having ascertained that billets in Brigade Area were not obtainable and that to have huts & ALBERT is inter fronts was premier the 11th Canadian F. Amb having accented to SCHOOL there and A.D.M.S. having authorised the completion I have returned hereto. The unit arrived to retenet to Day and F.A. were for 11th Canal F. Amb. ammun O.C. dusk. Reports to Brigade N.Q.	
do	27/7/16		Opened main Dressing Station ins St Division. A Cars, No 20 M.A.C. attached for Rations. Evacuation to Div Rest Station SENLIS, 9 C.C.S. Contay. Off Nur Pod. GEZAINCOURT Sedes came nots 35 sick ?. cast & Sick, 420 men attached from and unit 29th C.C.S. rejoined until on the 20th inst	

140/1900

51st Div.

2/1st Highland Field Ambulance

Dec 1916

COMMITTEE FOR THE
MEDICAL HISTORY OF THE WAR
Date 31 JAN. 1917

A D M S
51 H Div

Herewith, please, my
War Diary as O.C this Unit
during December, for necessary
action.

M Martin
LT COL
O C 2/1 High Fd Amb

31.12.16

WAR DIARY
INTELLIGENCE SUMMARY

Army Form C. 211

Unit: 21 K.F.Amb / 31st Division

Place	Date	Hour	Summary of Events and Information	Remarks and references to Appendices
ALBERT	11th Dec		Sent about 150 men under O.M.S. Davis & then sent out tentage and Pack-transport to repair the build at Chateau AVELUY for occupants of The unit at Fieus, as not indicated but.	
"	11th		Major J.H. STEPHEN R.A.M.C. 12th Hussars F.M. Amb. joined the unit for duty. Lt. Col. J. Robinson newton-dean till 23rd inst. Major J. Pringle took over command in his absence.	M.3527 A.D.M.S.
"	12th		Under orders from D.M.S 5th Army through A.D.M.S. 37th Div. evacuated Field and Hospital in ALBERT and moved to CHATEAU AVELUY. Move was completed by 2.30 p.m.	
AVELUY	15th		Capt. G.D. FAIRLEY R.A.M.C. joined field ambulance as a reinforcement.	
"	16th		MAJOR J.H. STEPHEN left under orders to rejoin 89 F. Field Ambulance.	
"	17th		Capt. T.B.A. TITMAS proceeded England on leave	
"	19		Capt. J.S. McConachie proceeds on leave & joined today	
"	24th		R.A.M.C. O.O. No 33. Copy No 27. Providing for the relief 1/13 Hyd F.A. and 2/1 W.R. Amb by contenth- exchange Duties	
"	26		This unit therefore took over the collecting ground from the front area and one today Hospital as follows.	

Army Form C. 2118.

WAR DIARY
or
INTELLIGENCE SUMMARY

(Erase heading not required.)

Army Form C. 2118.

L IV / 1/12 1/1 Auste / 2/1 1/12 Wheeler Ward / Convoy

Place	Date	Hour	Summary of Events and Information	Remarks and references to Appendices
OVILLERS HUTS	29/8/16		Having handed over the Ambulance Quarters at AVELUY CHATEAU to the 1/3 N.F.Amb. the Unit H.Q. & the unit were moved to OVILLERS HUTS. W.13.a.4.6. Advanced Dressing Stations were taken over at R.8.O.C. and R.29.d.5.F. These serve regimental aid posts at RED CHATEAU & R.29 Central respectively. There are the only regimental aid posts for ordinary infantry in the line held by 51st Div. They also serve the working parties who have no M.O. in the neighbourhood. Medical Aid Post at POZIERES X.4.b.8.5. Tramway convoy X.4.c.5.4. Motor Ambulance Station at POZIERES just the West Ambulances for transport of sick evacuated from M.D.S. the Main M.D. 2/3 N.F.Amb. here are taken over. Ordnance & Medical stores there were known, and the kits of Salvaging the Dressing Station at TARA HILL proceeded with. Evacuation from POZIERES for sick wounded is by OVILLERS VILLAGE ROAD & thence to AVELUY. The N.F.Amb. are employed in fatigue parties from H.Q. N.F.Amb. making a dug out at R.29.d.5.F. (Creighton Post) putting up huts here & in making a dug out at R.29.d.5.F. (Creighton Post)	Sheet 57.D. SUNKEN R.d / CREIGHTON'S POST / Reference

S

51st Div.

2/1st Highland Field Ambulance

149/9+1

Jan 1917

COMMITTEE FOR THE
MEDICAL HISTORY OF THE WAR
Date 13 MAR. 1917

WAR DIARY or **INTELLIGENCE SUMMARY**   Army Form C. 2118.

Sheet 1 January '17

Place	Date	Hour	Summary of Events and Information	Remarks and references to Appendices
OVILLERS HUTS	5.1.17		During the first week salvage operations by the acting Quarter Master & a party of men had proceeded rapidly. During several months the TARA Hill main dressing station had been in use by medical units of V Army although it was in IV Army Area. It is now to be demolished. The Hut at Ovillers being used instead. Enormous stocks of Medical Stores Ordnance Stores &c have to be inventoried & disposed of — Stores buried in trenches of Engineers of the Ambulance in this part & acknowledged by the Territorial Division. A new shelter at CREIGHTON'S POST completed and occupied. Box latrine with lid fitted at Ovillers Huts and Sunken Road Advanced Dressing Stations. Also supply of forms for cleaning dug outs of Gas put in each Advanced Dressing Station. Wounded from Front line to AVELUY main Dressing Station proceeds satisfactorily, notwithstanding enormous heavy lorry [traffic] so far as the A.D.S. It takes eight men to bring a stretcher case to the R.A.P. and onwards 8 — 9 hours three hundred to Taria to A.D.S.a and Cars can almost always be employed from there onwards. Light is good when there is no moon. Frequent shelling by the enemy renders the roads hard to POZIERES dangerous. Frequently ambulances are thrown in their [work] of Sdor [?] fire which makes it necessary to do my cars/line at night. one Ford Ambulance car was hit at POZIERES and almost completely demolished in the lorry [?] G.C. Carmichael	

WAR DIARY or INTELLIGENCE SUMMARY

Army Form C. 2118.

Place	Date	Hour	Summary of Events and Information	Remarks and references to Appendices
VILLERS HUTS	6/1/17		51st High Div Order No 126 Copy No 14 received. Provision for the relief of 51st Div by 2nd Div on 12-13th January. Attached March table shews 2/1 Wrgts 49 Amb moves on 13th inst from HUTS to PUCHEVILLERS on relief by 2nd Division. Move ambulance to accompany 152nd Brigade. Amendments to H.D.O.O. 126 received.	
	7/1/17		51st (H)D No 8700 Q received. Provision for handing of stores by 51st on 10th inst in order to lighten transport.	
	8/1/17		ADMS No 3308 orders the dispatch of 1 officer & 7 NCO, 54 men by Motor Ambulance to NOUVION-EN-PONTHIEU to take over billets from a Field Ambulance.	
	10/1/17		Dispatched three G.S. wagon loads of equipment & billeting by rail to Ley N. Oesley via Doullens. Capt. G. Dick who rejoined unit yesterday from Hospital at GEZAINCOURT to NOUVION-EN-PONTHIEU, will supervise party. 153 Inf Brig's A.T. No 20, Cap 2517 reinforced.	
	12/1/17		Under ADMS No 3306, 1 motor lorry & 1 G.S wagon to be attached for transport of Plant & Equipt in morning of 13th inst. Advance party of the 6th Field Ambulance arrived about 6 pm. C/C about parties were ambulated to various advanced dressing stations to relieve posts in relief of ourselves. Relief carried out, receipts for stores & ammunition handed over by 11 P.m.	

Army Form C. 2118.

WAR DIARY
or
INTELLIGENCE SUMMARY
(Erase heading not required.)

Sheet 3   LVII
January 17   N.F. Amb 9/11   Amb Maj
                              J Robertson
                              Cmdg

Place	Date	Hour	Summary of Events and Information	Remarks and references to Appendices
OVILLERS HUTS.	13/1/17	8.30 am	Major G.F. WHYTE having been granted leave to United Kingdom did not march with the unit but remained behind to obtain receipts from the 6.H. R.A.T. Ambulance for all stores taken over handed over, between units, & duplicate forms. Unit marched off	
PUCHVILLERS	to	4pm	Arrived PUCHVILLERS having had dinner & tea en route. 2nd Musical incident.	
			153 Infantry Brig OO no 173. Copy no 14 provides for the move of 153 Bgde Arrived. 3/1 H.F.Amb, is temporarily attached on 14- inst to GEZAINCOURT area. Also A.I. no 21.	
	14/1/17	12 noon	marches off destination LONGVILLETTE	
LONGVILLETTE	"	4 pm	Arrived. part of the road from Sezaincourt to Longvillette being impassable for transport The Main completed the journey by the route laid down. Transport was turned out back to Bagneux.	
			153 Inf Brigade OO no 174 Copy no 176 duly received ordering move to CRAMONT on 15th inst	
do	15/1/17	8.30 am	Marches on Brigade to LES MASURES de CRAMONT. About half way on account of blockage of traffic to Brigade had to be broken up and ORs H.Q. trans- sent to destination by BERNAVILLE instead of by Dom QUEUR Arrived without incident from units of 63rd Division on their way forward	
CRAMONT	3 pm			

Army Form C. 2118.

WAR DIARY
or
INTELLIGENCE SUMMARY

(Erase heading not required.)

Unit: 4th H.F. Amb LVIII 91 H.F.Amb
Month: January 1917

Place	Date	Hour	Summary of Events and Information	Remarks and references to Appendices
LES MASURES de CRAMONT	15/1/17		153 Bgde O.O. 207/5 Auf Recied Schedules No 2/1 H.F.Amb will move under orders 154 H.F. Brigade on 16th. 153 Brigade moves to DRUCAT area. A.I. No. 22. received. Extract from 51st H.Div. O.O. No 129 received from ADMS. Giving march table of this medical units on 16th instant, with destinations and detailing personnel accompanying Brigades to billets conveying from the front. 154 Inf Bgde O.O. No 96 Appx No 15 received furnishing station of this unit at NOUVION-EN-PONTHIEU with this Brigade on 16th instant.	
do	16/1/17		Marched off at 7.45 am. Joined 154 Inf Brigade at NEUILLY-LE-HOPITAL at 11.30 am.	
NOUVION	19/1/17	3pm	Arrived and opened out for receipt of Sick. Ambulances billeted in CHATEAU.	
do	23/1/17		Continue Brigade the duty of 154th Inf Brigade and to carry out Refitting and sanitation of all personnel & other proceedings of the unit. Also engaged in recreation & training.	
do	29/1/17		As far as materials was available from R.E. repairs improvements to Field Hospital with clean Water Huts at Le CROTOY taken over from 63rd Division and for an isolation hospital for cases of Diphtheria opened and placed under the medical charge of Capt J. STA. TITMAS of the unit on this date.	

2/1st Highland Field Ambulance

COMMITTEE FOR THE
MEDICAL HISTORY OF THE WAR
Date 4 - APR. 1917

WAR DIARY or INTELLIGENCE SUMMARY

Army Form C. 2118.

Staff 2/1 H'ld Mtd Amb
February INTELLIGENCE SUMMARY Moheston HU.
1917   Crawf

Place	Date	Hour	Summary of Events and Information	Remarks and References to Appendices
MOUVIEN EN PONTHIEU	2/2/17		ADMS instructions. The party at LeCrotoy with the new B.H.Q. & the rest take the transport & the only prison Huts were occupied by us. No patients admitted. The villages were handed over to Town Major Knox and borrowed with 154 Brigade out of 5th Army Area.	
do	3/2/17		152 & & Brig O.O. no 95 Coty 2570 received. This unit & move northwards to GUESCHART on 5th February.	
do	5/2/17		Having left a small rear party behind with the rest of Brigade having moved S-6 Captain AREO this unit moves HQ at 2.45 p.m.	
GUESCHART	6/2/17		at 9 p.m. had arrived here yesterday, a good deal of trouble was found in getting the transport along on account of the ice on the roads – during the first hour moving of the road. no more today as the Brigade reached us a few feet across and passed in column about GUESCHART. Detachmts. Bttalns formed in reasonable slack for C.R.E., 60 Divilllers & Reserve ARGYULE on 6th about 2.5 miles away, and the MDS Transport rode to Lt G. Luard Lieut. Alderman has taken over from BRAILLY.	
"	7/2/17		154 by Brig & 90. 99 Prisoners. Some men of Brigade here & H.Q. and C Coty, and O.O. 100 Provides for men wedding this unit to FROHEN area no 2. The Res Amd. move to WILLENCOURT today 7.2. The Brigade Major of this unit found all billets occupied & County in WILLENCOURT and referred him to the Major General him to Staff Captain for different orders	
BUIRE AU BOIS	do			

Army Form C. 2118.

WAR DIARY or **INTELLIGENCE SUMMARY**
(Erase heading not required.)

Sheet 2

41 Highland Mtd.
Wilkinson Lt Col
Engr

IX

February 17

Instructions regarding War Diaries and Intelligence Summaries are contained in F.S. Regs., Part II. and the Staff Manual respectively. Title Pages will be prepared in manuscript.

Place	Date	Hour	Summary of Events and Information	Remarks and references to Appendices
RUITZ AU BOIS	7/11/17		Indications seemed to point to NOEUX about 7 miles further on arrival found we were all occupied by 41st Inf Bn who cleared for the unit in good order Distributing Building given to B's HQ for orders. In his absence the Staff Captain 154 Bde offered and Stated that he had left the holding that took to ACQUET (6 mile back towards Stating point). As time seemed incessant & a very long march next day through up with the Brigade. I decided that whilst moved to fund full Sound and proceeds to RUITZ AU BOIS when the GS Royal Subs and billets out with much apparent suc space arriving 3.45 after having no formal dep. hospital and the days seeming such the Brigade reporting attention and comfort I decided to rather the Men hard left at GUESCHARE and Arty to for attendance on AD Corps for some days before. The arrangement on GUESCHARE and Army Field Artillery were about 5 km we left in charge of the Rear party Captain GAGARKO who died of Pneumonia in the 5th M. U.S. Station. His brother are here here 5 mo. are J SCOTCH him been, That was once he spans from history of sick & sick and fell from Rifleman on the line of march were Placed of Captain arms ammunition from Chevin & J.C.S. alopinee Army Sargt the units at RUITE about 9 P.M. Building of the unit had been attempted in four Detached major GRANTE to the change of billets and inoculation of sick on the movement of the unit on Reginall about my when station OC 101 reads	

Army Form C. 2118.

WAR DIARY or INTELLIGENCE SUMMARY

(Erase heading not required.)

About 3 Infantry Brigade February 1917

Place	Date	Hour	Summary of Events and Information	Remarks and references to Appendices
RUINE AU BOIS	8/II/17		Unit moves to FRAMECOURT.	
FRAMECOURT			FRAMECOURT. 1.30 pm went into Billets. During the move a 3 ton lorry has been at the disposal of the Unit for surplus Kits & Blankets. This is a distinct luxury as without blankets injuries and being many steps authorised by G.R.O. and Scales of charges of unused to Battalions and Intermediary stores, officers mess & officers private kits to OSTREVILLE Camp. The equipment which remains is about what is made a Divisional Table Equipment. Remainder of sick to transit.	
FRAME COURT	9/II/17		Road 80. 102. Marais. Unit and horses to OSTREVILLE today.	
OSTREVILLE	10/II/17	1.30 p.m.	Arrived 1.30 p.m. Billets arranged scattered. One room for hospital. Infantry hospital formed at GUESNART about today. Thermometer registered about zero.	
			W.D. D.D. to 103 marines. This must leave 5 FREVILLERS the Brigade to OCC on 11th. No move on 10th either. This is 153 Inf. Bde. Area. Minor difficulties formed in getting a suitable place for unit to as 153 A.D. had already billeted the place leaving no room for the Unit anyhow. As the North end of the present move, proceed the Brigade for leave and Manual a vertable house at the West of the Village. During the future move hard front & wintry weather prevailed.	
FREVILLERS	11/II/17	2 pm	arrived 2 p.m. at FREVILLERS, and took over Nicoles: 32 (AQ) 35. 44. 46. 23, 2, 4, 19.	

Nicoles B.D. B.D. 3.w. Copy 29. duty incurred

Army Form C. 2118.

WAR DIARY
or
INTELLIGENCE SUMMARY
(Erase heading not required.)

Sheet 4

LXII

February 9/1 Mgt 7th Arms
J. Robertson M Coly, Comdg

Place	Date	Hour	Summary of Events and Information	Remarks and references to Appendices
FREVILLERS	18/2/17		Have were continued to training. The local Sch. of the Arm - Capt ARGO. will personnel & equipment of 13 section attended to Inst Corp. Kent (Takes BERLETTE. Haning started firmness and tunes out Rebt no 1. as a word, the exceptions of Lewis from the Hit. Palso COCOVET began the training. Mens came in 9 J.C.T. and also not address on our officers mess.	
	20/2/17		Capt. Ser. Divish returned from leave on 11.7 inst. He was also on 5th but absente of Kindiana Transport, 97. home of The dis. strays 3 has. He was taking attached to CAMBERING and 1 M Corp. making to perform trainance duties with the 51st Div. Sch.ett.	
	27/2/17		Home OP. 35 Cpt M Q and various services for the hydrangea of trenches 1/2 T/3 Hq Davel. to be notified. The whole of Company has taken over, 1/3 H.Q. assuming the work of main during March.	

2/1st Highland Field Ambulance.

COMMITTEE FOR THE
MEDICAL HISTORY OF THE WAR
Date 11 MAY. 1917

Army Form C. 2118.

2/1 Highland F.A.
G Wharton M.Ry

WAR DIARY
or
INTELLIGENCE SUMMARY

Sheet 1. March 1917

LXXI

Place	Date	Hour	Summary of Events and Information	Remarks and references to Appendices
TRENILLERS	7/III/17		During the past week there was continues to receive the sick of bad arm and coughing cases from the Divisional Rest Station CAVEOURT. The preparing of a large convalescent Bns. R. Static for XVIII Corps was proceeded with under Capt'n S.H.E. ARGO, with B Section Tent & Horse Subsections. Major Murray of the Ambulance attended South African Brigade 9th Divn. in absence of Lt Col. C.D.R.S. Ltn.	
do	14/III/17		Yesterday Captain ARGO was admitted to L.C.S (30th) suffering from Appendicitis. Today transferred to 72 # Stationary Hospital and his attending Revmd Fors G Colonel Wright. Gray will the functions of Capt ans meanwhile.	
"	16/III/17		Captain J.B. MILNE. R.A.M.C T.C. arrived as a reinforcement. Ands of Highland Divn Pro. S.G. 2.14/105 inj. Instructions for Offensive Operations Various Sections.	V Machine Arrangements with Amendment I
				VI Store Ration & water Dumps
				VIII B Police & Stragglers posts
				XV Accommodation in Front Areas & Front Line Reports
				XII Salvage
				VII Sanitation kit
				XVI Ammunition
				XVIII Trench Railways
				IX Canalets & Runners
				XX Soup Kitchen. Veterinary Services, Special Notes.

WAR DIARY or INTELLIGENCE SUMMARY

Army Form C. 2118.

Sheet 2
March 1917

2/1 Highland Field Ambulance
2 November 1917
L/Col Anderson
Cmdg

LXIII

Place	Date	Hour	Summary of Events and Information	Remarks and references to Appendices
FREVILLERS	16/11/17		Under date 13th March a Draft of Machine Arrangements for Constants and a meeting of MOs with OC 2/1 F.Amb in connection Field Ambulance of the Division called for 15th At this meeting when Major Croft attended with me the whole of the arrangements were discussed. Capt J.B. Milne sent to 2/4 Seaforth Hrs in relief of the M.O. sick	
	18/11/17		Under this date arrangements made for the dumping of Surplus kits of units of the Division for the Event of sudden move	
	20/11/17		Under ADMS No 3467 Extracts from Medical Arrangements Third Army were received. Also Continuation of Third Army Medical Arrangements Extracts with XVII Corps Medical Arrangements. First Medical Arrangements 57 & 16 Div Operation 3 with Amendments received. Two schemes of attack to Eastward are arrived upon. The adoption of one or other will depend on Events of operation entered and methods for this will be issued. The Army Scheme differs only in the Ambulance of the Reserve provision. In the Army Scheme the Reserve of two Reserve Divns will be entirely divided between two Regimental Aid Posts SABLIERE and ABRI de MOUTON, Reserve HQ H & Amb. being placed in Reserve in the Corps Scheme and handing of 2/1 FA to SABLIERE	
	22/11/17		2/1 go to SABLIERE ready to LILLE RCMC, part	

Army Form C. 2118.

Sheet 3

WAR DIARY
or
INTELLIGENCE SUMMARY

(Erase heading not required.)

LXIV
2/1 Wfk 3d Amb.
March 1917
J Roberts W/Col Comdg

Place	Date	Hour	Summary of Events and Information	Remarks and references to Appendices
	22.III.17		Today B. Section under Major Whyte was sent to ANZIN to prepare the walking wounded collecting station. C Section under Capt McCormack was sent to BERLETTE to prepare for receipt of cases of tho Div. at the Andrews Rest Station. XVIII Corps A Section continues the hospital at FREVILLERS.	
	30.III.17		On receipt of instructions A Section will take over to D.R.S. CAUCOURT from the 1/2 Highland Fd Amb. and all reserve of the three Sections will proceed to LA SABLIERE. Severest wounded from the RE to the Colliery Pont LILLE ROAD and from any [?] R.A.P. [?] during the active operations. They will be in Command of an Officer. Motor Ambulances will be parked at Corps main Dressing Station HAUTE AVESNES. A & D Bosho O.R. kept at walking wounded Stat. Corps Rest Station & Field Ambulance CAUCOURT. - All Three Sections of this unit to Section have active use to [?] and all personnel will use LAS Battle. Positions on land before 2 ends. Arrangements medical Operations B. & D and in 3487 preparation of trenches continues. O.R. made. Gradual evacuation of hospitals proceeds with	

40/026

51st Div.

2/1st Highland F.A.

COMMITTEE FOR THE
MEDICAL HISTORY OF THE WAR
Date -6 JUN. 1917

WAR DIARY or INTELLIGENCE SUMMARY

Army Form C. 2118.

LXV
2/1 High(?) Amb.
1/1 Cdn Corps(?)

Month: April

Place	Date	Hour	Summary of Events and Information	Remarks and references to Appendices
FREVILLERS	2/4/17		Route, Co. & 36. (SIGNED) Copy will travel table attached. received.	
	3/4/17		A.D.M.S. no. 3467. received indicating that the events of his scheme (next) will be undertaken 2nd line bn the subject below (With Div. Med. Arrangements Op. 3)	
CAUCOURT	5/4/17		Reme Division under Captain G.L. PILLANS proceeded to ACQ to lever for the night. A section with H.Q. having destined 7 as patient to Div. Rest Station FRES. proceeded to CAUCOURT and took over Div. Rest Station from the 1/2 West 3/1 Amb.	
"	6/4/17		All moves for today cancelled.	
"	7/4/17		Bearers moved from ACQ to ANZIN St BUBIN.	
"	8/4/17		Bearers moved from ANZIN to SABLIERE. Motor Ambulance reports to HASTE AVESNES. also an Horse Ambulance on relief. Gale's reports to washing horses. Evacuating Station ANZIN for use of major WH&E. This completes the moving of this unit to battle position. The Dressing rooms are as follows.	

WAR DIARY or INTELLIGENCE SUMMARY

Army Form C. 2118.

Sheet 2

Army Corps: LXVI
2/1 14/2 Fd Amb
Mehertown W.C.L. Enoy
Month: April

Date	Hour	Summary of Events and Information	Remarks and references to Appendices
2/4/17		**Advanced Division** under Capt. PILLANS. Consists of 92 other ranks. SABLIERE Brigade Aid post. Instructions to carry wounded from Regimental Bearers to Collecting post. LILLE ROAD and to supplement Regimental Bearers when called upon. 50 men of Trench mortar Artillery are attached here from Zero hour. They ad rations for the 2nd day from HQ, & after that they draw rations from Divisional Ration Dump at ROCLIN COURT. Supplies are Stored at Sabliere Aid post. Reserve supplies at LILLE ROAD post. Men billeted their picks with articles not required, in clump of Cupola behind. They are fitted out as laid down for "Fighting kit." W.D. no 214/108 Sept III 65 fin an overcoat. **Tent Subdivision B Section** — kept with Equipment. Major G.F. WHYTE & Capt. GEO. DICK. 34th & 9th. — The XVII Corps training Wounded Collecting Station stationed at ANZIN MAUSIN. Equipment was supplements by various articles such as Tables, Crocks, Spoons by British Red Cross Society, Lady Leslie Otaman Comment Supplies of Rations, Biscuits, Medical Comforts & Medical Stain, from in Inspection. Field Ambulance Supplied. Biscuits. Chocolate were given to the Soldiers Churches Tent Ammunition	
CAUCOURT.			

2449 Wt. W14957/M90 750,000 1/16 J.B.C. & A. Forms/C.2118/12.

WAR DIARY or INTELLIGENCE SUMMARY

Army Form C. 2118.

Sheet 3
April

XVII
9/1. W.F. Amulgement
J. Newton Lt Col
AandQ

Place	Date	Hour	Summary of Events and Information	Remarks and references to Appendices
CAUCOURT	9/4/17		All walking wounded of the Corps will proceed to the Station by Cross Country Routes marked by own troops. A+D Both will be kept. A 36 Rendres daily and also Daily Stats for each Section of the Station. Cases will be evacuated in motor lorries & trains in order & made in importance, by walking & lit train. Stabling of Railway MAROEUIL. M.N.W. Station is a main Dressing Station for walking wounded. Major G.F. WHYTE has supervision of the whole Station. Major W.A. TAYLOR from the 5TH DIV A.S.C. will report to our Section of the walking wounded Station at 7 a.m. on 2 day & also attaches to our Section of the walking wounded Station. By order of A.D.M.S. dated today A Bearer Tent. will ht R. Main Station at CAUCOURT with instructions to receive all the sick of 51st Division. Convoys of a Tent Detachment two line OMC Kentro, will two Officers ng. Co. + Cpt. B.C. Runneder of Quarto M. and C. Station by unions with a [illeg] sent division of an RE, Ambulance. The Corps a town Platoon called XVII Corps Combined Divisional Rest Station was formed, under the Charge Major Clark manning Rest Station. They are instructed to receive the sick of Corps troops materials for formation of the Station in addition to Section M.R. Tent Sup recruited from 5TH XVII Corps	

Army Form C. 2118.

WAR DIARY
or
INTELLIGENCE SUMMARY.
(Erase heading not required.)

Army of
April

LXVIII
2/1 1/2 Fd Ambulance
J Mitchelson Maj
Cmdg

Place	Date	Hour	Summary of Events and Information	Remarks and references to Appendices
CAVCOURT	8/4/17		Four other ranks were withdrawn from C Section for the army with 5 of A section, at the 42nd C.C.S. AUBIGNY. Capt Bryan Rance, being in charge of the party. This party reported to O.C. 42 C.C.S. as apt 1st army to instructions received.	
do	9/4/17	5.30 a.m.	2nd day Zero hour 5 a.m. in concert with Corps to right & left the XVIII Corps advanced about 4.6·5 kilometres. Regimental aid posts were advanced into German trenches, and the Ambulance bearers worked in relays from the most front line backwards to LITTLE ROAD# where motor ambulances received the lying cases. Walking cases from the whole corps proceeded to ANZIN 2 No hospital + main transport was the centre of operations that I knew of 2 No hospital. No enemy shelling was encountered till late in the day. The weather was very stormy with squalls of snow. The walking wounded Station was divided into return compartments to the three Divisions 9th 34th & 51st and representatives of each working independently keeping their own A.D.S. busy. After dressing + feeding they were handed on to motor chara-bancs and despatched by the motor ... ... to AUBIGNY only. Our ... was to ... the ambulance ... to ho 72 Stationary St Pol. Today 11 officers + 675 O.R. (all same 31 O.R. were 52nd H.D) up to 6 P.m.	BULL ROAD for 51st Div. only

Army Form C. 2118.

Sheet 5
April 1917

LXIX
41 Fd. Amb. 1st and
2nd N. Midland Cav.
Canadian

WAR DIARY
or
INTELLIGENCE SUMMARY.
(Erase heading not required.)

Place	Date	Hour	Summary of Events and Information	Remarks and references to Appendices
CAUCOURT	9/4/17	6 P.M.	One section at Corps Rest Station & Officers' hospital AUBIGNY have had practically nothing to do today. The D.R.S. at CAUCOURT full 240/patients but about nine wounded, 1 trench German prisoner.	
do	10/4/17	6 A.M.	Working personnel 51st Div. Section joined through 6 Officers & 357 other rankings. Since 6 p.m. yesterday, this included 136 Germans. The other sections were correspondingly busy. Of these 4 Officers & 203 O.R. belonged to H.D.	
		6 P.M.	Very little doing at AUBIGNY Rest Station or CAUCOURT. The personnel however being very much needed were fully employed and extensive use of Convalescent Sick was made as regards statistical means. Covering none of Sick. One of rifles & packs also to a certain extent in Dressing Sores.	
do	11/4/17	6 P.M.	During last 24 hours working wounded O.R. 22 passed to Div. Rest stn (49 now H.D.) Recn. E.O.D. nis 37. Cdy nil 34 - Relay of 512th (UK 5A) & the 2nd Division. Bretton Brown at AMLIN	
do	12/4/17	6 P.M.	Since last entry 2 Officers & 223 O.R. only 4 were H.D. personnel went Cavalry (1st Div.) and 4th Division. 51st Div. having been relieved back began to arrive at Caucourt & Aubigny. This 6 Cans & Cavs B72 Cans to AUBIGNY, CDRS. 17 Officers 7,626 O.R.	
do	13/4/17	6 P.M.	Last twenty four hours. Division joined through working wounded. Also 3 Officers & 52 O.R. of H.D. Division. Today the section from 9 A Div. took over our department & working wounded Station AM2 IN Caucourt & to 1 ST NICHOLAS	

WAR DIARY or INTELLIGENCE SUMMARY

Army Form C. 2118.

Wad 6
April 1917

LXX
2/1 West, Yo Ambulance
J. Ashton H.A. RAMC

Place	Date	Hour	Summary of Events and Information	Remarks and references to Appendices
Couvent	14th		During the action near 9 a.m. met the Bearer Division of this Ambulance under Captain G.L. Pillans was at the disposal of the O/C Forward Evacuation. No casualties among them took place and today they rejoined Head Quarters. The personnel of B Section Tent Subdivision rejoined H.Q. during the day out they had two men wounded, one was wounded slightly by a shrapnel piece which came through their billet but not outside, the other was wounded by a shrapnel splinter just outside the billet from an own gun. C & C Section Tent Subdivisions at COUCOURT & BERLETTE respectively continued clearing rich of this Division. Many Corps Troops were also admitted at COUCOURT. The Horse Ambulance and 1/3 W.F. Amb. horse drawn Motor Ambs are at R. M.O.C Ambulance disposal, without having had any accident. Today R.A.M.C. Operation Order No. 35 was received. The Highland Division takes over the battle front of the 9th Division from this SCARPE H.24.a.4.7. S. Ingoalaz Redoubt (H.12.c.1.9.) inclusive on the night of 15-16 April. Similar arrangements as in Para 3. The working parties' locating hut at ST NICHOLAS, will be stopped by a test Ambulance from H.Q. and B Sect. detailed for this duty.	

WAR DIARY or INTELLIGENCE SUMMARY

Army Form C. 2118.

Sheet 7
April 1917.

LXXI
2/1 Highland Field Ambulance
Welcome War Diary

Place	Date	Hour	Summary of Events and Information	Remarks and references to Appendices
CAUCOURT	15/4/17		Advance party of Bearer Section Tent proceeded to ST NICHOLAS and took over from 9th Division a Summary of Stores was made and valuation made out for whatever articles to attach. A walking wounded Station similar to the one at ANZIN. Major WHYTE with Capt. GEO. DICK in charge of B Section Tent & 36 Pers. Removed from 12 noon today, ready to take in (B for all wounded). ADMS number 3606 received ordering the dispatch of the Bearer Divn. J. Stn unit to report on 16 – to O.C. 1/2 High Fd Amb. at CAVERNES during Stalin ST NICHOLAS. It is at the disposal of Major G.W. MILLER 1/3 High Fd Amb. Wm evacuants from the front.	
do	16/4/17		All battle positions taken up at 12 noon today.	
do	19/4/17		New Medical Arrangement position to secured. Divn fronted by Indian Sub Division of the Division fronting affecting this unit. Bearer post FAMPOUX Walking post L'ABBAYETTE. Relay Bearer post BLANGY, Walking wounded collecting Station ST NICHOLAS. Advanced Dressing Station also Rear & Main Dressing Station HAUTE AVESNES. Field Ambulance CAUCOURT. Corps aid post BERNETTE (Sheet 51 B VG The Rear Division of this Ambulance under Captain PILLANS B.L. distributed at 36 B I – 40000 Regimental aid Posts, at FAMPOUX and L'ABBAYETTE	

Army Form C. 2118.

WAR DIARY
or
INTELLIGENCE SUMMARY.

(Erase heading not required.)

Sheet 1   April 1917

LXXII
2/1 Highland Field Ambulance
Ellerton M'Culloch Captain

Place	Date	Hour	Summary of Events and Information	Remarks and references to Appendices
Couturelle	21/4/17		The wounded were anxiously expected and Zero hour intimated to be during 2 days being 2320. All in readiness by midnight on	
do	22/4/17	22—23	LIEUT. 7 Q.M. A.A. PROSSER reported from U.K. & assumed duty as Q.M. of this unit all "Parties" for attack moved up & the 51st Division and by evening of night and Lieut. Captains Murphy & Fenton of 2/4th Division reported to major WHYTE of this unit for duty at Walking Wounded Station. B section worked in conjunction with a Tent Subdivision of the 4th Division. The station counted 7 Marquees (6). Captain WILSON Kemp 17th section also reported for duty at Walking Wounded Station. [Lt. Tent pursuance of the 4/4 Division was ordered & those from the 37th Division this received on the 20th inst] Volume of transports as before but at ADISIGNY as above & bonus were short bag 10.	
do	23/4/17	4.45 am.	Zero hour. Total casualties passed through this station for walking wounded for totals 9 officers + 373 O.R. (including Stretcher Sick O.) & 312. O.R. also 2 German officers + 45 O.R. None serious 259 Prisoners & a long convoy for an adverse dies to walking W. Station	
do	24/4/17		Total casualties to date (6 P.M. to 6 P.M.) 4 Officers + 227 O.R. This morning M2/049868 Corpl T ASHTON was found dead in a Horse lines the W.W. Station. He had fallen in in the dark from his mech. Major Whyte held a court of Inquiry preceedings of which have been filed.	

A 3834 Wt. W4973/M687 750,000 8/16 D. D. & L. Ltd. Forms/C.2118/13

Army Form C. 2118.

WAR DIARY
or
INTELLIGENCE SUMMARY.

Sheet 9 LXXIII
2/1 Wst. Field Ambulance
April 1917 Yorkshire Wes. Cavalry

(Erase heading not required.)

Instructions regarding War Diaries and Intelligence Summaries are contained in F. S. Regs., Part II. and the Staff Manual respectively. Title pages will be prepared in manuscript.

Place	Date	Hour	Summary of Events and Information	Remarks and references to Appendices
CAYEUX	25/4/17		Today B. Section Tent Sub-div was ordered at mid-day by the 102nd & 3rd Can: 34th Division thereupon to Scots Fort Nyoma. WR Coy Major Whyte who remained for another day to meet any incoming wounded. The Bearers of this unit. During this action evacuated during 23rd Post to billet wounded. The situation was apparent, no covers available. 10 bearers were slightly wounded and three severely, one killed. The Kean Division Nyomo WQ today. 50th Div has been relieved by 34th Div.	
do	26/4/17		During the action A.Y.C. active customs became the sick of the Division. Major WHYTE Nyoma WR Today, having taken one command of W.W.C.S. & Captain ROSS 104th Field Ambulance. During this tour of duty from 16th to 25th Apl. 17 officers and 683 O.R. pass through our section of the walking wounded Station. Captain STEWART McNAUGHTON Name T.C. joins them round in doubt.	
do	28/4/17			
do	29/4/17		Capt. S. McNaughton withdraws to relief to a Dress 3rd Div and proceeds today.	

B.E.F.

SUMMARY OF MEDICAL WAR DIARIES of

2/1st Highland Field Ambulance,

51st Division,
17th Corps,

3rd Army.

WESTERN FRONT, APRIL - MAY 1917.

O.C. Lt.Colonel J. Robertson.

Summarised under the following headings:-

PHASE "B" - BATTLE OF ARRAS. APRIL - MAY 1917.

1st Period, April 1917. Attack on Vimy Ridge.
2nd Period, May 1917. Capture of Siegfried Line.

B.E.F.   1.

2/1st H.F.A., 51st Division,   WESTERN FRONT,
O.C. Lt.Col. J. Robertson,   APRIL 1917.
17th Corps, 3rd Army.

Phase "B" - Battle of Arras. April - May 1917.
1st Period, April 1917. Attack on Vimy Ridge.

April.   H.Q. at Frevillers.
5th   Evacuation, Moves & Moves det. All patients evacuated to
         D.R.S. and C.C.S.
         H.Q. to Caucourt and relieved 1/2nd High. F.A. at D.R.S.
         1 & Br. Divn. to Acq.

7th   Moves det. Brs. moved to Sabliere.
         Transport M. Ambs. to Haute Avesnes also H. Ambs.

8th   Med. Arr. & Evacuation 1 & 92 brs.- Sabliere Bde. A.P.
         These Brs. carried W. from R.S.B's to Coll. P. Lille Rd.
         and supplemented R.S.B's when called on.
         0 & 50 Trench Mortar Artillery attached from zero hour.
         2 & T.S.D. "B" sect. Complete with equipment.
         These with sections from each of Divns. of Corps (34th
         and 9th) formed 17th Corps Wlkg. W. Coll. Stn. at
         Anzin St. Aubin. All Wlkg. W. to this Stn. by cross
         country routes marked by sign posts. W. evacuated by
         lorries and buses when possible, or from siding of rail-
         way Maroeuil. Wlkg. W. Stn. also M.D.S. for Wlkg. W.
         2 & "A" sect. Tent. With H.Q. of unit at Caucourt and
         dealt with all Sk. of 51st Divn.
         "C" sect. In unison with "a F.A. of each Divn. of the
         Corps" formed 17th Corps Combined Divisional R.S. under
         charge of Major Chas. Murray, S.A.M.C. of the 9th Divn.
         S. African Bde. 0 & 9 at 42nd C.C.S. Aubigny.

9th   Operations. Zero day. Attack opened at 5.30 a.m. In
         concert with Corps on R., and L. the 17th Corps advanced
         4 - 5 kilo-metres.
         Med. Arr. & Evacuation   R.A.P's advanced into Ger.
         Trenches. Brs. worked in relays from new front line
         back/

B.E.F.

2.

2/1st High. F.A., 51st Division,   WESTERN FRONT,
O.C. Lt.Col. J. Robertson,   APRIL 1917.
17th Corps, 3rd Army.

Phase "B", continued.
1st Period, continued.

April. 9th (contd.) — H.Q. at Caucourt.

Med. Arr. & Evacuation (contd.) back Lille Rd. (51st Divn. only.) where M.Ambs. were loaded. Wlkg. W. for whole Corps preceeded to Anzin. So swift and interrupted was advance that ½ hour after zero practically no enemy shelling was encountered till late in day. Wlkg. W. Stn. was divided into sections corresponding to the 3 divns. and worked independently, each keeping A. & D. books. They shared Corps Troops. First Wlkg. W. arrived 7 a.m. Wlkg. W. evacuated by Motor Char-a-bancs to Aubigny.

Casualties   11 & 675 W.

10th   Wlkg. W. 51st Divn. sect.   6 & 357 including 136 Ger.

11th   0 & 22 -

12th   2 & 223 Mostly Cav. and 4th Divn.

13th   17 & 626 Mostly 9th Divn.

Casualties R.A.M.C. 9th/13th   0 & 2 W.

14th   Operations R.A.M.C. "A" & "C" sections T.S.D. at Caucourt and Berlette respectively continued to receive Sk. of Divn. Many Corps troops admitted at Caucourt.

15th-16th   Military Situation 51st Divn. took over line. R. Scarpe H.24.a.4.7. to Hydrabad Redoubt H.12.c.1.9. exclusive from 9th Divn.

Moves det. "B" sect. T. to St. Nicholas and took over from 9th Divn.

B.E.F.

2/1st High. F.A., 51st Division,   WESTERN FRONT,
O.C. Lt.Col. J. Robertson.   APRIL 1917.
17th Corps, 3rd Army.

Phase "B", continued.
1st Period, continued.

April.

16th   Moves det. Br. Divn. to 1/2nd High. F.A. at A.D.S. St.
Nicholas to be at disposal of Major Miller 1/3rd High. F.A.
for evacuation from Front.

19th   Med. Arr. All battle positions taken up at noon.
    Br. P.   Fampoux.
    Coll. P. L'Abbayette.
    Relay P. Blangy.
    Wlkg.W.Coll.Stn. - St. Nicholas.
    A.D.S.   "
    M.D.S.   Haute Avesnes.
    C.R.S.   Berlette. Sheets 51 B. & C. 36 B.

22nd   "B" sect. worked in conjunction with T.S.D. 4th Divn.

23rd   Operations Zero 4.45 a.m.
Casualties Total 9 & 373 Wlkg. W.
Evacuation As before. Only 10 Char-a-bancs available.
Operations Enemy. Some shelling of St. Nicholas with long
range guns.

24th   Casualties 4 & 227 W. (?Wlkg.)

25th   Moves det. Br. Divn. and "B" sect. T.S.D. rejoined H.Q. on
relief by 102nd F.A.
Casualties R.A.M.C. & Ops. R.A.M.C.
23rd/25th O & 13 W.
The situation was difficult and no cover available.

B.E.F.

2/1st H.F.A., 51st Division, WESTERN FRONT,
O.C. Lt.Col. J. Robertson, APRIL 1917.
17th Corps, 3rd Army.

Phase "B" - Battle of Arras. April - May 1917.

1st Period, April 1917. Attack on Vimy Ridge.

April. H.Q. at Frevillers.

5th Evacuation, Moves & Moves det. All patients evacuated to D.R.S. and C.C.S.

H.Q. to Caucourt and relieved 1/2nd High. F.A. at D.R.S.

1 & Br. Divn. to Acq.

7th Moves det. Brs. moved to Sabliere.

Transport M. Ambs. to Haute Avesnes also H. Ambs.

8th Med. Arr. & Evacuation 1 & 92 brs.- Sabliere Bde. A.P. These Brs. carried W. from R.S.B's to Coll. P. Lille Rd. and supplemented R.S.B's when called on.

0 & 50 Trench Mortar Artillery attached from zero hour.

2 & T.S.D. "B" sect. Complete with equipment.

These with sections from each of Divns. of Corps (34th and 9th) formed 17th Corps Wlkg. W. Coll. Stn. at Anzin St. Aubin. All Wlkg. W. to this Stn. by cross country routes marked by sign posts. W. evacuated by lorries and buses when possible, or from siding of railway Maroeuil. Wlkg. W. Stn. also M.D.S. for Wlkg. W.

2 & "A" sect. Tent. With H.Q. of unit at Caucourt and dealt with all Sk. of 51st Divn.

"C" sect. In unison with "a F.A. of each Divn. of the Corps" formed 17th Corps Combined Divisional R.S. under charge of Major Chas. Murray, S.A.M.C. of the 9th Divn. S. African Bde. 0 & 9 at 42nd C.C.S. Aubigny.

9th Operations. Zero day. Attack opened at 5.30 a.m. In concert with Corps on R., and L. the 17th Corps advanced 4 - 5 kilo-metres.

Med. Arr. & Evacuation R.A.P's advanced into Ger. Trenches. Brs. worked in relays from new front line back/

B.E.F.

2/1st High. F.A., 51st Division,   WESTERN FRONT,
O.C. Lt.Col. J. Robertson,   APRIL 1917.
17th Corps, 3rd Army.

Phase "B", continued.
1st Period, continued.

April.   H.Q. at Caucourt.
9th   Med. Arr. & Evacuation (contd.)
(contd.)   back Lille Rd. (51st Divn. only.) where M.Ambs. were load-
                ed. Wlkg. W. for whole Corps proceeded to Anzin. So
                swift and interrupted was advance that ½ hour after zero
                practically no enemy shelling was encountered till late
                in day. Wlkg. W. Stn. was divided into sections corres-
                ponding to the 3 divns. and worked independently, each
                keeping A. & D. books. They shared Corps Troops. First
                Wlkg. W. arrived 7 a.m. Wlkg. W. evacuated by Motor
                Char-a-bancs to Aubigny.
                Casualties   11 & 675 W.
10th   Wlkg. W. 51st Divn. sect.   6 & 357 including 136 Ger.
11th   0 & 22 -
12th   2 & 223 Mostly Cav. and
                                                         4th Divn.
13th   17 & 626 Mostly 9th Divn.
                Casualties R.A.M.C. 9th/13th   0 & 2 W.
14th   Operations R.A.M.C. "A" & "C" sections T.S.D. at Caucourt
                and Berlette respectively continued to receive Sk. of
                Divn. Many Corps troops admitted at Caucourt.
15th-16th   Military Situation 51st Divn. took over line. R. Scarpe
                H.24.a.4.7. to Hydrabad Redoubt H.12.c.1.9. exclusive from
                9th Divn.
                Moves det. "B" sect. T. to St. Nicholas and took over from
                9th Divn.

B.E.F.

2/1st High. F.A., 51st Division,   WESTERN FRONT,
O.C. Lt.Col. J. Robertson.   APRIL 1917.
17th Corps, 3rd Army.

Phase "B", continued.
1st Period, continued.

April.

16th   Moves det. Br. Divn. to 1/2nd High. F.A. at A.D.S. St. Nicholas to be at disposal of Major Miller 1/3rd High. F.A. for evacuation from Front.

19th   Med. Arr. All battle positions taken up at noon.

     Br. P.   Fampoux.

     Coll. P.   L'Abbayette.

     Relay P.   Blangy.

     Wlkg.W.Coll.Stn.   - St. Nicholas.

     A.D.S.   "

     M.D.S.   Haute Avesnes.

     C.R.S.   Berlette. Sheets 51 B. & C. 36 B.

22nd   "B" sect. worked in conjunction with T.S.D. 4th Divn.

23rd   Operations Zero 4.45 a.m.

     Casualties Total 9 & 373 Wlkg. W.

     Evacuation As before. Only 10 Char-a-bancs available.

     Operations Enemy. Some shelling of St. Nicholas with long range guns.

24th   Casualties 4 & 227 W. (?Wlkg.)

25th   Moves det. Br. Divn. and "B" sect. T.S.D. rejoined H.Q. on relief by 102nd F.A.

     Casualties R.A.M.C. & Ops. R.A.M.C.

     23rd/25th 0 & 13 W.

     The situation was difficult and no cover available.

140/2161

51st Div.

2/1st Highland F.A.

May 1917

COMMITTEE FOR THE
MEDICAL HISTORY OF THE WAR
Date 10 JUL. 1917

Army Form C. 2118.

WAR DIARY
or
INTELLIGENCE SUMMARY.

LXXIV
2/1 Highland Field Ambulance
1/1 Wellington MGA Cmdy

May 1917   Sheet 1.

Place	Date	Hour	Summary of Events and Information	Remarks and references to Appendices
CAVOURT	7/5/17		During the past week the Division being out of action to receive the Sick of the Division at the Hospital. Lieut. M. Hooper, R.A.M.C. attached. 3rd Res. An inspection of the transport of Brigade was held by the G.O.C. The transport of this unit paraded with the 154th Infantry Brigade at TINQUES. Today A.D.M.S. A.P. 3650 was received warning that the 51st Division would take over from the 4th Division the Battle front on 13-14th May.	
	9/5/17		R.A.M.C. operation order no 39 copy no 25 received. Proceeded at once to prepare. The 2/1 H.F. Amb. move in 10 A. instr to ARRAS. The 2/3 H.F. Amb move over to the 2/3 High 2d Amb.	
ARRAS	10/5/17		This morning patients were taken over & all surplus stores by armoured party 2/3 H.F. Amb.: paraded at 1 p.m. and marched to Arras where we were billeted by the Commandant ARRAS in the buf & dine district. A halt was made for tea half way near Haut Avesnes. The unit arrived in ARRAS at 7 p.m. Sick of 152 Inf. Brigade were collected & no to Haut Avesnes. 152 Infantry Bgd. O.O. no 141 copy no 19 received providing for movement of the Brigade into "Reserve" for 4th Division.	
do.	11/5/17		Visited the 11th Field Ambulance from which we are to take over and find out the System of Evacuation from ROEUX front with the O.C. 11/72 Amb.	

WAR DIARY or INTELLIGENCE SUMMARY

Army Form C. 2118.

May 1917 Sheet 2

LXXV
2/14½ 7th Annual
Midnight 1/2th Cmdg

Place	Date	Hour	Summary of Events and Information	Remarks and references to Appendices
ARRAS	12/5/17	10 p.m.	The suspicion of Huns shelled slightly by a long range rifle released from the evacuation. The transport as parked by the Convent Bands just outside the town beside ARRAS gas works. During visited some of forward Advance position at 152 Brigade H.Q. Then I learned that the relief had been accelerated and was to be completed tonight as 4th Div personnel commanded the coming. Communicated this to ADMS and made arrangements to take over the front line positions from 11th Field Ambulance this afternoon. Capt. B. G. BEVERIDGE with 16 bearers dispatched to FAMPOUX LOCK. Captain G. PILLANS with 40 bearers to FAMPOUX VILLAGE POST. 4 bearers to be attached to each battalion of 152 Bay Brigade. These two are Bearer Relay Posts. Capt. J. S. McCONNACHIE and Captain H. E. McDOUGAL will C Section Tent Subdivision to L'ABBAYETTE to form a Collecting Post. Go the 4th Div was removing their Onations from the Scarpe Canal and the gun Durham had not taken over the working of the Canal from FAMPOUX to ATHIES, evacuation of wounded was arranged by road from FAMPOUX to L'ABBAYETTE + thence by Railway embankment & bridge in front of FAMPOUX to our Two Bearer Relay Posts. Hence by road in FORD CARS to L'ABBAYETTE + thence to usually cars to advanced Dressing Station ST NICHOLAS, thence to HAUTE AVESNES from Dressg Static.	

Army Form C. 2118.

WAR DIARY
or
INTELLIGENCE SUMMARY.
(Erase heading not required.)

LXXVI
2/1 Highld. F.A. Amb.
9th Division Wm Crombey

Place	Date	Hour	Summary of Events and Information	Remarks and references to Appendices
ARRAS	12/5/17		O.C. RAMC O.O. dated Copy No 21 received. Orders of Cmdt accelerating Relief. Unit moved to reponsible for Evacuation from front to Advanced Dressing Stat. St NICHOLAS and for despatch of cases from there by M.A.C. Convoy, to main D.S. Station, Transport moved to St Nicholas near walking wounded Collecting Stat. by STEARINERIE there.	
"	13/5/17	7 am	Moved H.Q. to ST NICHOLAS and took over the walking wounded Collecting Station. A Section Tent Subdivision with Lieut M. HOOPER to m.o. B Section TENT Subdivision with Major WHYTE & myself took over the Advanced Dressing Station ST NICHOLAS. Relief of 11th Field Ambulance completed 5.8 pm. Friday. Record numbers of Cases sick & wounded passed through various forward A & D Posts for walking wounded kept and daily stat. Y A 36 received daily at both Reports 6 am to 6 pm & 6 pm to 6 am. at Advanced Dressing Station – my Stretcher cases are taken and 2 u A.D. Posts Kept. with a nominal Reserve of all Cases. Admin MEDICAL ARRANGEMENTS received. A large dump of all forms of Medicine Stores and Serum Rations formed at L'ARRAYETTE	
St NICHOLAS	14/5/17	10 am	See the heavy of this Unit am now detailed in front Lines from 7.30 pm last night & Station were sent up last night from reserves of 1/3 H.F. amb Where have drawn New returns from for future status at Aux. Dress. Stat.	

WAR DIARY / INTELLIGENCE SUMMARY

Army Form C. 2118.

May 1917   LXXVII   2/1 High: 3rd Aust. Division R.E. Coy.

Place	Date	Hour	Summary of Events and Information	Remarks and references to Appendices
ST NICHOLAS	14/5/17	10 a.m.	The turning of the pipe 12 ord. who reported went to Capt. H. Brown for Infm. Actual and as reserve of reserves for front area. At 10 p.m. last night the 8th Aus H'rs & 5th Suffolks attack's Rouxville housed Roeux heavy damage. Successfully all right no delay or lack of tools secured. The wounds had to be moved from FAMPOUX Post via Corons Senile being 250 [?] been notified. The DECAUVILLE RAILWAY to returned from BR working from ATHIES to the Orion. ARRAS. I am today investigating the one and line to work it serving thus. I visited also the forward posts with Capt. Macdonald. This morning ... instructing the two N.C.Os at FAMPOUX mine withdrew O.H.Q, Leaving there in charge of N.C.O. under the daily supervision of Captain Macdougal who stays at L'ABBAYETTE a maintains lines between Brown Post & N.C.Ps.	
		6 p.m.	The Station — a collecting post L'ABBAYETTE is being cleaned up and a satisfactory progress. During Station might be made there the first of the RE tending of the division went up from ATHIES the afternoon, no orders have been given to the RE Officer in charge that wounded are to begin as if at the output below in pipes bodied may be brought down the way out the Roeux — Fampoux Road from FAMPOUX to L'ABBAYETTE	

WAR DIARY or **INTELLIGENCE SUMMARY.**
(Erase heading not required.)

Army Form C. 2118.

LXXVIII
2/1 Highland Field Ambulance
Multiplies War Diary

Place	Date	Hour	Summary of Events and Information	Remarks and references to Appendices
St NICHOLAS	14/5/17	6pm	All the cars of the B/S/B Hgr. F.A. Amb. reported today except this Head Qrs. & returned with their H.Q. (Mid. amounts to Hqrs.) Relay post at the ATHIES end of the Cause from FAMPOUX. The wounded evacuated from patients bays and post in Ambulance Cars thence by road to L'ABBAYETTE and St NICHOLAS. There is a Telephone at ATHIES available for communication with St NICHOLAS, at the Office of the 22nd H.A.G. The Decauville Railway is working from Athies lock to St Nicolas and arrangements made today for taking seven stretcher cases & some walking on to Railway trains. The Railway runs from the North bank of the Canal to Arras and is connected from Malvoisin, near the Armoured Dressing Station, 50 Metres or so also connected for the walking wounded.	
	15/5/17	10 am	At the request of the O. 5th Leinster at ALS Highest 6 bearers were employed last night in each Aid Post. The night was quiet. During the past 24 hours 60 Other Ranks wounded and 3 officers wounded have been handed over + 24 O.R. Sick, 12 Sickness wounded. Pontoon Barges are now carrying cases from FAMPOUX to ATHIES. R.E.s are mowing	

WAR DIARY or INTELLIGENCE SUMMARY

Army Form C. 2118.

LXXIX

May 1917

Sheet 6

9/ Winslow Field Ambulance
M. Wholin R.N. Comdy

Place	Date	Hour	Summary of Events and Information	Remarks and references to Appendices
St NICHOLAS	15/5/17	10 a.m.	L'ABBAYETTE. An amusement of Decauville Trams has been made from the huts at ATHIES LOCK for all cases to our dressing station at ST. NICHOLAS. As need so proposed. Walking wounded. ST NICHOLAS. This station works in conjunction with our main and aid at St Nicholas. It is at the junction of the BLANGY & ROCLINCOURT roads to ST NICHOLAS and proposed to make a main dressing station here by motor of Marquis on ground adjacent when this has been Lewis's returns. St Nicholas the habit of the house of the picard Avenues. Ambulance. Dressing Station here to Ambulance.	
		6 p.m.	This afternoon sharing commenced by the Enemy on ROEUX and west of it. Roads being night block to BLANGY. Continued very heavy. Shellst. Incts L'arosette. No alarm in evacuation of wounded & as ammunition her houses here has been met. The M.O. I/c A.T.S.14 reports that a counter attack was imminent & tomorrow, sent who had for 12 hours to 7 A.T.S.H. on that prevention of wind and to retrieve casualties among Infantry Reserves. A further total by F Keenan and out to reinforce FAMPOUX LOCK White is having the Chief heavy shell in account of the Canal Service.	

WAR DIARY
or
INTELLIGENCE SUMMARY.

Army Form C. 2118.

LXX 7
Appx 7
Map

2/1 High: 2d Amb
Materlain Lt Col: RC

Place	Date	Hour	Summary of Events and Information	Remarks and references to Appendices
St Nicholas	15/5/17	6pm	The pontoons are working regularly now with a horse for haulage. The R.E. are endeavouring to get a motor boat. This evening intimation was received that Capt Gilpillan J 5th Seaforths was wounded. Capt B.G. Beveridge cannot proceed at once to take his place and Capt Machell to aid post before Capt GILFILLAN left.	

[Hand-drawn map showing: CHEMICAL WORKS & STATION, FRONT, ROEUX, CANAL, "aid post", outpost, aid post, FAMPOUX VILLAGE, FAMPOUX POST, Lock POST, FORD EMRS, L'ABBAYETTE, CANAL, ATHIES PONTOONS Lock, BAILLEUL Rd, FEUCHY, DOUAI RAILWAY, SCAUVILLE Rly, ROAD, CANAL, W.M.G.S., A.D.S. ST NICHOLAS, ARRAS, Collecting Post]

Army Form C. 2118.

LXXXI

WAR DIARY
or
INTELLIGENCE SUMMARY.
(Erase heading not required.)

9th Infy. Bde. 9th Bde.
Wilkinson Lt.Col. Comdg.

Place	Date	Hour	Summary of Events and Information	Remarks and references to Appendices
ST NICHOLAS	12/4/17	10 am	At midnight last night we had passed through 94 Coys including washing kennels. Gen. Armings for reasons not clearly not have increased the strength of Reserve at FAMPOUX to 10, and FAMPOUX LOCK to 96. The work is being done in prolongation of way post and barricade communication tramway. A few are carrying stores to the stable of the village which is extremely shelled. Troops not at the West end of the village. None of 2nd very urgent. They are and to the LOCK both trenches and there by Canal & ATHIES, very occasionally the inspired area come down of find Car & L'ABBAYETTE. FAMPOUX VILLAGE is under a Maxim M.G. on Case the Canal is very heavily shelled on the trooper heavier. 21 German prisoners were helping to carry from R.A.P.s. At Nichola, this morning the Enemy continues to shell the roads + batteries as far back as BLANGY. And numerous Lewis from the road + Battery are strong in L'ABBAYETTE. At 6 am this morning Captain Kennedy D.A.A.Q.M.G. 51st Div called as informed me that 152 Infy Brigade who had just captured the Remainder of ROEUX had cut off and primarily a total loss. The Enemy 52nd Battn of Guards the frontier, an last order entered our trenches in front and come in behind during the night. He also told me the 153 Infantry Brigade (in support) were attack the Situation at 7.30 to take back the lost ground.	

Army Form C. 2118.

WAR DIARY
or
INTELLIGENCE SUMMARY.
(Erase heading not required.)

LXXXII
2/1 Highrs. 74 Amb.
Wilson Lt Col Comdg

Sheet 9

Place	Date	Hour	Summary of Events and Information	Remarks and references to Appendices
St Nicolas	16/5/17	10 am (ctd)	This attack did not materialise so any stretcher bearers/squads who were available to any stretcher squads were maintaining the old front. Brigade cut off this Germans in the new while maintaining the old front. Through the afternoon were continuously arriving by German troops. Cpl W.G. Gell of this unit was hit by a piece out L'ABBAYETTE. This morning cut various parts of rear to ATHIES from ambulance cars have been put out of action by shell fire (2 wounded) at L'ABBAYETTE. A shell made a direct hit - In an underground Gallery and wounded within two Kemmel veterans Pt McKay & Sinclair. Some other R.B's were wounded at the front. A sergeant Clerk was slightly wounded. Capt McDougal & reports all relay posts working smoothly. Portions have been flying refuglants.	
		6 P.M.	The Barbarans & Entrances most of the day with intermissions. The repository of Fampoux & the Fampoux road escaped serious injury. The reserve battalion relieved FAMPOUX manned a number of S.A.A. sheets 20 S.A.A. cases been sent over to hospital burns. This afternoon have had home ambulances plying between L'ABBAYETTE & ST NICHOLAS. An orderly in going up was hit by a shell and both horses killed & driver seriously wounded. The ambulance was but slightly of returns, the one of your M.A.C. cars from D.D.M.S. Reference had continued.	

Army Form C. 2118.

WAR DIARY
or
INTELLIGENCE SUMMARY.

(Erase heading not required.)

LXXXIII
2/1 Wessex F.A. Amb.
Wellington Ho. Coy.

Place	Date	Hour	Summary of Events and Information	Remarks and references to Appendices
ST NICHOLAS	16/5/17	6 p.m.	In account of the known snipers activity, brought down today, in the employment of heavy calibre shells. The town of hand Ambulance always in of employment have ceased today. This was necessitated by	
	17/5/17	10 a.m.	Up to 6 p.m. today from 6 p.m. yesterday 136 Stretcher cases have passed down and 100 walking wounded. Enemy Shortened off last night activity & today there was hardly any. Intend to Shortly open a + The Cars from Drag onto + ROEUX + the CHEMICAL WORKS are being reserved including a number of Severely wounded Germans. They have been no further calls for Bearers. I have a Corpl who was with the 1/5 seaforth H? during the night 15/16 had him with me + SIMMONDS To Survey had been all round this aid post when Capt B.G. BEVERIDGE was [crossed out] This aid post of 1/5 seaforths was in Batt. HQ, the aid post Dugout having been hit by a Shell.	
		6 p.m.	5 of the Public Nurses for walking wounded here today. Returns to 4/11 Corps who 5 f the 15 M.A.C. Cars. Plans arranged to form an advanced Dressing Station at the Coulotte post L'ABBAYETTE	

WAR DIARY or INTELLIGENCE SUMMARY

Army Form C. 2118.

Sheet 11

LXXXIV

1 May
2/1 Highr FD Amb
[signature]

Place	Date	Hour	Summary of Events and Information	Remarks and references to Appendices
ST. NICHOLAS	18/5/17	10 am	The bearers of 1/2 H.F. Amb & 1/3 H.F. Amb. have been gradually relieved from duty for forward area work, and so 1/3 is now remain at L'Abbayette as a first call. They are sheets partly at the Collecting Post & partly behind the BAILEUL Railway Embankment.	
do.	19/5/17		Stahli graduates relieves them by 154th. The 153. have taken on a piece of line of 17th Div. north of Railway. Aid posts the same. ADMS O.O. No 41 Copy 207 received. Transfer for relief of 2/1 bearers in the Relay posts & R.A.Ps. by the bearer Division of 1/2 Highr FD Amb. Rely completes today. Capt H. BROWNE & 1/2 Highr. H.F. Amb. relieved Capt MACDOUGAL as bearer Officer.	
do.	20/5/17		The Tent subdivision 1 A section and C section at Collecting Post L'ABBAYETTE replaced the Tent Subdl. of 1/3 H.F. Amb. in the Battn action in the line are now in one. The Aid posts of the 1st and the 2nd Brigade - the Triple Arch Bridge over the Scarpe River and the Somme place – under the DOUAI Railway. The Bridge immediately in front of the (East) has become a Battalion H.Q.	

WAR DIARY or INTELLIGENCE SUMMARY

Army Form C. 2118.

Sheet L X X V / 12

2/1 Highland F? Amb
(Attached to 51st Div Cav?)

Place	Date	Hour	Summary of Events and Information	Remarks and references to Appendices
ST NICHOLAS	24/4/17		The 1/1 Highland F? Coy RE have instituted a service of pontoons from FAMPOUX lock as far up as the Triple Arch Bridge. Wounded are now floated on pontoons at the Regt Aid Post and taken to FAMPOUX from thence by motor ambulance to ATHIES from thence to base. This new scheme has stopped all the pontoons at FAMPOUX lock thence by teams of Royne to reground the pontoons. As carrying work is practically no longer work by day or by night. The wounded have been the first returns since attempt at the former hamstred which first returns since and are now far the above, Latrine Battalion have drag the pontoons a name could have in boat. During the whole day no pontoon was patiently to come to bring either by stretcher or otherwise. There have been several wounded evacuated however. The Corner Grig dim'd by high trees is probably all easily seen by the enemy. The services of Captain N.E. McDOUGAL & Capt? H. BROWNE (M.C.) in daily helping tends with all of the relay posts has contributed much to success although men fairly & stale. The Evacuation has required no further interference except to increase the Staff during presence of work.	

Army Form C. 2118.

WAR DIARY
or
INTELLIGENCE SUMMARY.
(Erase heading not required.)

LXXVI
9th High'd Co. R.E.
(Mtd. to LGpCoy)

Place	Date	Hour	Summary of Events and Information	Remarks and references to Appendices
St Nicholas	13 May /17		The work at L'ABBAYETTE has been largely that of an Advanced Dressing Station, & except during previous tours most Caves were cut on 5 May at to A.D.S. St Nicholas much fresh aid has been done in Caves from the Batteries including The Amputation during the past week. R.E. personnel with the mines leavers are improving the accommodation and complete lino heating of the place has been done. Where the shell has through the gallery a new entrance has been made to this and little installation of this Gallery and convenience for loading Cars has thereto. St Nicholas A.D.S. Much labour has been done in levelling the road, for direction of wagons with the intention of opening a main Dressing Station there. Space for 16 wagons has been prepared.	Scheme of main Dressing Station Marquees

[Diagram showing layout with labels: Orchard, Officers, Reception, Orderlies, Addison Cars, Marquee, Chant, HQ Office, MAC Cars, Field Staffs dump, To MAC's, Evacuation]

LXXXVII

Army Form C. 2118.

WAR DIARY
or
INTELLIGENCE SUMMARY.
(Erase heading not required.)

Sheet May 14.

2/1 Highland Field Ambulance
Milestone W.Col. Cemy

Place	Date	Hour	Summary of Events and Information	Remarks and references to Appendices
St Helbro	26/5/17		Evacuation proceeding normally. Following movements of Officers: Capt. S.B. MILNE rejoins. Lieut. W. SHAW. rank Capt. W. SHAW rank have been attached to this unit. LIEUT. M. HOOPER to Officers Rest Station Sick 20th W.F.C.S. On 20th Capt. B.G. BEVERIDGE returns to unit & Capt. N.F. MACDOUGAL (25th May) took his place as no. 5th Sergeant O.C.	
do	27/5/17		Heavy Brown. 9½ W.F.Amb. relieves from duty on the front by Heavy Brown. 9 2/1 High Fd Amb under Lieut W. SHAW. Capt. B.G. BEVERIDGE relieves Capt. 9 L. PILLANS at Collecting Post L'ABBAYETTE	
do	28/5/17		Heavy Brown. 9½ W.F.Amb. relieves 9 ½ K.F.Amb. 9 2/1 High Fd Amb reports this unit today as per orders, with the Stretcher Carriage and Ambulance Cars & ADMS orders. AD ms OC 2/5 & 2/6 High Fd Amb which have been an hour ADMS O.O. 2482 means provided for man of the A&S CHEVERS. 9 of Riding L 27th Fd Amb, 9 Div St NICHOLAS position to be taken 5 102 L Fd Amb, 34 Div.	

A5834 Wt. W4973/M687 750,000 8/16 D.D. & L. Ltd. Forms/C.2118/13.

Army Form C. 2118.

WAR DIARY
or
INTELLIGENCE SUMMARY.

LXXXVIII
Sheet 15
MAY.

Place	Date	Hour	Summary of Events and Information	Remarks and references to Appendices
St Nicolas	30/5/17		Today the following reliefs of medical units in forward area took place. Pampoux Village — 25th Fd Amb — 26th Fd Amb } 9th Div. Athies Lock — 27th Fd Amb L'ABBAYETTE St Sauv Dn Hotel — 103rd Fd Amb Nicholas 55th Dn Lot. Walking wounded Coll. post 102nd Fd Amb } 34th Fd Amb Dublin Heights for Stretcher	
CHELERS.	31/5/17		All complete by 5.30 p.m. Today D.M.S.L.S. Transport & Horses were moving. Unit moved today to Mullin Bro, near Coupette entret advance of main Corps.	

B.E.F.

SUMMARY OF MEDICAL WAR DIARIES of

2/1st Highland Field Ambulance,

51st Division,

17th Corps,

3rd Army.

WESTERN FRONT, APRIL - MAY 1917.

O.C. Lt.Colonel J. Robertson.

Summarised under the following headings:-

PHASE "B" - BATTLE OF ARRAS. APRIL - MAY 1917.

1st Period, April 1917. Attack on Vimy Ridge.
2nd Period, May 1917. Capture of Siegfried Line.

B.E.F.

1.

2/1st H.F.A., 51st Division. WESTERN FRONT,
O.C. Lt.Col. J. Robertson. MAY 1917.
17th Corps, 3rd Army.

Phase "B" - Battle of Arras. April - May 1917.
2nd Period, May 1917. Capture of Siegfried Line.

May.	H.Q. at Caucourt.
1st-7th	Operations R.A.M.C. Unit in rest. Sk. of Divn. treated.
10th	Moves To Arras.
12th	Operations Enemy. Arras shelled by long range H. Vil. gun.

Moves det. 1 & 16 to Fampoux Lock.
     1 & 40 " " Village P.
     O & 4 attached to each Btln. of 152nd Inf. Bde
     2 & C. sect. to L'Abbayette to form Coll. P.

Evacuation As 4th Divn. removed their pontoons and 51st D Divn. had not taken over working of canal from Fampoux to Athies, W. were evacuated by road from R.A.P's in Rly. embankment bridges in front of Fampoux to (2) Br. Relay P's thence by road in Fords to L'Abbayette and thence by Wolsely Cars to A.D.S. St. Nicholas, thence to Haute Avesnes M.D.S. 2/1st High. F.A. responsible for evacuation from front to A.D.S. St. Nicholas and for despatch of W. by M.A.C. to M.D.S.

13th Transport Moved to St. Nicholas rear Wlkg. W. Coll. Post.
    Moves H.Q. to St. Nicholas.

14th Assistance Brs. of 1/3rd High. F.A. attached to 2/1st High. F.A. for duty at A.D.S. 1 & Brs. of 1/2nd High. F.A. also attached.

Operations 13th/14th At 10 p.m. 13th, 8th A. & S. Highrs. and 5th Seaforths attacked successfully.

Evacuation No delay or lack of touch occurred.

B.E.F.

2/1st High. F.A., 51st Division,   WESTERN FRONT,
O.C. Lt.Col. J. Robertson.   MAY 1917.
17th Corps, 3rd Army.

Phase "B", continued.
2nd Period, continued.

May.
15th

H.Q. at St. Nicholas.

Evacuation From L'Abbayette and Athies lock by Decauville to St. Nicholas.   Attached App. 1.

Accommodation St. Nicholas - Very well made dugouts lit by electricity. Situated at junction of Blangy and Roclincourt Roads.

Operations Enemy. At 6 p.m. shelling commenced on Roeux and west of it. Roads and Canals R. back to Blangy very heavily shelled.

Casualties R.A.M.C. Capt. Gilfillan, M.O. 5th Seaforths, W.

16th

Casualties Total to Midt. 15th   94 W.
                "   "   6 p.m. 16th 126 L.D.W. & 100 wlkg. W.

Med. Arr. Brs. at Fampoux increased to 40 and Fampoux Lock to 76. Lock became principal Relay P. Most W. came that way.

Evacuation A few W. carried along streets of village, which was shelled continuously, to Post at W. side of village. Thence, if not urgent, to Lock to the pontoons, thence by canal to Athies. Occasionally urgent cases came by Ford to L'Abbayette. Fampoux Village used as reserve post in event of canal being heavily shelled or the bridges broken. 21 P.O.W. helped to carry W. from R.A.P's to Lock.

Operations Enemy. Enemy continued to shell Blangy. Enemy got round and cut off 152nd Inf. Bde. at Roeux and it was expected they would be a total loss.

Operations 153rd Inf. Bde. made an attack on lost ground but the surrounded Bde. cut off the Gers. in rear while it maintained the old front, though its flanks were temporarily over-run by Gers.

B.E.F. 3.

2/1st High. F.A., 51st Division,   WESTERN FRONT,
O.C. Lt.Col. J. Robertson.,   MAY 1917.
17th Corps, 3rd Army.

Phase "B", continued.
2nd Period, continued.

May.
16th
(contd.) Casualties R.A.M.C. Shell made direct hit on underground gallery and penetrated. O & 2 killed.

O & 1 wounded.

Empty H. Amb. hit, both horses killed also

O & 1 killed. driver

O & 1 Wounded. Orderly.

Operations Enemy, Gas. Res. Btln. behind Fampoux shelled with gas shells. No casualties, Gas.

17th Operations Enemy. Shelling slackened off considerably.

Evacuation Proceeded steadily. Cases evacuated from dugouts in Roeux and Chemical Work including a number of seriously W.

Transport 5 Motor Buses and 5 M.A.C. Cars returned.

18th Med. Arr. Brs. of 1/2nd and 1/3rd High. F.A. gradually relieved in forward area.

19th Military Situation 152nd Bde. relieved by 154th.

153rd Bde. took over part of line of 17th Divn. N. of Railway.

20th Med. Arr. Brs. of 2/1st High. F.A. relieved at Relay P. and R.A.P's by Brs. of 1/2nd High. F.A.

T.S.D. "A" sect. relieved T.S.D. of "C" sect. at Coll. Post L'Abbayette.

A.P's of the 2 Btlns. in line at Triple Arch Bridge over R. Scarpe, under Douai Railway.

21st Evacuation 1/1st High. Fd. Coy. R.E. instituted a service of pontoons from Fampoux Lock to Triple Arch Bridge. W. placed on pontoons at R.A.P. and taken to Fampoux. Transhipped into other pontoons at Fampoux Lock thence to Athies.

B.E.F.

2/1st High. F.A., 51st Division, WESTERN FRONT,
O.C. Lt.Col. J. Robertson. MAY 1917.
17th Corps, 3rd Army.

Phase "B", continued.
2nd Period, continued.

May. 21st (contd.)   Evacuation (contd.) Pontoons worked night and day, thus obviating the necessity of any carrying by brs.

W. expressed satisfaction at smooth method of transit. Labour Coy. men hauled pontoons. The whole service was carried out without mishap throughout Ops.

22nd   Accommodation Attached App. A.

27th   Med. Arr. Br. D. 2/1st High. F.A. relieved 1/2nd High. F.A. brs. at front.

28th   Moves dets. B.D's of 1/2nd and 1/3rd High. F.A's rejoined their H.Q's with Str. carriages and Amb. Cars.

30th   Med. Arr. Following reliefs took place :-

Fampoux Village	28th F.A.	9th Division.
" Lock)		
)	27th F.A.	" "
Athies ")		
L'Abbayette.		
St. Nicholas. (A.D.S.		103rd F.A.
(		
(57th Divn. Sect. W.W.Coll.P.		102nd F.A.
(both 34th Division.)		

31st   Moves To Chelers.

B.E.F.

2/1st H.F.A., 51st Division.   WESTERN FRONT,
O.C. Lt.Col. J. Robertson.   MAY 1917.
17th Corps, 3rd Army.

Phase "B" - Battle of Arras. April - May 1917.
2nd Period, May 1917. Capture of Siegfried Line.

May.   H.Q. at Caucourt.
1st-7th   Operations R.A.M.C. Unit in rest. Sk. of Divn. treated.
10th   Moves To Arras.
12th   Operations Enemy. Arras shelled by long range H. Vil. gun.
            Moves det. 1 & 16 to Fampoux Lock.
                        1 & 40 "   "   Village P.
                        0 & 4 attached to each Btln. of 152nd Inf. Bde
                        2 & C. sect. to L'Abbayette to form Coll. P.
            Evacuation As 4th Divn. removed their pontoons and 51st D
            Divn. had not taken over working of canal from Fampoux
            to Athies, W. were evacuated by road from R.A.P's in Rly.
            embankment bridges in front of Fampoux to (?) Br. Relay
            P's thence by road in Fords to L'Abbayette and thence
            by Wolsely Cars to A.D.S. St. Nicholas, thence to Haute
            Avesnes M.D.S. 2/1st High. F.A. responsible for
            evacuation from front to A.D.S. St. Nicholas and for
            despatch of W. by M.A.C. to M.D.S.
13th   Transport Moved to St. Nicholas rear Wlkg. W. Coll. Post.
            Moves H.Q. to St. Nicholas.
14th   Assistance Brs. of 1/3rd High. F.A. attached to 2/1st
            High. F.A. for duty at A.D.S. 1 & Brs. of 1/2nd High.
            F.A. also attached.
            Operations 13th/14th At 10 p.m. 13th, 8th A. & S.
            Highrs. and 5th Seaforths attacked successfully.
            Evacuation No delay or lack of touch occurred.

B.E.F.

2/1st High. F.A., 51st Division,   WESTERN FRONT,
O.C. Lt.Col. J. Robertson.   MAY 1917.
17th Corps, 3rd Army.

Phase "B", continued.
2nd Period, continued.

May.   H.Q. at St. Nicholas.
15th   Evacuation From L'Abbayette and Athies lock by Decauville to
            St. Nicholas.   Attached App. 1.
            Accommodation St. Nicholas - Very well made dugouts lit
            by electricity. Situated at junction of Blangy and
            Roclincourt Roads.
            Operations Enemy. At 6 p.m. shelling commenced on Rœux
            and west of it. Roads and Canals R. back to Blangy very
            heavily shelled.
            Casualties R.A.M.C. Capt. Gilfillan, M.O. 5th Seaforths, W.
16th   Casualties Total to Midt. 15th 94 W.
                        " " 6 p.m. 16th 126 L.D.W. & 100 wlkg. W.
            Med. Arr. Brs. at Fampoux increased to 40 and Fampoux
            Lock to 76. Lock became principal Relay P. Most W. came
            that way.
            Evacuation A few W. carried along streets of village, which
            was shelled continuously, to Post at W. side of village.
            Thence, if not urgent, to Lock to the pontoons, thence by
            canal to Athies. Occasionally urgent cases came by Ford
            to L'Abbayette. Fampoux Village used as reserve post in
            event of canal being heavily shelled or the bridges broken.
            21 P.O.W. helped to carry W. from R.A.P's to Lock.
            Operations Enemy. Enemy continued to shell Blangy. Enemy
            got round and cut off 152nd Inf. Bde. at Roeux and it was
            expected they would be a total loss.
            Operations 153rd Inf. Bde. made an attack on lost ground
            but the surrounded Bde. cut off the Gers. in rear while it
            maintained the old front, though its flanks were temporarily
            over-run by Gers.

B.E.F.

2/1st High. F.A., 51st Division, WESTERN FRONT,
O.C. Lt.Col. J. Robertson., MAY 1917.
17th Corps, 3rd Army.

Phase "B", continued.
2nd Period, continued.

May.
16th (contd.) Casualties R.A.M.C. Shell made direct hit on underground gallery and penetrated. O & 2 killed.
  O & 1 wounded.
Empty H. Amb. hit, both horses killed also
  O & 1 killed. driver
  O & 1 Wounded. Orderly.

Operations Enemy, Gas. Res. Btln. behind Fampoux shelled with gas shells. No casualties, Gas.

17th Operations Enemy. Shelling slackened off considerably.
Evacuation Proceeded steadily. Cases evacuated from dugouts in Roeux and Chemical Work including a number of seriously W.
Transport 5 Motor Buses and 5 M.A.C. Cars returned.

18th Med. Arr. Brs. of 1/2nd and 1/3rd High. F.A. gradually relieved in forward area.

19th Military Situation 152nd Bde. relieved by 154th.
  153rd Bde. took over part of line of 17th Divn. N. of Railway.

20th Med. Arr. Brs. of 2/1st High. F.A. relieved at Relay P. and R.A.P's by Brs. of 1/2nd High. F.A.
  T.S.D. "A" sect. relieved T.S.D. of "C" sect. at Coll. Post L'Abbayette.
  A.P's of the 2 Btlns. in line at Triple Arch Bridge over R. Scarpe, under Douai Railway.

21st Evacuation 1/1st High. Fd. Coy. R.E. instituted a service of pontoons from Fampoux Lock to Triple Arch Bridge. W. placed on pontoons at R.A.P. and taken to Fampoux. Transhipped into other pontoons at Fampoux Lock thence to Athies.

B.E.F. 4.

2/1st High. F.A., 51st Division, WESTERN FRONT,
O.C. Lt.Col. J. Robertson. MAY 1917.
17th Corps, 3rd Army.

Phase "B", continued.
2nd Period, continued.

May.
21st Evacuation (contd.) Pontoons worked night and day, thus
(contd.) obviating the necessity of any carrying by brs.

    W. expressed satisfaction at smooth method of transit. Labour Coy. men hauled pontoons. The whole service was carried out without mishap throughout Ops.

22nd Accommodation Attached App. A.(attd. 1st copy.)

27th Med. Arr. Br. D. 2/1st High. F.A. relieved 1/2nd High. F.A. brs. at front.

28th Moves dets. B.D's of 1/2nd and 1/3rd High. F.A's rejoined their H.Q's with Str. carriages and Amb. Cars.

30th Med. Arr. Following reliefs took place :-

    Fampoux Village   28th F.A.   9th Division.
    " Lock)
)   27th F.A.   " "
    Athies ")
    L'Abbayette.

    St. Nicholas.   (A.D.S.   103rd F.A.
                 (57th Divn. Sect. W.W.Coll.P. 102nd F.A.
                (both 34th Division.)

31st Moves To Chelers.

St Nicholas
Scheme of M.D.S. 22-5-17
4/1 Highland F.A.

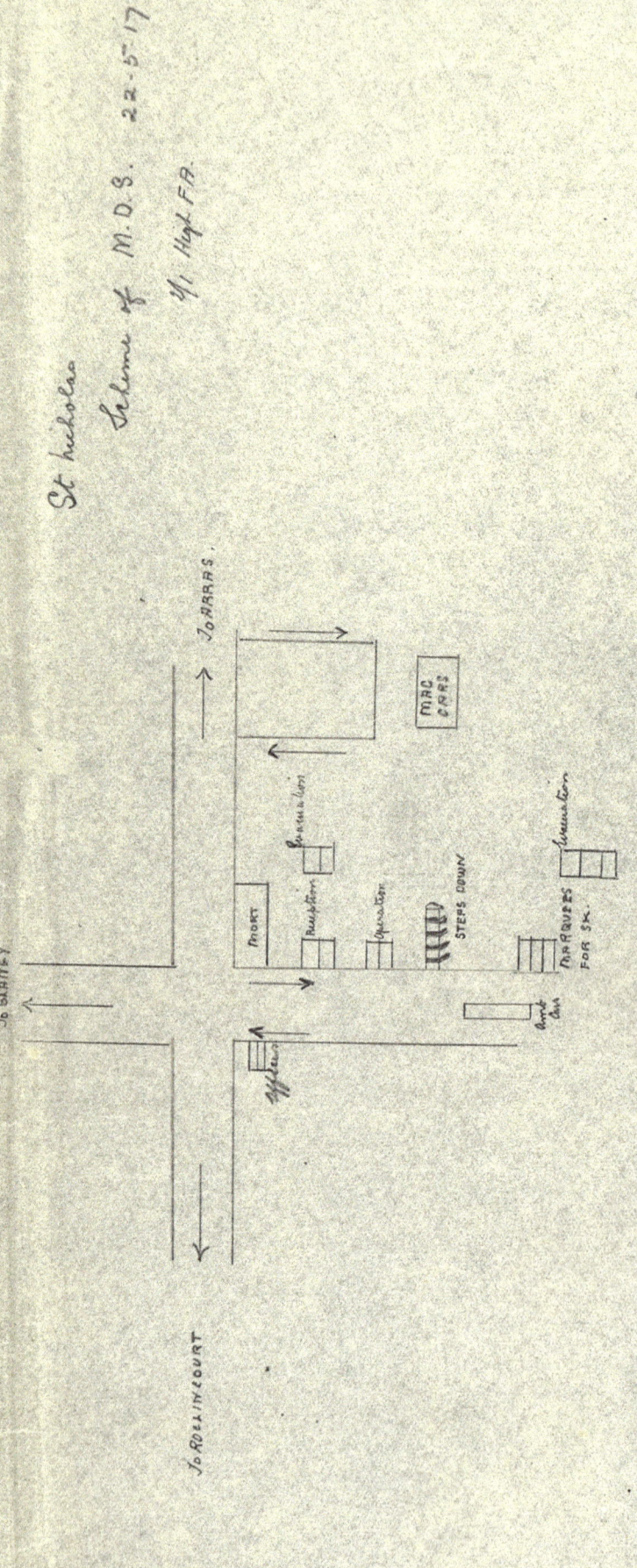

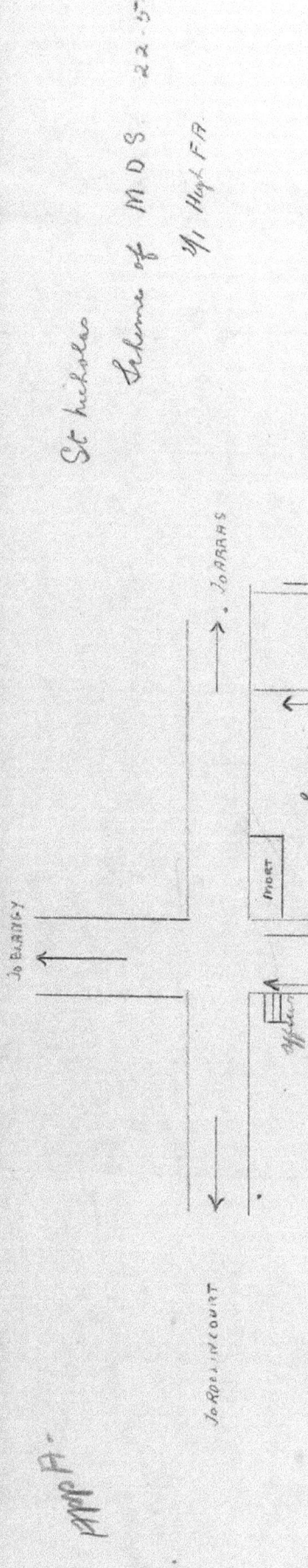

App 1

2/1 H.F.A.
15-5-17

FRONT

8th Durham Works of Staffs
R.P.
FAMPOUX
FAMPOUX LOCK
R.P.
FORD CARS
PONTOONS
FEUCHY
ATHIES LOCK
CANAL
EMBANKMENT
DOUAI RLY
DETRUVILLE RLY
RD R.D
N.W.P
A.D.S. STRONGHOLD
ARRAS

2/1st Highland F.A.

COMMITTEE FOR THE
MEDICAL HISTORY OF THE WAR
Date -7 AUG. 1917

Army Form C. 2118.

WAR DIARY or INTELLIGENCE SUMMARY.

(Erase heading not required.)

LXXXIX 2/1 Highland Field Ambulance

Place	Date	Hour	Summary of Events and Information	Remarks and references to Appendices
CHELERS	1/6/17		RAMC O.O. 43, Copy no 1. received. 154 Bf. Brigade orders received under Brigade orders. Ambulance to have under Brigade orders. Capt. G. Dick shall return from 42 C.C.S. to which he was temporarily attached to 29. 57th N. Div. Sino Quinine arrangements. 154 Bf. Brigade A.I. to S.S.5 duly received. 2/1 H'ld F.A. Amb moves forward to HUCLIER on 4th June. A.I. S.S.6 - Provides for move of this unit to LUGY on 5th June. A.D.M.S. do 3650 gives a resumé of moves of units within the Division.	MAP LENS 11
	2/6/17		154 Brigd O.O. 119 Copy 20 10. received with march tables for 4th & 5th June as above.	
	3/6/17		154 Brigd O.O. 120 Copy no 10. received orders move of Transport by road on 4th & 5th & NORDAUSQUE holts the night at WIZERNES. Dismounted personnel by motor Bus to 7 & NORDAUSQUE AREA	
HUCLIER	4/6/17		Moved unit to HUCLIER. H.Q. in School. Capt Gh. Pillans to be Billeting Officer during forward move. HQ was Estaminet there	
LUGY	5/6/17		Moved unit to LUGY. Received S.S.7. Brigade A.I. as C Entrainment. 3 Buses 652 at LUGY Church at 7 A.M. for movement of this unit to GUEMY	MAP DJ HAZEBROOK DJ S.A. do
do	6/6/17	7.30 am	Transport under charge of Capts B.g. BEVERIDGE proceeds to WIZERNES. Dismounted personnel reaches LUGY	

WAR DIARY or INTELLIGENCE SUMMARY

Army Form C. 2118.

2/1 H.Sx. F.A. Amb.   LXL

Place	Date	Hour	Summary of Events and Information	Remarks and references to Appendices
GUEMY	7/5/17		Move of Amb. completed without incident of note. Transport arrived about 3 p.m. Hospital for 25 sick opened in tents in accordance with W.O.ms 3698 of 5th June.	
do.	14/5/17		Since leaving St Nicholas repitition. Clothing of Staff & Personnel has been carried out of the whole unit. All the sports, exercises with trainings in drill & First Aid have been made use of for improvement of physique & efficiency of the unit.	
do.	21/5/17		Captain G.L. PILLANS awarded Military Cross for gallantry between 23rd April & 15th May (Authority Third Army H.R.S.I dated 24/V/17) Capt. PILLANS proceeds on 14 days leave today.	

Movements of Officers

5 June   Lieut W. SHAW. assumed Temp Medical charge to Sordeum W.Q's
14 June Capt G. DICK   do   do
14 June Capt H E Medreyal proceeded to base on expiring of contract, struck off strength
15 June Capt G.L. PILLANS granted leave to U.K.
20 June Capt E. DICK rejoined H.Q.
25 June Capt G. Dick assumed temp med charge 51st W.D. Train A.S.C.
28 June Capt T.B. Milne assumed temp med charge 74th A.F.A. Bde

Army Form C. 2118.

WAR DIARY
or
INTELLIGENCE SUMMARY.

(Erase heading not required.)

Army Form C. 2118.

1 X L 1
2/1 H'ghs. Field Ambulance
Major H.A. Craig

Place	Date	Hour	Summary of Events and Information	Remarks and references to Appendices
GUEMY	21/5/17		Rame O.O. no. 1 of 19th received previous for the lifting up of the Div. front by a brigade from division. 1/5 Highrs. 79 Amb. to be moved with 163 Brigade to this purpose.	Marshals SA
	22/5/17		Rame O. no. A14 of 21st received previous for the movement on 22nd of the unit to LEDERZEELE area with the 154th Inf. Brigade.	
		7 P.M.	15th Inf. Brigade O.O. no. 121 Aug. received 7 P.M. here on Brigade to LES CINQ RUES from starting point at 5.40 a.m. (am roads NORDAUSQUE)	
LES CINQ RUES	22/5/17		here complete. Yesterday afternoon Major G.F. WHYTE proceeded to HERZEELE to take charge of XVIII Corps Rest Station in process of erection. Capt. Hutchinson & two men in charge at HERZEELE for duty.	
	23/5/17		15 Station Tent Subdivisions	
	27/5/17		40 ORs proceeded to HERZEELE for duty at Corps Rest Station.	
	28/5/17		Unit at Corps Rest Station. Erection of Marquees & tents almost complete. Kitchens, Stoves & tents erected with Labours.	

B.E.F.

SUMMARY OF MEDICAL WAR DIARIES OF 2/1st Highland F.A.

51st Division.   8th Corps.   5th ARMY.

18th Corps from 22nd-23rd June 1917.

Western Front Operations - June - 1917.

Officer Commanding - Lt.Col. J. Robertson.

SUMMARIZED UNDER THE FOLLOWING HEADING :-
Phase "D" - Battle of Messines - June.- 1917.

B.E.F.

<u>2/1st Highland F.A. 51st Div. 8th Corps. 5th ARMY.</u> WESTERN FRONT.
June 1917.

<u>Officer Commanding - Lt.Col. J. ROBERTSON.</u>

<u>18th Corps from 22nd-23rd June 1917.</u>

<u>PHASE "D" - Battle of Messines - June - 1917.</u>

<u>Headquarters at GUEMY.</u>

June 21st.   <u>Decoration.</u>   Capt. G.L. Pillans awarded M.C. for gallantry between 23/4/1917 and 15/5/1917.

22nd-23rd.   <u>Transfer.</u> Unit transferred to 18th Corps.

B.E.F.

2/1st Highland F.A.   51st Div. 18th Corps,   5th ARMY. Western Front
                                                         June 1917.
Officer Commanding - Lt.Col. J. ROBERTSON.

PHASE "D" - Battle of Messines - June 1917.

June
22nd-23rd. Transfer. Unit transferred to 18th Corps.

           Moves. To Les Cinq Rues.

23rd.   Moves Def. "B" Sect. T.S.D. to Herzeele C.R.S.

27th.   O & 40 to C.R.S. Herzeele.

B.E.F.

SUMMARY OF MEDICAL WAR DIARIES OF 2/1st Highland F.A.

51st Division. 8th Corps. 5th ARMY.

18th Corps from 22nd-23rd June 1917.

Western Front Operations - June - 1917.

Officer Commanding - Lt.Col. J. Robertson.

SUMMARISED UNDER THE FOLLOWING HEADING :-
Phase "D" - Battle of Messines - June - 1917.

B.E.F.

2/1st Highland F.A. 51st Div. 8th Corps. 5th ARMY. WESTERN FRONT.
June 1917.
Officer Commanding - Lt.Col. J. ROBERTSON.
18th Corps from 22nd-23rd June 1917.

PHASE "D" - Battle of Messines - June - 1917.
Headquarters at GUEMY.

June 21st. Decoration. Capt. G.L. Pillans awarded M.C. for gallantry between 23/4/1917 and 15/5/1917.

22nd-23rd. Transfer. Unit transferred to 18th Corps.

B.E.F.

2/1st Highland F.A.   51st Div. 18th Corps,   5th ARMY.   Western Front
Officer Commanding - Lt.Col. J. ROBERTSON.   June 1917.

PHASE "D" - Battle of Messines - June 1917.

June
22nd-23rd. Transfer. Unit transferred to 18th Corps.

            Moves. To Les Cinq Rues.

23rd.   Moves Det. "B" Sect. T.S.D. to Herzeele C.R.S.

27th.   O & 40 to C.R.S. Herzeele.

2/1st Highland F.A.

COMMITTEE FOR THE
MEDICAL HISTORY OF THE WAR
Date 10 SEP. 1917

WAR DIARY or INTELLIGENCE SUMMARY

Army Form C. 2118.

LXII / 2/1 Hqrs 1st Aus / Stationary / November

Vol 23

6 JULY

Place	Date	Hour	Summary of Events and Information	Remarks and references to Appendices
1-VII-17 LES CINQ RUES	5/7/17		Capt. J.B. MILNE rejoined H.Q. Capt J.W. BENNET joins the unit for duty	
do	6/7/17		Col. G.L. PILLANS. returns from leave yesterday, today assumes Temporary medical charge 1/6 Seaforth Hdqrs vice Capt. A.G. PETER killed in action. Recd. Copy of Medical Arrangements XVIII Corps Part I	
do	7/7/17		Capt. J.W. BENNET R.A.M.C. assumes Temporary med. charge of 1/5 Royal Scots during the absence on leave of their M.O. Captain L.R. SHORE. R.A.M.C. (Repatd.) joins for duty	
do	10/7/17		XVIII Corps Medical Arrangements Part II (Z Scheme) Corps no 29. Being the Corps arrangements for Aid Posts & duties of Medical personnel of from Divisions 39th, 51st, 11th, 1/6th A.F.A. Division. The Corps will attack the Enemy with his Divisions 39 and 51, also two divisions in support. The duty of Zonals troops from the firing area rise in carried out to to Divisions in the line. Corps D.D.M.S. is responsible for medical arrangements for advanced Dressing Stations backwards. A.D.M.S. from front to advanced Dressing Stations	

WAR DIARY or INTELLIGENCE SUMMARY

Army Form C. 2118.

July 1917
No 2.

LXL(111)

2/1st F. Ambulance
(Scottish N.C. Coy)

Place	Date	Hour	Summary of Events and Information	Remarks and references to Appendices
LES. CINQ RUES.	14/7/17		R.A.M.C. O.O. no. A5 Copy no 13 duly received. Provides for the Relief of 1/3 W.F. Amb. in forward area by the 33rd Field Amb. 11th Division has consequently taken over the Div. Front.	
			The following Instructions for Offensive Operations 51st Div. have been received.	
			No. SG. 279/15. Section V. with amendment I. Formation of Stone Relay Truck Dumps	
		do	Sect. VI. Medical Arrangements	
		do	Section VII with amendment Fighting kit.	
		do	Sect. XVIII Trench Tramways	
		do	Sect. XIX Salvage	
		do	Sect. VIII Police	
		"	Section XX Burials	
		do	Sect. XVII Prisoners	
	15/7/17		Capt J.S. Mackenzie proceeds to C. Rest Station vice him G.E. WHYTE attached O.C. XVIII Corps W.W.C.P.	
			51st Highl. Div. medical arrangements for Operation 4. received	Med. Ref. Belgium & France sheet Passchendaele 52
	16/7/17		The Bearers of this unit will be Attached at follows at following Shelt 27 & 28	

Army Form C. 2118.
WAR DIARY
or
INTELLIGENCE SUMMARY. 1/1 Highland Field Ambulance
(Erase heading not required.)

Sheet 3

Place	Date	Hour	Summary of Events and Information	Remarks and references to Appendices
LES CINQ RUES	15/VII/17		Disposition of Bearers of H.F. Amb. 8 Bearers to each Battalion, 152 Brigade, + 8 to each of the Battalions 154 Bde. Remainder 32 in Reserve at Advanced Dressing Station. (C.19.c.4.1.) in 40,000 (Snoy Farm) Tent Divisions 1 Tent Subdivision at walking wounded Collecting Post 2 Tent Subdivisions at Advanced Dressing Station Snoy farm Horse and motor wagons 5/2 horses at B 26.a.2.5. Wheeled Stretcher Carriers will be parked at Advanced Dressing Station Head Quarters of the unit will be at G.2.a.2.4. along with H/3 High. F. Amb. (Private letter from H.Q.N.S.) The personnel of this unit will therefore work under O.C. Advanced Dressing Station and O.C. Corps walking wounded Collecting Post	
do.	16/VII/17		R.A.M.C. O.O. no 46 and no 12 received. Provides for distribution and moving up of the unit to forward area given below and forms	
	17/VII/17		Medical arrangements operation to amendment 25T. 6 N.C.O.s duly received. Capt. L.R. Shore R.A.M.C. proceeded to HERZEELE. C.M.W. Station. & reliefs. Capt. J.S. McConnachie returned to H.Q.	

Army Form C. 2118.

WAR DIARY
or
INTELLIGENCE SUMMARY.
(Erase heading not required.)

LXLV 2/1 Highl. Field Ambulance

Place	Date	Hour	Summary of Events and Information	Remarks and references to Appendices
LESCINE RUES.	21/VII/17		152 Inf. Bnigd. order 160 pants 1 O 2 with Affendicis A V B. recurs. Provides for the men of this unit on 23rd to St JANSTER BIEZEN & motor transport to General hummer day halls on night at WORMHOUDT Addendum Medical Arrangement XVIII Corps recurs 152 Inf. Bnigd. A.I. no 26 recurs	
do	22/VII/17		153 Inf. Bnigd. OO 2115 C/m USA recurs provides for move of this unit to Camps near STIENJE CABARET preparatory to going into the line First lunus of this unit were today dispatched to east of the following Battalions 1/6 A.Y.S. Har'n.'; 1/6 Batt Gordon Ht'rs.; 1/5 Seaforths, to Dragoths; 1 Batt. Th Royal Scots to Natt. Seaforths.	
St. JANSTER BIEZEN	23/VII/17		152 Inf. Bnigd. A.I. no 27 recurs Moved the unit to "N" Camp. Tents along with 16 BlackWatch to London US D 33 M. G. C. A.Dms. O.O. no 47 nes. This unit will relieve yesterday 12 first Scottish am and running (heavy) to relieve 33rd Field Ambulance at ESSEX FARM. Advance Dressing Station in night of 26 T. 27 th July B. Lect. Lieut Bd Lumin from HERZELE to M.D.S. XVIII Corps to report to Major G.F. WHYTE preparatory to going to washing wounds arrivals of rests	
	24/VII/17			

A.5834. Wt. W4973/M687 750,000 8/16 D.D. & L. Ltd. Forms/C.2118/13

WAR DIARY or INTELLIGENCE SUMMARY

Army Form C. 2118.

LXLVI
H/Hya. 1st Army
Malcolm Nev. C(...)

July 5
Sheet 5

Place	Date	Hour	Summary of Events and Information	Remarks and references to Appendices
ST JANSTER BIEZEN	24/7/17		Captain Thur became attached for duty with XVIII Corps under Colonel Clancy. Major Whyte and until the attachment of 1/132 = 2nd Army, the tent subdivision with from this XVIII Corps walking wounded Collecting Post near VLAMARTINGHE (H.3.a.) marched on the eleven later hours at the M.D.S. (A.23.c.2.9.) Sheet 25 and been up to the wound at M.S.d. and hires a carrying corps for attendance on walking wounded from XVIII corps. This party will be supplied by Corps Troops Supply Column except for ordinary ration. Until I rise be on the strength of this unit strictly. This unit is a provisional arrangement of Major Whyte with me. In addition to Major Whyte, Capt. J.S. McCormack, Capts J.B. Hellis, Revd. from this unit are of the party. Major Whyte is responsible to Corps direct.	
do	25/7/17		B.M. 153 to 247 notifies the cancellation of all moves till further orders.	
do	26/7/17		K.A.M.C. O.O. 45 of 25th inst received. This unit less attachments will move independently to Camps at A.30.Central. Transport to H.Q. G move to POPERINGHE and be quartered along with the 1/3 = Ship of Amb on 27th inst leave 62 suspects by 10 a.m.	
do			K.A.M.C. O.O. no. 49 Cpr 3 received. Personnel for A.D.S. will move there from A.30 Central at 9 p.m. on 28th inst	

LXLVII

WAR DIARY or INTELLIGENCE SUMMARY.

Army Form C. 2118.

Sheet 6   July   9/1 1/xt, 7th Ambl.
         J. Mackenzie M.Cdr. Comdg.

Place	Date	Hour	Summary of Events and Information	Remarks and references to Appendices
POPERINGHE	27/7/17		Starting about 6 am. The unit proceeded to POPERINGHE and formed a camp on the S.W. side at 6.11.b.9.9. (Sheet 27) After a short halt the personnel fell in & proceeded during station. Proceeded to A.30 Central & practiced in Rules near the Commandant Office. During Capt. GUYTORRANCE M.C. Junr E. N.S. omm reported in dbs.	
do.	28/7/17		in accordance with M.Orders. O.O. No. A.9. The pants at A.30 Central Journals to ESSEX FARM at 9 p.m. The half numbers 72 o'orns, broken down (Capt). B.G. BEVERIDGE. (Came under the command of the O.C. Advanced (Capt). - Major G.W. MILLER 3 Inft. 7d Amb. During Station -	
do.	29/7/17		This is around 6 to 7 day as orders have been received for all cars to report to O.C. M.A.C. at A.23.C.29. and More Ambulances to proceed to B.26.S. and fork there two called for by O.C. advanced Dressing Station, With 2 ford Ambulances forward & Advanced Car park near the washing Winnie Station at 10 p.m.	
			All personnel in Position for Zero hour	
do.	27/7/17		In the night of 27th July, DDMS. XVIII Corps. O.O. No 3 was received. At 12 noon a I.C. Divisional Medical units-wire wire close to receipt of met numbered and to for with return Para 2 pensions were annual at that hour.	
		11 p.m. corps OO. N°4 received about 11 pm which had in account of a withdrawal of the heavy guns the V any bdq 2 hours was to advance with in manually in respect of a telegram. All personnel to "stand to" hendung receipt of this telegram	
	31/7/17	4.30 am	Cancelled - more to 2nd line	
		2 May		

B.E.F.

SUMMARY OF MEDICAL WAR DIARIES OF 2/1st Highland F.A.

51st Division.   8th Corps.   5th ARMY.

Western Front Operations - "July - 1917.

Officer Commanding - Lt.Col. J. ROBERTSON.

SUMMARISED UNDER THE FOLLOWING HEADINGS:-

Phase "D" 1. Passchendaele Operations,"July - Nov. 1917."

   (a) - Operations commencing 1/7/17.

   (b) - Operations commencing 1/10/17.
        Canadians attaked Passchendaele, Oct 30th.
        Canadians took Passchendaele, Nov. 6th.

B.E.F.   1.

2/1st Highland F.A.   51st Div. 8th Corps. 5th ARMY. WESTERN
                                                            FRONT.
Officer Commanding = Lt.Col. J. ROBERTSON.   July 1917.

PHASE "D" 1. Passchendaele Operations, "July - Nov. 1917."

   (a) - Operations commencing 1/7/17.

Headquarters at Les Cinq Rues.

July 5th.   Casualties R.A.M.C. Capt. A.G. Peter attached 1/6th

            Seaforths died of wounds.

   22nd.   Moves. Detachment.) 8 bearers proceeded to each battalion
            Medical Arrangements.)
                       of 152nd Brigade and 2 Battalions

            of 154th Brigade.

   23rd.   Moves.   To St. JANSER BIEZEN.

   24th.   Moves. Detachment.) "B" Section T.S.D. moved from
            Medical Arrangements.)
                       HERZEELE to VLAMERTINGHE H.3.d.

            (Sheet 28) and formed walking wounded Col. Post with detach-

            ment of 132nd F.A.

   27th.   Moves.   Unit less detachments to POPERINGHE.

   28th.   Moves. Detachment.) 1 & 2 T.S.D's to A.D.S. Essex Farm
            Medical Arrangements.)
                       under command of Officer Commanding

            A.D.S. Major G.W. Miller 1/3rd H.F.A.

   30th.   Moves. Transport. Horse ambulances to B.26.C. and Ford

            Cars to Adv. Car Park near W.W.C.S.

   31st.   Operations. Z day.

B.E.F.

SUMMARY OF MEDICAL WAR DIARIES OF 2/1st Highland F.A.

51st Division. 8th Corps. 5th ARMY.

Western Front Operations - "July - 1917.

Officer Commanding - Lt.Col. J. ROBERTSON.

SUMMARISED UNDER THE FOLLOWING HEADINGS:-

Phase "D" 1. Passchendaele Operations,"July - Nov. 1917."

   (a) - Operations commencing 1/7/17.

   (b) - Operations commencing 1/10/17.
       Canadians attaked Passchendaele, Oct 30th.
       Canadians took Passchendaele, Nov. 6th.

B.E.F.   1.

2/1st Highland F.A.   51st Div. 8th Corps. 5th ARMY. WESTERN
                                                                                    FRONT.
Officer Commanding = Lt.Col. J. ROBERTSON.   July 1917.

PHASE "D" 1. Passchendaele Operations, "July - Nov. 1917."

(a) - Operations commencing 1/7/17.

Headquarters at Les Cinq Rues.

July 5th.   Casualties R.A.M.C. Capt. A.G. Peter attached 1/6th
            Seaforths died of wounds.

22nd.   Moves. Detachment.   ) 8 bearers proceeded to each battalion
        Medical Arrangements.   )
                                   of 152nd Brigade and 2 Battalions
        of 154th Brigade.

23rd.   Moves.   To St. JANSER BIEZEN.

24th.   Moves. Detachment.   ) "B" Section T.S.D. moved from
        Medical Arrangements.   )
                                   HERZEELE to VLAMERTINGHE H.3.d.
        (Sheet 28) and formed walking wounded Col. Post with detach-
        ment of 132nd F.A.

27th.   Moves.   Unit less detachments to POPERINGHE.

28th.   Moves. Detachment.   ) 1 & 2 T.S.D's to A.D.S. Essex Farm
        Medical Arrangements.   )
                                   under command of Officer Commanding
        A.D.S. Major G.W. Miller 1/3rd H.F.A.

30th.   Moves. Transport. Horse ambulances to B.26.C. and Ford
        Cars to Adv. Car Pk. near W.W.C.S.

31st.   Operations. Z - day.

140/2364

21st Highland F.A.

Aug 1917

COMMITTEE FOR THE
MEDICAL HISTORY OF THE WAR
Date −1 OCT. 1917

Army Form C. 2118.

WAR DIARY
or
INTELLIGENCE SUMMARY.

(Erase heading not required.)

2/1 Highland Field Ambulance
J. K. Morton Lt. Col. Comdg.

Vol 24

August 1917
Sheet 1.

Place	Date	Hour	Summary of Events and Information	Remarks and references to Appendices
POPERINGHE	16/8/17		Yesterday the 51st High. Division attacked with the 39th Div. on their right and the 38th Div. on their left. Zero hour was 3.50 a.m. & whilst time & amount of further advance was complete the Division prepared to & began occupying & extending which was the East bank of the STEENBEEK RIVER where posts were established. 5 Tk & 6 P Black Watch Casualties came freely in many being Germans. The advanced dressing station at Kachin Wounded or main Dressing Station were were enemies prisoners. By there has been much rain and sick on stretcher. Lt Elwood T Robertson was employed at the Corps Sick Convoy Station and the XVIII Corps Sick Convoy Station. The Remaining of the unit 9th Wacking huts at Were the XVIII Corps (1 East Butcher, 132nd 2 Field Amb.) was evacuated through 2/1 High. Fd Amb. All personnel employed at K Forward Dressing Station (Saint Jans) was relieved 5&3 H.T. Fd Amb. Fd. Medical Supplies were drawn from the XVIII Corps main Dressing Station. The front having been held against all enemy attacks but further the Continued rain a further attack was planned for 6th inst. R.A.M.C. O.O 50 Copy 11 Wanlockhead.	
	26/8/17			

WAR DIARY or INTELLIGENCE SUMMARY

Army Form C. 2118.

LXXIII
51st Highland Field Ambulance
/Robertson (R.H. Smith)

Place	Date	Hour	Summary of Events and Information	Remarks and references to Appendices
POPERINGHE	4/8/17		No alteration of Medical posts in 51st Div. was notified to Rgmmd.Sd. Lt Watt Reynolds Aid Posts have been established at C.9.6.32 and C.10.c.15. Will relay posts between these & Essex Farm. The Bearers are well on wilnasse for Wheeled Transport. 150 men of Trench Mortar Batteries are available on Stretcher Carries. The A.D.M.S. informed me today that the operation's intended for 6th inst will not come off.	
	5/8/17		51st Div. Opns Operation order No.6 of 3rd Aug. Bn to 25th received. The 39th Division takes relieve on 5-6th Aug by the 48th Div. H.Q Staff. 1 Offr W.W.R.F & C.M.D.S. remain. Major G.F. WHYTE wire Thorpe Vermin. Capt J.B. MUNE + Capt McCONNACHIE with Tent Subdivision came to health at C.M.D.S. being a good at the MSDS.C.P. 51st Div. R.A.M.C. ops. to 51st Copy of record provides for the relief of the Advanced Dressing Station personnel on 4th Aug. by personnel from the 11th Division. The Tent Subdivisions St Ems W.W.C.P. are to relieve on the 5th August by similar personnel of 11th Division.	

WAR DIARY or INTELLIGENCE SUMMARY

Army Form C. 2118.

August 1917
Sheet 3

2/1 Highland Field Ambulance
J. Knowlton Lt. Col. Cmdg.

Place	Date	Hour	Summary of Events and Information	Remarks and references to Appendices
POPERINGHE	5/8/17		The personnel & vehicles were again warned which will be moved to TUNNELLING CAMP. St JANSTER BIEZEN on the 8th inst. The Advanced Dressing Station tents were billed on night of 7th inst at A.30 Central (sheet 28) DIRTY BUCKET CAMP and will remain pegged. HQ under orders of 154 Infantry Brigade on 8th inst. Transport of Coy moves on morning of 8th under orders of O.C. to TUNNELLING CAMP. D.D.M.S. XVIII Corps OO. No.7 Copy No. 34 received. The 11th Div. was relieved 51st Div. in the line. Ambulance, two Major G F WHYTE R.A.M.C. 2 senior N.C.O. + 2 Clerks of 2/1 High. F.A Ambulance who will remain at W.C.P. will accompany their respective affiliated Brigade. Sufficient personnel will be left behind by A.D.M.S. to bring 11th Div. up to strength in RAMC. The provision of Tent Subdivisions as Army Reserve allocated to 11th Div. by Medical Arrangement of XVIII Corps / out 2 Z Sektren 9/10th July are from 2/6/1st Division. Any individual not brought will be renamed by ambulances of 39th Div.	Shed 26
	6/8/17		51st H. Div. RAMC OO. 52 Copy 3 rcvd. All FA duties to the 1/2 High F? Amb and 2/1 HFA.	

WAR DIARY or INTELLIGENCE SUMMARY

Army Form C. 2118.

2/1 Highland Field Ambulance
Y. Section 2/C. Coy. (Crews)

August 1917

Place	Date	Hour	Summary of Events and Information	Remarks and references to Appendices
POPERINGHE	6/viii/17		On the 9th inst. the 2/1. H.F.Amb. will proceed to L'EGGE FARM (F.29.d.5.9.) & the parties and remain ready to move. The loans of the 1/3 H.F.Amb at present at the Advanced Dressing Station (party) will remain at St JANSTER BIEZEN under orders of 1/2 H/o/s. F.Amb. Advance to Raine O.O. 52. Convoy point 2 & 3. The 2/1. H.F.G. will not proceed to L'EGGE FARM but will remain ported at F.29 & 5.9. with the 1/3 party attached. 51st H.D. A.I. on Div Order 183 Copy no 36 received at Tunnelling Camp St JANSTER BIEZEN. R. Amb. e. addendum to O.O. 51. Copy no 3 received.	(Sheet 27)
ST JANSTER BIEZEN	8/viii/17		LIEUT COLONEL D. RORIE, D.S.O. having been appointed to Command XVIII Corps M.D.S. vice Lieut Col. HILDRETH, will remain in Command 1/2 H.F. Amb. D.D.M.S. O.O. no. 7. XVIII Corps received. The 39th Division will proceed to Second Army. HQ 2/1 Highld F. Amb. move from Today and St Tanshor camp. The advance Dressing Station Parties & the A.D.S. Relief by B Section from the 1/W.C/3. joining HQ. This unit removed parties & loads to Cairo Station to Relieve the W.W. C.P. Major Whyte and Captain M.C. Cameron with 3 Sergts. & 1 Private proceeded at W.W. C.P.	

2353 Wt. W2511/1454 700,000 5/15 D.D.&L. A.D.S.S./Forms/C. 2118.

Army Form C. 2118.

WAR DIARY
or
INTELLIGENCE SUMMARY.

(Erase heading not required.)

2/1 Highland Field Ambulance
51st (Highland) Division

J. Robertson Lt Col
Commanding

Place	Date	Hour	Summary of Events and Information	Remarks and references to Appendices
St JANSTER BIEZEN	9/VIII/17		1 Corpl. 98 O.R. Ranks of this unit attached for duty to 35th F. Amb. 11th Division whilst Cpl. C.R. McKAY was hit in action on 31st July 17 at Advanced Dressing Station on GWALIA FARM. Whilst whilst loading a Car. He was buried at the Cemetery near Dressing Station on GWALIA FARM. ELVERDINGHE - POPERINGHE ROAD. No. 2 101495 Private W.H. PLAYER one of the M.T. A.S.C. attached this unit died at 47 C.C.S. of wounds received on 31st July probably 2:2:2. H.D. RAIN C.00.53 C(b) 2:4 received. The 154 Inf. Brigade moves on 10th to EPERLEQUES AREA. In Tent Subdivision of 2/1 H.F. Amb. will accompany with Equipment. Also wire has been received for 50 patients and Army Ophthalmic, Dental & Expedition to ST. OMER & ARQUES Inhabit at PROVEN, between WATTEN. Transport to move by road under Brigade transport Officer. (2 day march). C Section Tent with Equipment & 2 large Cars proceeded as advance will on 9.8.17 and opened Hospital at BAYINGHAM (Wastahook 5A) Capt. GEO. DICK, who reported on 8th inst with Captain TORRANCE, stand in command. Captain Dick proceeds to Inhabit at 7 a.m. Capt. Torrance proceeds by car with Existing notions 15 a.m. on arrival forty West Staff Captain in EPERLECQUES.	
	10/8/17		ADDENDUM to M.E.D. arrangements XVIII Corps part 2. Operations 2 Selects dated 75th July 17 received. Copy 30 also attached Div. F.C. for Unit only. 1 Ford Car will be supplied to 11th Div by the unit who cares for.	

2353 Wt. W2544/1454 700,000 5/15 D.D.& L. A.D.S.S./Forms/C. 2118.

Army Form C. 2118.

WAR DIARY
or
INTELLIGENCE SUMMARY.

(Erase heading not required.)

2/1 Highland Field Ambulance
Wolverton H.Q. Convoy

August 1917   Sheet 6

Place	Date	Hour	Summary of Events and Information	Remarks and references to Appendices
St. JANSTER BIEZEN	11/8/17		Operation order No 9 DDMS XVIII Corps 6/8/16 received. Duties in trenches "Z" Scheme 910th Inf. will be assumed at 12 noon on 12th inst and Convoys work about then to be what is later.	
do	12/8/17		Duties of the unit on 12th to be tanks ready to move forward. All in order for this. Captain Geo. Dick to hospital sick. Today. Major W. HAIG, D.S.O. from 1/13 Highland Field Ambulance in command. Charge of the Tent Subdivision at BAYENHAM which has been hospital for 154 & 27 Brigs. Capt GUY TORRENCE injured W.E. but was immediate posts for duty with 1/2 H. F.Amb.(Bayeux) Memoral of Ypres	
do			9th Aug. 1st Lieut W.F. WILLIAMS U.S.A. M.O.R.C. attached for duty and instruction 1st Lieut H.T. WICKERT U.S.A. M.O.R.C. attached for duty and instruction 3rd Aug (about) Capt. B.G. BEVERIDGE attached. He became N/C as M.O. vice Capt Van C. BENNET sick evacuated to base. (Admin authority) Orders given to Major Huddle OC Advanced Dressing Station	
do	23/8/17		Copy of 51st Highland Div. order No 188 dates today received. Provides for the relief of 154th Inf. Brig'd to 2nd JANSTER BIEZEN Line on 22nd & 23rd - Aug. Transport by road infantry by rail. The Bus Scheme of this unit will rejoin H.Q. on 23rd	

Army Form C. 2118.

WAR DIARY
or
INTELLIGENCE SUMMARY.
(Erase heading not required.)

August 1917 #1 Highland Field Ambulance 51st Div. (Whitton)

Place	Date	Hour	Summary of Events and Information	Remarks and references to Appendices
ST JANSTER BIEZEN	23/VIII/17		The Tent Subdivision of this unit under major Haig moved from BAYENHEM to ST JANSTER BIEZEN today. Transport & two days moved by road staying the night at WORMHOUDT. Remained by rail on 23rd. Arrived about 5 P.M. Detraining ABEELE STATION. Major Haig then informs 1/3 High F.A. Amb. This morning the 70th Bgde of Infantry 23rd Div. which has been camped here is what is called TUNNELLERS Camp, moved & their place was taken by 154 Inf. Bgde of this Div.	
do.	24/VIII/17		Intimation appears in D.R.O. 2/836 that the following O.R. of this unit has been granted the MILITARY MEDAL by XVIII Corps Commander under powers delegated to H.M. 307417 Pte ALEX. M.F. SILVER 301535 Pte JAS. MCINTOSH 55742 Pte S.A. HOGG Royal a.M. 301262 Pte A.M. TAYLOR 301308 L/Cpl JAS. AITKEN "for gallantry displayed between 2nd July & 7 August 1917." Informer S.M. JOHN CURRIE of this unit appointed R.M. & Hon Lieut? RAMC dated 20. Aug. 1917. (Intimation from Base Records.)	

WAR DIARY or INTELLIGENCE SUMMARY

Army Form C. 2118.

August 1917
Sheet 8

CV
2/Lt Stephens Field Ambulance
Richardson R.S Lr Comdg

Place	Date	Hour	Summary of Events and Information	Remarks and references to Appendices
Nr. Bng. POPERINGHE	27/VIII/17		D.D.M.S. G.O. No 10. intimating relief of 11th Division by 51st (High.) Div. holding posts of 11th Div to be taken over by relieving units. O.C. Corps Main & Walking Wounded Dressing Station Brewery Rames. N. Div. OO. 54 Copy 13 received. Par 2/1 Utility Tr. Amb. will take over duties of Evacuation from front area and leaving of the 1/2 + 1/3 H.C. Amb. were to attend for duty. Move up on 29th Aug. Today visited posts in front area will D.D.M.S. and cond over the Route of evacuation with officers 1/Lt 33rd & 1st Amb.	
do ESSEX FARM	28/VIII/17		Under 152 Inf Bing's order No 16) Copy of which was previous this went entrained at POPERINGHE until two Motorlillus Provision Lony and Motorcas at RIGERSBURG station near BRIELEN personnel marched then to ISLY FARM at the South End of BRIELEN where there is a billet. In Morning of Journey to the advance tour at Pumping Station ESSEX FARM. 3 S.B. Bearer Ambulance and Artifates two officers and 80 O.R. to MINTY FARM (C.10.c.2.3) to take over the Div. Collecting Post thus ambulance bearer at forward	Sheet 2T Sheet 2T

Army Form C. 2118.

WAR DIARY or INTELLIGENCE SUMMARY.
(Erase heading not required.)

August 1917   CVI
Sht 9.   2/1 1st H. F. Amb.
    Nicholson A.D.M.S. Corps

Place	Date	Hour	Summary of Events and Information	Remarks and references to Appendices
ESSEX FARM	30/8/17		Relay Posts. 4 horses now attached to the M.O. 1 each of the 3 battalions going into the line tonight, not individuals to carry to the first relay post.	
		6 P.M.	1st Lieut. GERSON, U.S.A. M.O.R.C. and 81 horses of the 1/3 High. F.T. Amb. arrived to train and was billeted at ISLY FARM. G.R.	
			An Officer of the 35th F. Amb. remained one night.	
			Relief completed of advanced Dressing Station & forward posts at 9 A.M. today. Reports to A.D.M.S. bearers of 1/2 H.F. Amb. runs to billets at XVIII Corps M.D.S. 24 personnel are distributed as follows:-	
			ESSEX FARM - 4 Officers and 55 other ranks. (Tent personnel & 10 bearers)	
			ISLY FARM. 1 " (Q.M.) 110 OR. 2/1 H.F. Amb. 12. A.S.C. H.T. 3 M.T. A.S.C. 1.3 FORD Cars	
			SMITH. " 12 " 23 OR. 1/3 H.F. Amb.	
			MINTY FARM. 2 " 59 OR.	
			SPENCE POST 1 " 23 OR. Tent accommodates at the WILLOWS.	
			RED FARMS 1 " 21 OR. (4 at Ryl. Aw/post MONT. BULGAR	
			RUDOLPH. — 9 OR.	

Army Form C. 2118.

WAR DIARY
or
INTELLIGENCE SUMMARY.

(Erase heading not required.)

August 1917

C VII
(Sheet 10) 9/1 North, 92 April
Oppelduim 18th Corps

Place	Date	Hour	Summary of Events and Information	Remarks and references to Appendices
ESSEX FARM	1/8/17		COMEDY. Relay post 13 O.R. C4 at Regimental Aid Post WELLINGTON HOUSE FRANCIS d. 10/pm. 9 O.R. The attached sketch maps shows the relative positions of these. The route of carriage is shown in orange. By hand carriage in stages from Regimental Aid Posts along overland Duck board tracks, on the right to Divisional Collecting Post MINTY FARM through RELAY posts at RED FARM (S.) and RUDOLPH Relay posts. (whilst stretcher carriage from Relay posts (stretcher COMEDY, FRANCOIS to MINTY) a hand carriage in a From MINTY to SPENCE's post evacuation is by hand trolleys on a tramway running between the two posts. From Spence to Essex on returning light Railway Track to Tramex trolley by hand carriage up the track to ESSEX. After dressing & attention cases are dispatched to C.C.S., C in D.S. and a Car of walking wounds mile lorries parked at Essex. Lift F. then to C.W.W.C.P. The motor ambulances are parked at Essex farm and BRIELEN and are under orders of O.C. 94 M.A.C.	

2353 Wt. W2544/1454 700,000 5/15 D.D.& L. A.D.S.S./Forms/C. 2118.

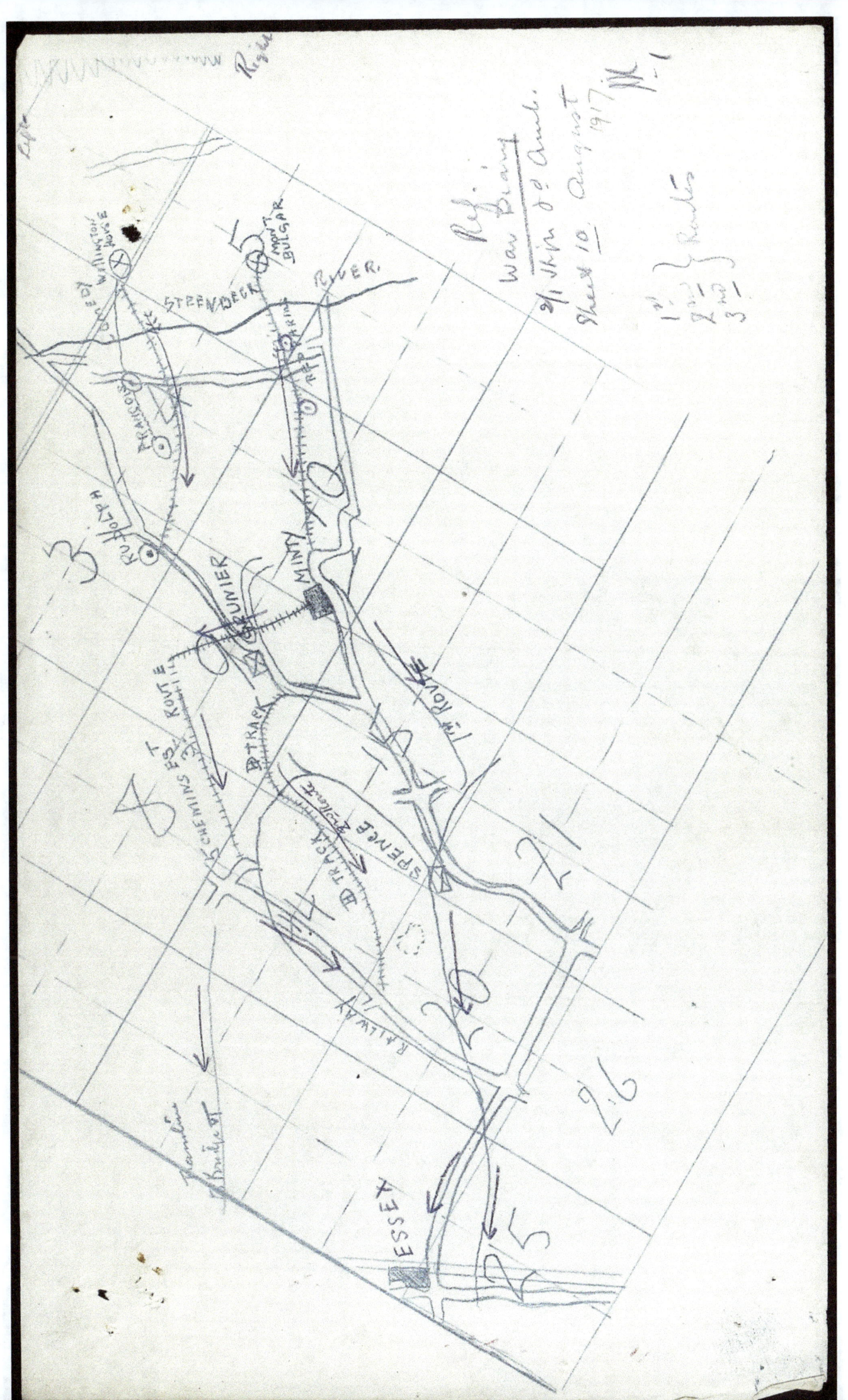

140/2438.

21st Highland F.A.

COMMITTEE FOR THE
MEDICAL HISTORY OF THE WAR
Date -5 NOV.1917

8/11/1917

WAR DIARY or INTELLIGENCE SUMMARY

Army Form C. 2118.

2/C Offiel 2/4 Devit
1/1 Stephens
Arblame
Morton

Place	Date	Hour	Summary of Events and Information	Remarks and references to Appendices
ESSEX FARM.	7/9/17		Harassing fire continued. The evacuation of sick and wounded from the forward area of 51st Div. Brain 7/2 & 7/3 W.E. Dvi. have continued. We attacked. Improvement of delay bearer posts and advances Dressing station things for working nature. The road communications with the forward area have been refused and have stressed by the material for the building in now advanced dressing station 2½ miles in front JESSEX FARM has been set up. 5th Chatry Post MINTY FARM very morning. Three elephant shelters being littered round posted with a truck, lain on top of 2 Steel shelter sand bags have been completed. The Dutch cure accommodates in now 20. The Sanitation of the 50th Bde area & the Canal Bank has been directed and some reference improvement has been made & several & shelter latrines which much of incinerators. A good deal of use directed every attention here has in terrain with the work.

Many to hardwork the Anuday of Ammunition Dumping overheads, and | |

Army Form C. 2118.

WAR DIARY
or
INTELLIGENCE SUMMARY.
(Erase heading not required.)

2/7 Highland F.A.
Authors Marked Trench
Coy S.

Place	Date	Hour	Summary of Events and Information	Remarks and references to Appendices
ESSEX FARM	14/9/17		At MINTY FARM and a R.D. ambulance Car has been bringing over from this to Essex Farm & the Relay post at WILLOWS has been kept pumped out and the shrapnel of 51st A.S. area of Canal Bank has been repaired. Before 6 inches of the dugouts were entered. The new E. He Subway water mains and roads	
do	15/9/17		15th Sept. Same as on 14. wind S wind is now more west than anywhere Search parties for the teams of Du Coliacty put at ROBERT FARM and the steenwerck horses of 3rd 7 More ambulance to sundown. The kept enemy dead uncovered no horses. He attached copy of map & Co. 2/1 H.F. A.B. and others for inspection of dugouts. The plans works out on an attempt of destroying No 7 dugouts.	Appendix A 21.IX.17
do	16/9/17		Same as on 15. Recon Fly horses for use if the mov. of Field Ambulance / M.T. Divns on 20th. inst.	
	17/9/17		The 33 F.A and trans ESSEX FARM N.S and 35th and MINTY FARM + Relay posts, transports were taken to operate for all Stores loaded must arriving at Div.- Y Cyclist Camp today.	

2353 Wt. W2544/1454 700,000 5/15 L.D.&L. A.D.S.S./Forms/C. 2118.

WAR DIARY or INTELLIGENCE SUMMARY

Army Form C. 2118.

September 1917
Sheet 3

2/1 83rd (3rd West Lancs) Field Ambulance

Place	Date	Hour	Summary of Events and Information	Remarks and references to Appendices
	Sept 25-9-17		Proceeded today to X camp	
	27.9.17		Capt. Torrence with 3 other ranks proceeded on advance party to new area - ACHIET LE GRAND.	
	28.9.17.		Motor Ambulance Ay moved to ABLAINZEVILLE.	
	29.9.17		Unit entrained HOPOUTRE at 15.45. Detrained BAPAUME MAIN at 1 a.m. 30/9/17.	
	30.9.17.		Marched to billeting area COURCELLES LE COMTE leaving BAPAUME MAIN at 2 a.m. & reaching area at 4 a.m. Took over from a walking party - 9/111th Fd. Amb.	
	27.9.17.		G.O.C. & Hon Lt H.A. PROSSER was evacuated from No 46 CCS to the Base on 6/9/17 from which ⅌ stough.(?) on that club(?): (Authority ADMS 57th Div No 3969/ADG/9/17 and OAG. List 899?) 24.9.17. Lt Shannon R.D.M.S.M.C. detailed for temp duty with 1/7 A&S. 11th from 27.9.17	

APPENDIX A
21 IX 17.

At zero hour the following will be the disposition of R.A.M.C. in "forward area"

RIGHT REG. AID POST. NEAR "MONT DE RASTA"

    8 MEN BATTALION "NOAH"   30 STRETCHERS AND ONE DOUBLE DECKER
    8 MEN   "   "   "NOISY"   TROLLEY

LEFT REG. AID POST NEAR "WILLINGTON HOUSE"

    8 MEN BATTALION "NOTION"   30 STRETCHERS
    "   "   "   "   "NOBLE"

RELAY POSTS "RIGHT-SECTOR"

    RED - FARM :-   1 SERGT AND 8 BEARERS
    PALACE-FARM :-   1 "   "   "   AND 2 TROLLEYS
    OUSE - DUMP :-   1 SERGT AND 8 BEARERS

MINTY FARM ("DIV COL POST")

    2 MEDICAL OFFICERS, 10 TENT PERSONNEL, 30 BEARERS,
    100 STRETCHERS   200 BLANKETS   3 HORSED AMB, 2 FORD CARS
    8 TRAMWAY TROLLEYS.

LEFT SECTOR

    COMEDY FARM :-   1 SERGT AND 8 BEARERS
    VARNA   "   :-   1 "   "   "

RADOLPH FARM (DIV COL POST)

    2 MED OFFICERS   6 TENT PERSONNEL, 30 BEARERS   100 STRETCHERS
    6 STRETCHER CARRIAGES, 200 BLANKETS. 3 HORSED AMB, 2 FORD CARS
    AND 1 MOTOR CYCLIST.

GOURNIER FARM "RESERVE BEARER POST"

    2 OFFICERS AND 60 MEN OF ROYAL ARTILLERY ALONG WITH 2 NCOS
    AND 60 MEN OF R.A.M.C. BEARERS

TRAMLINE RELAY BOUNDARY RD FOR LOADING TRUCKS

    1 SERGT. 1 CORPL. AND 12 BEARERS. 6 RAILWAY TRUCKS FITTED FOR
    8 STRETCHER CASES EACH AND ONE ENGINE

KEMPTON PARK SIDING

    2 TROLLEYS WITH 6 MEN TO BE DETAILED BY O.C. MINTYS FARM
    DIV COL POST WHEN REQUIRED FOR CASES FROM RADOLPH
    DIV. COL. POST.

ADVANCED DRESSING STATION

    4 MED OFFICERS   2 TENT. SUB. DIVS. 50 BEARERS 300 STRETCHERS
    300 BLANKETS. RESERVE SUPPLY OF DRESSINGS, 2 FORD CARS 8 HORSED
    AMB. 4 LARGE CARS IN RESERVE. SIX STRETCHER CARRIAGES FOR
    MOVING CASES FROM AMBULANCE TRAIN, (VIA No 3 BRIDGE) TO
    ESSEX FARM.

REPORTS & INDENTS

    URGENT REPORTS OF NUMBERS OF STRETCHER CASES AWAITING BEARERS AT AID POSTS, REPORTS OF
ALTERATION OF AID POST WITH CORRECT MAP POSITION AND INDENTS. ALSO ANY OTHER URGENT MESSAGE TO BE SENT
TO O.C. CORRESPONDING DIV COL POST FOR TRANSMISSON TO O.C. ADVANCED DRESSING STATION

    REPORTS INDENTS FROM O.CS DIV. COL. POST. BY TELEPHONE OR CYCLIST TO O.C. ADVANCED
DRESSING STATION EVERY FOUR HOURS AND WHEN REQUIRED. IN ALL CASES THE HOUR OF DISPATCH
DATE & M.OS. SIGNATURE MUST BE PUT ON MESSAGES.

DUTIES

    N.C.Os I/C RELAY POSTS WILL DIRECT THE TRANSPORT OF WOUNDED BY TRAMWAY OR HAND
CARRIAGE FROM RELAY POST TO THE ONE TO THEIR REAR AND WILL ENSURE THE RETURN OF STRETCHERS
TO REG. AID POSTS. THEY WILL ALSO REPORT ANY UNUSUAL OCCURRENCE TO O.C. DIV COL POST OF THEIR
SECTOR & TRANSMIT MESSAGES FROM THE POST.

    M.O's I/C DIV COL POSTS WILL SUPERVISE TRANSPORT OF WOUNDED FROM REG. AID. POST. TREAT
CASES WHERE NECESSARY AND SUPERVISE LOADING OF CONVEYANCES BOUND FOR ESSEX
FARM. REPORTING IN WRITING OR BY TELEPHONE AT LEAST EVERY FOUR HOURS TO
OC ADVANCED DRESSING STATION.

O.C. ESSEX FARM :-

    RECEIVE AND TREAT ALL CASES REQUIRING SUCH AND DISPATCH TO THE REAR
ARRANGE TO MEET ANY DIFFICULTIES IN TRANSPORT BETWEEN ESSEX FARM AND DIV COL POSTS.
ALL REPORTS AND RETURNS TO A.D.M.S. AND INDENTS FOR MATERIAL TO REPLACE ISSUES.

MEDICAL SUPPLIES :-

    DEMANDS FOR REG. AID. POSTS WILL BE SUPPLIED FROM DIV. COL. POSTS AND
REPLENISHMENT OBTAINED FROM ESSEX FARM.

    MEDICAL OFFICERS AND O.C. DIV COL POST WILL REPORT AT ZERO, THAT PERSONNEL FOR THEIR
AS ABOVE DETAILED IS IN POSITION TO O.C. ADVANCED DRESSING STATION.

ACKNOWLEDGE.

COPIES TO :- A.D.M.S.   N.C.Os I/C SPENCERSPOST   18-IX-17.
    NOISY   O.C.   ESSEX FARM
    NOTION
O.C. RADOLPH - FARM
O.C. MINTY

2/1st HIGHLAND FIELD AMBULANCE

2/1st Highland F.A.

COMMITTEE FOR THE
MEDICAL HISTORY OF THE WAR
Date -8 DEC. 1917

WAR DIARY or **INTELLIGENCE SUMMARY.**
Army Form C. 2118.

(Erase heading not required.)

Place	Date	Hour	Summary of Events and Information	Remarks and references to Appendices
COURCELLES	Oct/1		L.M. J. ROBERTSON proceeded on 10 days leave to U.K. on 28th Sept. Major G.F. WHYTE acting in his stead. 51st W.D. R.A.M.C. O.O. 7st 57 C.Py No 15 received. The 2/1 Wyr. 29 And will relieve 1/1 Northumbrian Field Ambulance at the main Dressing Station BRICKFIELDS (S.2.L.7.4.) on 4th inst. 40 Beans including a Sergeant & 2 Corpls. Sheet/51B this unit received Benjack (1/54) & local Siek during hours of Stay in COURCELLES. Recvd Turkey 154 2/1 Army O.O. 142 Copy No 17. also A.T. 2843 and MEDICAL ARRANGEMENT'S 51st Wyr. Division dated Oct 2 = 17.	
	2/17		Moved to Brickfield S.2.6. and took over from 1/1 Northumbrian 8th Amb. The position is close to 28th, 143rd C.C.S. and to 16 Advanced Depot Medical Stores Medical Arrangements 57 Div support the position & all medical installations in Div Area	
to S.2.b.	4/17		and the sorrt institution affecting the work of field ambulances. All cases of Serious illness will be sent to C.C.S. held a ticket marked "To be retained to the Corps Rest Station". They will remain on the M.V.D. book of the Bria Amb till discharge from C.C.S.	

CXII

Army Form C. 2118.

2/1 Highland Field Amb.
M. Neilson Lt.Col
Comdg

WAR DIARY
or
INTELLIGENCE SUMMARY.
(Erase heading not required.)

October
Sheet 2

Place	Date	Hour	Summary of Events and Information	Remarks and references to Appendices
S.2.b.	4/10		2 large cars be attached to 1/2 Sec 3rd Amb. for duty. All wheels Stated Carriers to be attached to R 1/2 H.F. Amb. Provision made for disposal of all special cases.	
do	6/10		The party (20 O.R.) was despatched and large cars x 5 1/2 H.F. Amb. NCOs 39/56 orders 10th 17 Oct. to 43 O.Rs. for duty. (1 Lieut M. Smith U.S. M.O.R.C.) Report for duty at ACHIET LE GRAND S.2. 10th 18 Oct. to 45 OCs. Scheme intend for trained Despair building & separate proceeded with.	
do	12/10		N/Lt J. Robertson returned from leave U.K. having been granted an extension of leave by War Office for the purpose of attending an interview with Home Authorities, Western Command, Edinburgh between 5th & 11th Oct.	
do	15 Oct		The preparation of Ambulance trains, Quarters, huts) on during past week and patients removed from huts to NISSON HUTS.	
do	29/10		Information received that C in C has awarded MILITARY CROSS to Captain B.G. BEVERIDGE and Captain J.S. McConnachie of this unit. Military Medal to Sergt. ANGUS GORRIE, Sergt DAVID JACK & Sergt P.B.ELMSLIE. Authority XVIII Corps.	

WAR DIARY or INTELLIGENCE SUMMARY

Army Form C. 2118.

CXII

2/1 Highland Field Ambulance

October Sheet 3

Place	Date	Hour	Summary of Events and Information	Remarks and references to Appendices
S.2.C.	27/oct		154 Infantry Brigade O.O. No. 145 Copy No. 17 received. Instructions to man an advance party being issued by the 12th Division, to Avesnes LES HAMEAU, AVESNES LE COMTE. LATTRE - ST. QUENTIN. Pnmo O.O. No. 59 Copy No 6 received. Instructions for an advance party being sent by 1/2 High Fd. Amb. to Y. Hutts (L.I.C.) to collect sick of High Div Units and evac them to C.C.S.	
do.	28/oct		Pnmo O.O. No. 60. Copy 15 received 2/1 Hd. Fd. And. Adv. nils to relieve Fy. 104 F Amb. (12th Div Bnd) on 31st Oct and moved to AVESNES LE COMTE and open a train dressing Station and collect sick from 154 Inf. Brigade. The 104 F. Amb. arrived and was accommodated in hospital buildings for last night. They arrived in small parties during the night. Lorry to evacuate rate & Co. went over the sleep ice, troublings. Supp Thoughts	
do.	29/oct		Today Ambulance party was sent by the road to AVESNE LE COMTE (by filled patients & Workshop Workshop for readjts) of sick. Warned at 7 pm for move from S.Z.C. and arrived at AVESNES LE COMTE in afternoon having hailed 12 hrs for buses on the way. Ambulance lorry was sent by D.H.R. for transport of blankets & supplies medicine stores & dressings	

14/2678

2/Lt. Hyllard T.A.

COMMITTEE FOR THE
MEDICAL HISTORY OF THE WAR
Date 17 JAN 1918

Army Form C. 2118.

WAR DIARY
or
INTELLIGENCE SUMMARY.
(Erase heading not required.)

Army Form C. 2118.

Place	Date	Hour	Summary of Events and Information	Remarks and references to Appendices
AVESNES LE COMTE	2/6/17		Horse Ambulance Car which had been placed at the disposal of D.A.C. for evacuation of sick of Div. Artillery reported here having been sent back as the 51st Div. Artillery was moving to 16th Div. area. Recd. instructions that 51st Div. Artillery offrs. & 10 Veterinary reinforcement dent. incl. Smith U.S. M.O.R.C. detailed for Div. Charge of 52nd D.A.C. in place of Capt. J.M. Stewart, R.A.M.C. on leave to U.K. Col. Smith observed a 6.2 How. Lorry was estimated as a general history tractor of the G.P.C. in ammunition of the nature of Beaumont Hamel when 5" w. Div. cobbles the shiny keys from the Germans. Push was organised by the Brigade and proved very successful. Sustained heard 75" Gives the man on the return Shrapnel, the prevision of push developments this top picture. A very good chairman was provided for Patients J personnel and in the evening a concert was given by the camel party of this unit.	
do	3/6/17		Attm. OO. on 61 attm. no 3 war news. Provision for the circulate the material limits of 51st Artillery will that happen in IV Corps area 14-17th June 17.	

Army Form C. 2118.

WAR DIARY
or
INTELLIGENCE SUMMARY.
(Erase heading not required.)

C XIV
Wiltshire Wilts. Regt

Place	Date	Hour	Summary of Events and Information	Remarks and references to Appendices
AVESNES LE COMTE	14/2/17		154 In. Brig. O.O. 10 No. Capt. W.P.J. Meares will march Battn. attached transport Group on 15th inst. by road to COURCELLES LE COMTE and thence on 16th – 17th – to BAPAUME. Returns to Brne on 17th from BEAUMETZ LES LOGES to BAPAUME. When they are join the transport. Battn. enters an extended march discipline with Special Regulations for men South of ALBERT-CAMBRAI ROAD also planned. S.S. 729/52. (H.D.)	
do.	15/2/17		The transport of this unit consisting of 17 Vehicles under Command Capt. GUY TORRANCE, parade at 5.30 p.m. and proceeds to join Brigade transport Column en route for MOYENVILLE (answered of O.O. 146 by Bn War Diary) This unit (headed) line transport at 11.45 today in accordance with Brigade O.O. Number 3 above (146) and proceeds to Brigade Bivouac to BEAUMETZ thence to Bivouac along with 4th Gordons & 7th A&S Highlanders. Detrains at 6 P.m.	
BAPAUME	16/2/17		on BAPAUME. Marches to Guards. Major G.F. WHYTE was assumed Military Officer. Capts. T.S. McCarnachi was detailed Stake down of 52nd Div. Wing (R Echelon) and remains at IZEL les HAMEAU.	

Army Form C. 2118.

WAR DIARY
or
INTELLIGENCE SUMMARY.
(Erase heading not required.)

Sheet 3 C xy
November 1st Aust. Field Amb. / Wheeler McAlpine.

Place	Date	Hour	Summary of Events and Information	Remarks and references to Appendices
BAPAUME	5/2/17		In course of the night the Transport proper McR at BAPAUME from MOYENVILLE. 15th Fld. O.O. No 147 received will move Ech. This unit proceeds to LECHELLE in Brigade tonight. Animals of 2/1. D. Trans. Dy. 147 received. Moved 10 a.m. and proceeds accompanied by Transport and equipment. Capt. Bevridge went in morning in advance party to LECHELLE. 6 miles long. Two stands from A.D.M.S. for many Fd Amb's of Mahamas Murphy, Pakros Shea. Arrived at 9 pm. Quartered in Room Hats on F. and S.E.	
LECHELLE	6/2/17		Mos. Medical arrangements Positions 6 Coy 14 Division. This unit are to remain parked next to Rear Forward in certain eventualities to For on new Burning Station, Latrines and Public Baths or places of disposal of OC 1/2 Wd. Fd. Amb. Medical arrangement IV Corps Copy 10 11. Received	
do	6/2/17		OA.D.M.S. writes use 9 always tent material for an advanced Dressing Station should be find is G Howard Ambulances and that motor with 3 units Carts and are tent personal except Tent repairs & Lorr after remainder of units equip next 2 trucks proceeds on receipt of instruction (hourly former 720½) to FLEISEU 10 C.C.S.	

WAR DIARY
INTELLIGENCE SUMMARY.

Army Form C. 2118.

CXVI Sh. 57A Pt. Fr[...]
Sheet 4 Hebuterne War-Crecy
Miraumont

Place	Date	Hour	Summary of Events and Information	Remarks and references to Appendices
20.XII.19 ECHELLE		5pm 8pm	No orders having been received today I visited ADMS and received verbal orders FLESQUIERES was supposed to be taken and orders to send my Third Wave Ambulance empty for duty with 1/2 W.F.Amb. Ambulances (in front Area).	
do	24.XII.17 7am		ADMS, A11S instructs the move Third Unit to Q14.d.1.5. now vacated as an Advanced Dressing Station, the same having proceeded forward to FLESQUIERES. Arrived at 9.50 am and took over. I proceeded forward to TRESCAULT and had two telegraph adv. Dr. Station. Communicates with ADMS by L/Tele & received instructions to take over the liaison station at TRESCAULT with an officer & 12 O.R., loading Ambulance train and attending bad cases. This was done at 6 pm. Capt. GUY TORRANCE to act at TRESCAULT.	(Lt. W.F.Amb) Asphalt 100 stretcher 300 blankets to Flesquieres
do	25.XII.17		Very marked difficulty is being experienced in transport of wounded from Advanced Dressing Station to Liaison Station at TRESCAULT. This is on account of the bad state of the road FLESQUIERES - RIBECOURT - TRESCAULT which has been destroyed by the enemy by means of mining. The difficult part two now RIBECOURT just West of the village. Detours have been made by the RE but much obstruction is caused by traffic & inequalities of the road. I formed the G.S. Light Railway Coy to	Start 576.

WAR DIARY or INTELLIGENCE SUMMARY

Army Form C. 2118.

Army: C XVII
Sheet 5 November
[Heading: 71 Hy. Fd Am.]

Place	Date	Hour	Summary of Events and Information	Remarks and references to Appendices
Audit. 8.	13/8/17		Work on the light Railway from TRESCAULT along the GRAND RAVIN to RIBECOURT but even today the two rails have been down. Chief reason as stated by the Eng. Section is that the Construction people work only from 9 a.m. to 3 p.m. It is also stated that at Sidney 54 near TRESCAULT the NCO i/c states that he had only 17 P.B. men. On 23rd (or yesterday) ammunition & petrol etc. the unloading had to be done in the main line the [unreadable] the Advance Gauge Line pretty up. On one occasion when a number of lorries had cribs at the line at TRESCAULT they were put in an ordinary empty train (probes) down to where the Ammunition train was unloading. Carried part time to load on to a waiting Ambulance train. The Bdmer Car & M.A.C. Car from ADCS from the neighbourhood of Gate Ave at RIBECOURT working at TRESCAULT. It was found after several accumulation of wounded had occurred at the two hundred place. Stopen land not turned on the Railway at one and three large elements on M.A.C. had to be made. Stones [party] of 16 under an NCO was stationed at the Rate Area to carry two more Ambulances across the lad piece of the road fixed Car. Tonight I was promised a biting was RIBECOURT 6th opens on 24th Gyshm by the Authority of OC 21 L. Railway Coy.	

2353 Wt.W2344/1454 700,000 5/15 D.D.&L A.D.S.S./Forms/C. 2118.

WAR DIARY or INTELLIGENCE SUMMARY

Army Form C. 2118.

Sheet 6 CXVIII 26 Inf. Bde
November Infantry War Diary

Place	Date	Hour	Summary of Events and Information	Remarks and references to Appendices
Q.W.d.I.9.	23/11/17		About 6 P.M. today received from Capt. TORRANCE a call up from "B.O.C. 2/1 Insp. to Amb." copy from H/q H.F.A. re orders – Please send up from 2/1 H.F.A. lorry to Cavalier Paraffin Candles Sandbags Medical Stores from 6 P.M. Please all cars have been ordered to remount by METZ, GOUZEAUCOURT, VILLERS PLOUICH, MARCOING, RIBECOURT, FLESQUIÈRES and returning same route "G TORRANCE Lieut Nomt TRESCAULT. I entered the orders ordered by the Cats now and in addition established a Station on the METZ – RAYUCOURT Road with a Sergt & 5 O.R. for helping wounded & loading on a Car (Ambulance which I accompanied via siding past by the enemy. This station did not operate at all as no cars came returning. It appears from information from Capt TORRANCE that all Cars parts were sent in use. The Cars however on new route from GOUZEAUCOURT by FINS direct STORES at YPRES. 154 Inf. Brigade 80, 150 Comp to 9 Received Transport Drawn to BEAULENCOURT tonight. Ammunits hurried to Embus at 3:45 P.M. METZ & Entrain at YPRES at 6 P.M. 50 Y.R. Div. Re-forms. Scouts Downier. Detrails 3,632 thingles	(P.15.d.) (Attached on/pinned)
Q.W.d.I.9.	24/11/17		BEAULENCOURT AREA. A.D.M.S. Telephone M. 223, 251, 253 Received Divison Instruction as in 6&9 OD. 150	

Army Form C. 2118.

WAR DIARY
or
INTELLIGENCE SUMMARY.

(Erase heading not required.)

CXIX 2/1 Hghd. F.A. Amb.
Atherton Mtn. Eng.

Place	Date	Hour	Summary of Events and Information	Remarks and references to Appendices
Qud. I.F.	24/2/17		Advance party of 4th H. Amb. Munro Ferrier arrived at 10.30 a.m. C.O. & remainder at 12 noon. SM2 dispatched relieving party to TRESCAULT in relief of Capt TORRANCE relay posts. Three at Canteen on RIDECOURT road. One outside to Capt TOTTENHAM to arrive on relief and dispatched Transport for his service Equipment. This unit arrived at 3 p.m. and marched to Entraining point. A Rear party was to be left behind to dispose of Stores belonging to this unit which could not be moved in requested transport - Ambulance Postal Carriers (15), 2nd Wounded for non-stretcher placed outside the Carrol, Pyjama Suits, Telephone, Packs of the Bearer Division.	1. K454 Ref. 69P 00. 150. This
BEAURICOURT	24/2/17		An approaching Entraining point was met by a messenger saying Convoyed the lorries and Guns instructions for a Cars something moved north by EQUANCOURT & YPRES. I was put in time to face into big place on Private road. Arrived YPRES and entrained. Made DERNANCOURT at 2.30 a.m. Transport was found under command of Major G. F. WHYTE & BEAULENCOURT who absorbs the expert Infantry 25th Brigade Transport Office there.	

Army Form C. 2118.

WAR DIARY
or
INTELLIGENCE SUMMARY.

(Erase heading not required.)

C.XX A/1 W.F. Scott
Malcolm H.Kts Cavalry
Bavincourt

Instructions regarding War Diaries and Intelligence Summaries are contained in F.S. Regs., Part II. and the Staff Manual respectively. Title pages will be prepared in manuscript.

Place	Date	Hour	Summary of Events and Information	Remarks and references to Appendices
BEAUVANCOURT	25/11/17		Motor convoy of transport enroute, personnel are without blankets or cooking utensils.	
			Received A.D.M.S. No. 4115, including medical Or'rs, No Spa. per side of 154 Brigade, Unmounted of men and Ambulance Cars arrived. Cars despatched to A/144.T.S. for stores. Left H.Q. now party. Initials for 60 cases opened in billet E.27. BEAUVANCOURT today. very few sick and to hospital. Mostly Scabie cases.	
do.	26/11/17	2.30 pm	A.D.M.S. No. 4115 intimates move of this unit will 154th Brigade by train to BAPAUME thence by road to ROCQUIGNY. Transport by road under B.T.O. Orders detailed.	
		2.40 pm	154. Brigade S.G. 375 intimate at EDGE HILL at 7:30 p.m. Invited brigade H.Q. & note final arrangements and ascertain that the enemy had made an infantry attack on the new salient near CAMBRAI, from three directions North of SOUTH, The whole attack failed except on South where they had pushed through and SW behind the VII Corps mounting artillery fighting and reaching to GENOSAUCOURT. This concentrates rapid move up of Reserve troops.	Attached 154th K.O.O. 151 Brass Band Sheet.
		(continued)	This unit arrived at 7:30 pm. and transport moved off at 4.15 under Capt. J.S. McBRIDE/DOHIE motor near party was Wm Capt of blankets & rations for which repacked Transport is not finished.	

2353 Wt. W2544/1454 700,000 5/15 D.D.&L. A.D.S.S./Forms/C. 2118.

COMMITTEE FOR THE
MEDICAL HISTORY OF THE WAR

Date −1 FEB. 1918

2/Lt. Highland R.A.

WAR DIARY / INTELLIGENCE SUMMARY

Army Form C. 2118.

M.T. Medical
41 Wpn 2? Amb.
December 1917
Sheet No. 1

Place	Date	Hour	Summary of Events and Information	Remarks and references to Appendices
ROCQUIGNY	1/12/17		S.C. 375 from 154 Brigade received. The Inspired Common car has arrived. S.C. 390 received having to proceed to BERTINCOURT billeting party to set forward at 9.30 a.m. R.E. 396 received. This unit were moving forward on and near BUS at 10.15. Ambulance brigaded. Orders at 11.15 a.m. for BERTINCOURT Many carried out. The aLMS [alarm] instruction. This unit carried BERTINCOURT to find no billets for its accommodation. In the afternoon the battalion moved to BEUGNY on the BAPAUME - CAMBRAI road as billets of 9th Royal Scotts divides between that Rocledon and 401/12 Coy RE and this unit. After dark troops all accommodated. Also a forward place for Sick in BERTINCOURT.	S.C. 405 S.C. 375
BERTINCOURT	2/12/17		Received M.O.O.D. 1062 Copy 15. The 57th H Bu. will relieve the 56th D.G. at MOEUVRES. This ambulance will relieve 2/4 London Field Amb. at N.11 Central (near BEAULENCOURT). Relief to complete by 10 a.m. on 3rd Dec. Great difficulty was experienced in getting this unit but into Billets in new camp city of hutmts and since 2 p.m. was asked by the Town Major to vacate all hutrs except a small one near centre 5th Town street that been trying as an Adv post, or the amount 1 decided to move the whole unit to N.11 Central and these total lack of accommodation available. Accordingly the March at H.Q.M. Branch Off a advance party left	Dec. 1576

WAR DIARY or INTELLIGENCE SUMMARY

Army Form C. 2118.

(Erase heading not required.)

A/ Wightman Field Ambulance
1 Canadian M/Cdn. Corps.
December 1917.
Sheet 2/1/

Place	Date	Hour	Summary of Events and Information	Remarks and references to Appendices
N.11 Central	4/12/17		Majr. Perry Smith sen by Car to make arrangements.	
do	5/12/17		Arrived at 7 P.M. and found billets in miners huts at BEAULENCOURT. Sent out from B/2 Trenton Field Ambulance, for including the Deauville Advancing Station between BAPAUME and GREVILLERS. When an officer and 5 other ranks Station H.Q. H.D.M.O. Cars are attached for duty there from 27 M.M.B., their convoy not station Lower to N.11 Central and C.C.S. convoy to 3 & 29 C.C.S. which is situated (GREVILLERS). The cars run from the Deauville Advancing Station and H.Q. armoured Dressing Station and situated where the main dressing Station and H.Q. armoured Dressing Station are situated. All Motor Cars and 2 Horse Ambulances allocated for duty with 1/2 (A.D.S.) H.P. Corps are all drawn off the units, one lorry on light for collecting field Am Reserve brigade. This New Station has been carried on for 3 months and 371 patients hang /5 there were evacuated. About 150 cases were cleared out by the R. London Ford before our take over. 14 Officers patients were taken over, will these onwards to B/2 London Camb. Hand off the morning to SIMONSCOURT near DOUILLENS	
do	6/12/17		All Cars, except one, and one horse ambulance returned to their respective units, the being arranged up the Air Prideaux returned. Patents in the Amb. Station evacuated rapidly and in Brackens arrived from the Corps to instruct Corps Returns of R.S.M. This is emergency establishment by D.D.M.S. Having two Quartermasters N. Capt. Ramsay acts in his stead. The	

2449. Wt. W14957/M90. 750,000. 1/16. J.B.C. & A. Forms/C.2118/12.

Army Form C. 2118.

WAR DIARY or INTELLIGENCE SUMMARY

(Erase heading not required.)

Effingham, Field Ambulance
Flanders 60th Army
Part 3.   December 1917

Place	Date	Hour	Summary of Events and Information	Remarks and references to Appendices
M.N. Cabel	6/12/17		The finding of 600-650 patients tonight must attain. It is a remarkable fact that there the plans to full we have no way of closing down or clearing the patient we have attended. It is impossible as the most of them further down the line to make room for others with practically the same affections. The treatment and proper shelter is clearly nothing but & interrupted. Here is an out-commencement with commencement to 51st N.D. Medical Arrangement (Admin. R.L. #138) received. Arrangement of the front line held by this Division having been made the medical position in forward area were altered. We now really assembly & plan the old British front line Advanced Dressing Station J.9.b.4.1. Westroosebeke 9 J. 16. a. 52. DOIGNIES	
N.11. E.n.t.	14/12/17		A large movement of Indian work was done since last entry, installing Dr. Combinations of a large incinerator with drying room. Water tank heater, & Steam Supplies Chamber. While this window broke works. Raining & whitening sheet home front. Disinfecting certain wards. In this act the 51st N.D. came under IV Corps without change of position. The Rest Station became Floges and a place for 51st Div. Rest Station is being sought. IV Corps Medical arrangements 2047 bh 29. duly received	

2449 Wt. W14957/Mgo 750,000 1/16 J.B.C. & A. Forms/C.2118/12.

1/1 Highland Field Ambulance

December 1917 WAR DIARY or INTELLIGENCE SUMMARY

Army Form C. 2118.

Place	Date	Hour	Summary of Events and Information	Remarks and references to Appendices
N 11 Cent	16/12/17		Ramie OO, no 63, A/py N.11. 4 A/Dvs 57th W Divs received Young with 13.HUCOURT along with the Orders (Capt Ramsbottom) and formed a suitable instruction been received for movement on 17th inst. from here. The 6th Field Ambulance 2nd Div. to billets today in rough country ready to take out.	
BIHUCOURT	17/12/17		I detailed Capt McCormick, 2/2 Pte, to remain at N.11 Central to keep in charge after Sect. N.H. this patients as we were not able to move today. By 3 P.M. this unit completed the move to BIHUCOURT being handed over ORBs F. and I.S.T.M. Humphstone. Men remained about 90 horses of H.D. Natubs 19.2 having been removed today to Large commodious Indian Huts. Vehicles &c Stores handed over at N.11. Cent. Station now at BIHUCOURT were assessed & given hut spread out hospital for 300 here.	
do	18/12/17		Capt. J.S. McCormick and the remainder of H.D. Corps moved here by h.at Amb. Rl. returned as to the premises of officers inspected Sgts. Quarters, Boyle Disinfecting Chamber, Bath hurt, Boilers for all, forwarded with. Army have heavy Aeroplane raid this evening. At least Bombs dropped from (hostile?) Bombs dropped near about 1 kiln from here in The Satingrave road. Three being reported taken prisoners	
	22/12/17		to the R.F. Corps.	

WAR DIARY
OR
INTELLIGENCE SUMMARY

Army Form C. 2118.

2/ Highland Field Ambulance
1st Division. 51st Division. Infantry.

December 1917

Sheet 5

Place	Date	Hour	Summary of Events and Information	Remarks and references to Appendices
Bihucourt 28.XII.17			The Canteen tented Divisional HQ. A direct hit on A Coy Officers Mess and BHQ Offices slightly one hit by a piece of bomb Practically, as Chart put above the head. BHQ Offices slightly hit in as side of the mud. tiers of the Elevated Shop wounded.	
" 29.XII.17			Joined the 3 COS. Whose HQ had been taken and was turned at the quoins by Col. Kerrs Store, at 11 a.m. The wound was dressed & the officers. Enfd by Ambulance. Col. Fleming died in the afternoon. (4 p.m.)	
" 30.XII.17			an excellent start has been arranged for patients has was previous. Sufficient being thanks of the Div. Canteen found a substitute was also made for the Canteen proper Station Hood and a gift of misc. crackers Christmas Cards came from the Bar. Red Cross Soc. a concert was held in the Evening for Patients.	
" 31.XII.17			Grateful for Whiney 050	
" 31.XII.17			Gratitude has been announced CAD & Infantry units for our temporary hospital and hands especially attached to Battery Patrols & Sections Patrols Sect. A Coy. G. 8 Convoy. This meant extra duty to B. & C. Convoy be confined to keep the list of the Division which had not been carried beyond little discussion. B TCS. After all Vehicles of 51st Div.	

140/2696

2/1st Highland F.A.

COMMITTEE FOR THE
MEDICAL HISTORY OF THE WAR
Date -4 MAR. 1918

WAR DIARY
INTELLIGENCE SUMMARY

Army Form C. 2118.

Sheet 1. 2/1 (Highland) Field Ambulance
1/Wellington M.R., Coy 29
January 1915

Vol 29

Place	Date	Hour	Summary of Events and Information	Remarks and references to Appendices
BAKLOORT	11/1/15		Medical Arrangement 27th (6)/12. Noted today received. As far as the duties of this unit are concerned the Medical use said to be over the hard work and efforts now made to ameliorate the patients. Surgical cases, serious pulmonary + pleural cases that were carried at with some effect. Arrangement of buildings and for probable Cases Airplane Bombs were proceeded with, keep us always on guard + vigilant for a more of attack was any between the lines. The ground had the make of battle debauch by opposing metal wires round them. Fairly frequent visits of hostile planes have been made by the Enemy but no bombs have fallen in the Camp. No British Red Cross have supplied hats + pillows for a small officers Hospital. This is not being much in use at present. This furniture for the relief of the sick and all 1947. Jan 14 + 25 and by 6th Dir: Dir: arrived down to BUCQUESSE & CONTE.	
"	12/1/15		Horse on 20 to BAILLEULMONT.	
"	13/1/15		The C.C. 9 No. F. Art Bly Q.M. Copped lines over the forenoon.	

SHEET II
January 1918

2/1 High.Rª Field Ambulance Army Form C. 2118.

G. W. by L. Meyer

WAR DIARY
or
INTELLIGENCE SUMMARY.
(Erase heading not required.)

Place	Date	Hour	Summary of Events and Information	Remarks and references to Appendices
BIHUCOURT	16.1.18		154 Inf Bde A.I. Nº SS115 dated to-day received. This contains instructions re billeting, baths etc in new area.	
do	18.1.18		154 Inf Bde O.O. Nº 4 Copy Nº 10 dated to-day received containing instructions for move on 19.1.18.	
do	19.1.18		Lt Colonel J. ROBERTSON RAMC was granted leave to U.K. from 21.1.18 to 20.2.18. Captain J.S. McCONNACHIE RAMC took over charge of Unit in place of Col Robertson on leave. Unit moved from BIHUCOURT at 11AM after handing over to 17ᵀᴴ FIELD AMB Bde Hospital + collected sick from 154 Inf Bde at ACHIET LE GRAND detraining centre and around at COURCELLES LE COMTE at 12 noon without incident. Opened up STN for Bde + transferred them to 6ᵀᴴ Div REST STN AT BIHUCOURT. 154 Inf Bde OO Nº5 Copy Nº12 received this evening. Instructions for Bde Move on 20ᵀᴴ contained herein - Unit to move with Brigade.	
COURCELLES LE COMTE	20.1.18		Collected sick from Bde in COURCELLES AREA + transferred them to 6 DIV REST STN BIHUCOURT. Unit moved at 9.15AM leaving party behind with surplus stores. Move delayed at start for over an hour with incoming Division. Picked up Bde at cross roads COURCELLES LE COMTE, roads very bad but transport managed to negotiate difficulties successfully	

SHEET III
January 1918

Army Form C. 2118.

2/1 Highland Field Ambulance
G. Ralph - Major

WAR DIARY
or
INTELLIGENCE SUMMARY.
(Erase heading not required.)

Place	Date	Hour	Summary of Events and Information	Remarks and references to Appendices
BAILLEULMONT	20.1.18		Unit arrived at destination BAILLEULMONT at 3·30 PM and took over Billets in Village previously arranged for by Advanced Party. Hospital opened by 'A' Section at Hospital Camp outside village. Surplus stores & cooking party arrived next morning	
do	21.1.18		Hospital Grounds & Buildings discovered to be in a bad condition, day spent in repairing buildings, clearing mud for paths, making up estimates for material duckboards &c to improve hospital site	
do	22.1.18		Major G. F. WHYTE RAMC T rejoined Unit from leave & took over duties as O.C 2/1 H'ghd' Fd Amb in place of Captain J S McCONNACHIE RAMC T.	
do	23.1.18		Captain B. C. BEVERIDGE RAMC T was granted 30 days leave to UK from 24.1.18 to 23.2.18	
do	do		In addition to carrying on hospital the Unit had lectures on First Aid in Regt Aid Post & Field Ambs, also Physical Drill & Route Marches.	

2/1st. Highland. F.A.

Army Form C. 2118.

WAR DIARY
or
INTELLIGENCE SUMMARY. 2/1 Highland Field Ambulance RAMC.TF
(Erase heading not required.)

FEBRUARY 1918 SHEET I

Vol 30

Place	Date	Hour	Summary of Events and Information	Remarks and references to Appendices
BAILLEULMONT	1.2.18		1st Lieut J E QUIGLEY M.O.R.C. U.S.A. who rejoined from temporary duty at 29 C.C.S. on 23.1.18 was detailed for temporary duty at IV Corps School BONES on 28.1.18. QM & Hon Lieut W. A. BUTTERY. RAMC.TF joined 2/1 Highland Field Amb for duty on 30.1.18 from ENGLAND and was taken on strength of Unit from that date No 301230 Q/Sgt Major DAVIS. W.T.J. RAMC.TF was promoted temporary Sgt Major for duration of War under ACI No 717 of 1917 & Special Bde Order No 30 TF dated 8.1.18. During Units stay at BAILLEULMONT the Hospital Grounds & Billets were improved also Brick Fireplaces were built in Hospital Cookhouse and Officers Quarters. 154 Inf Bde Group O.O. No. 9 received to-night.	
LOGEAST WOOD A/BLAINZEVELLE	2.2.18		154 Inf Bde Group Leo 401 (H) Field CY RE moved to-day to Billets in LOGEAST WOOD AREA. 2/1 Highland Field Amb left BAILLEULMONT at 9 A.M. Move completed without incident & Unit arrived & took over 20 Nissen Huts allotted to it just outside A/BLAINZEVELLE. Four Ruts were set aside as Bde Hospital and the rich of the Brigade was collected each day	GW GW
"	4.2.18		A party of 2 NCO's 32, OR's RAMC was detailed for Constructional Work at 29 C.C.S.	GW

Army Form C. 2118.

WAR DIARY
or
INTELLIGENCE SUMMARY.
2/1 Highland Field Ambulance RAMC TF

(Erase heading not required.)

FEBRUARY 1918 SHEET II

Place	Date	Hour	Summary of Events and Information	Remarks and references to Appendices
LOGEAST WOOD ABLAINZEVELLE	6.2.18		A thorough inspection of the KIT of all ranks of the Unit was held and notes taken of all deficiencies	4 zw
	8.2.18		1st Lieut M.K. SMITH. M.O.R.C. USA rejoined Unit from temporary duty as M.O. 1/6 BATT 1/6 ROYAL HIGHRS. Notification was received from the Base that 96/301230 Sgt Major DAVIS. W.T.S. RAMC TF of this Unit had been mentioned in despatches. Authority 3rd Supplement to the LONDON GAZETTE dated 21.12.17 96/30445.	
	9.2.18		The personnel of the Unit passed through a GAS TEST to-day under the direction of 51 DIV GAS OFFICER at DIV H.Q ACHIET LE PETIT. The working party at 96/29CCS of 2 NCO + 31 O.R returned to Unit this evening. RAMC. D.O. 96/63 received to-day containing Medical Arrangements for taking over line by 51st Highland Division. OC 2/1 Highland Fd Amb was detailed to take charge of evacuation from the Front Area	4 zw
				6 zw
	11.2.18		Captain GUY TORRANCE RAMC.T & 20 O.R including 2 Sgt alongwith 1 Ambulance Car left to-day to take over Adv Dress Stn at BEETROOT FACTORY and Relay Post at LOUVERVAL + Reg. Aid Posts in Left Sector of DIVISIONAL FRONT. Just as first Car arrived at BEETROOT FACTORY a shell burst immediately behind	

Army Form C. 2118.

WAR DIARY
or
INTELLIGENCE SUMMARY.
2/1 Highland Field Ambulance. R.A.M.C. T.

(Erase heading not required.)

FEBRUARY 1918 SHEET III

Place	Date	Hour	Summary of Events and Information	Remarks and references to Appendices
LOCEAST WOOD ABLAINZEVELLE	11.2.18		The Bar wounding four men of this Unit, two severely and two slightly. They were at once sent to Main Dressing Station at BEUGNY where three were transferred to CCS and one returned to duty. 154 INF BDE O.O. N°7 d 11.2.18 Received with details for move of the Unit on 13.2.18	L.P.W
	12.2.18		R.A.M.C. T. CAPTAIN, J.S. McCONNACHIE & 20 - OR' including 4 NCO along with 2 Ambulance Cars left today to take over Adv Dres Stn at DOIGNIES also RELAY POSTS at BEAUMETZ-LES-CAMBRAI & DEMICOURT + R.A.P's in right sector of Div Front. This was accomplished without incident.	L.P.W
BEUGNY	13.2.18		Unit left LOCEAST WOOD AREA at 9.15 this morning for Main Dressing Stn BEUGNY. March accomplished in wet weather without mishap and Unit took over Huts & Marquees alongside M.D. Stn. BEUGNY.	L.P.W
	14.2.18		"A" Section Tent Sub consisting of 2 NCO's & 14 OR" were detailed for duty with N° 29 CCS on this date.	L.P.W
	15.2.18		1st Lieut J.E. QUIGLEY M.O.R.C. U.S.A rejoined H.Q from IV Corps School to-day 1st Lieut M.K. SMITH. M.O.R.C.U.S.A was granted leave to PARIS from 15.2.18 to 1.3.18 Auth ADMS 51 D 9/2 429 d 11.2.18	L.P.W

Army Form C. 2118.

WAR DIARY
or
INTELLIGENCE SUMMARY.
(Erase heading not required.)

2/1 Highland Field Ambulance
RAMC TF
J Robertson Lt Col Comdg

Place	Date	Hour	Summary of Events and Information	Remarks and references to Appendices
BEUGNY	15.2.18		A new evacuation shelter is being constructed at DOIGNIES A.D Stn and a new R.A Post at DEMICOURT under supervision of 404 (H) Field C.RE	J.W.
	17.2.18		1st Lieut J.E QUIGLEY MORC USA was detailed for duty as temp "M.O" "1st Batt" GORDON HDRS	J.W.
	18.2.18		New work on Dug Outs at A.D Stn BEETROOT FACTORY is to be started tomorrow under supervision of 404 (H) Field C.RE The idea is to sink a fresh shaft and connect up present A.D Stn with Dug Out to the East of it	J.W.
	"		R.A.M.C. O.O. No 66 received to-night This order provides for the taking over of GROPI CAMP LEBUCQUIERE as Headquarters of 2/1 High. Fd Amb.	
	20.2.18		1 Sgt & 17 O.R's proceeded to GROPI CAMP as an advance party took over CAMP at 12 Noon. This party are preparing Camp for occupation by this Unit and for the reception of patients –	
	"		154 Inf Bde O.O No 8 received to-day. Contains nothing affecting this Unit	J.W.
	21.2.18		Lt Colonel J ROBERTSON. RAMC T. OC 2/1 High Fd Amb returned from months leave today	J.W.
	22.2.18		Carts even from Major in Wayte and proceeded to inspect Regimental Bearing Mahins at DOIGNIES and BEETROOT, also the intermediate Stations at BEAUMETZ, and Regimental Aid Posts & Relays in Erip Sector found all Correct JW

2353 Wt. W2544/1454 700,000 5/15 L.D. & L. A.D.S.S./Forms/C. 2118.

Army Form C. 2118.

WAR DIARY
or
INTELLIGENCE SUMMARY.

2/1 Midland. Field Ambulance,
48th (Sth Midland) Division.

(Erase heading not required.)

Instructions regarding War Diaries and Intelligence Summaries are contained in F. S. Regs., Part II. and the Staff Manual respectively. Title pages will be prepared in manuscript.

Place	Date	Hour	Summary of Events and Information	Remarks and references to Appendices
BEUGNY	2/7/15	3 pm	Afternoon inspected the new Head Quarters Camp at GROPI. near LEBUGVIERES. This camp is presently occupied by M.G. Corps & I.M. troops. It requires a great deal of repairs and duck boarding. Material indented for.	Sheet 57 C. (I 30. C.1.5)
BEUGNY	24/1/15		Today visited DOIGNIES and inspected routes and aid posts voluntary near Beam Valley Post at North End of DEMICOURT. Past near DOIGNIES both outposts to Shell fire the afternoon near nothing evacuated.	
GROPI CAMP	25/1/15		and CAMBRAI ROAD. Capt B.G. BEVERIDGE M.B., Referred from arrangements leave to U.K. Head Quarters of this unit with all equipment moved to GROPI Camp near LEBUCQUIERES. Map Ref Sheet 57C. I 30 c.24. This comment of 10 armies of Prison huts and other huts feet covered into Patients Patients against bombs from Aeroplanes. The camp is well laid out but is very insanitary. The force of Mission huts have been inverted through in several places and the commons in the windows leaving running almost entirely. The M.T. and H.T. M.S.C. were left in their previous billets in BEUGNY temporarily, as there were left hands beside GROPI camp. A private hospital was opened for Local cases. The position of GROPI camp is about 500 yards from the FREMICOURT road and the approach is a very bad road.	

Army Form C. 2118.

WAR DIARY
or
INTELLIGENCE SUMMARY.
(Erase heading not required.)

2/1 Wyndhm Field Ambulance
1/Robertson H/M. Army

Place	Date	Hour	Summary of Events and Information	Remarks and references to Appendices
GROUPI	24/11/18		Units DOIGNIES, BEAUMETZ & BEETROOT in company with Coast Guards and Army Mains Centre back from their stores Reserve of Camp regards forward with.	/c
do	25/11/18		Recd left letter RAMC. Consult Coast Guards received Talk to remove at BEETROOT intended entrance of Cas Ambulance with ADMS at his office FREMICOURT in which Scheme of defence was discussed and forward action in the event of a sharp retreat of our troops was decided that in the event of our 12th Reserve line having our front that DOIGNIES ADS fall back on GROUP I Camp and that a Rear Relay be made at BEAUMETZ; DOIGNIES having a Regimental Aid Post. That BEETROOT ADS. fall back on BEUGNY having a Rear Relay at 9 ELMS near MARCHIES; BEETROOT having a R.A. aid post. The M.D.S. at BEUGNY would fall back on LOCH CAMP. FREMICOURT during the long action thereby greater retreat the first would be known as two Section BEUGNY and GROUP Camp and provisional as Main Dressing Station — and close to C.C.S. from LEFT and RIGHT Sectors respectively	

J/Robertson Lieut t Colonel
O.C 2/1 Wysham Field Ambulance

140/2849

March
1918   2/Lor. Strickland Y a

COMMITTEE FOR THE WAR
CAL HISTORY OF THE WAR
2 MAY 1918

Army Form C. 2118.

WAR DIARY
or
INTELLIGENCE SUMMARY.
(Erase heading not required.)

2/1st Highland Field Ambulance
MARCH 1918

Place	Date	Hour	Summary of Events and Information	Remarks and references to Appendices
GROPI.	5/3/18		Today replaces the light trailers to forward area of 51st Div front and commenced with ADMS inspecting hand bogey bank for R.A.P.s ARDENICOURT and sent 100 back to DOIGNIES and 9 ELMs repairing. Also inspected 2 sources of ambulance from mid to BEETROOT from BEUGNY thus relieving the M.O.s of ambulance cars and receiving wounded cases from R.A.P.s. March. We cleared near GROPI Camp for shell proof shelters close by FREMICOURT road (I.29.6.8.5) for use as an advanced Bearers station in event of retreat. The place at BEUGNY is being studied so arrest by Bde Hd Qr Cmdr intends for arrangements for the sheltering of personal items tools, horse but in - but no orders received. Stores, Rations transports, and M.E. material. Lieut Morris K. Smith M.S.A.M.O.S. (retired) from Yarra's team to PARIS.	Front lug 100 feet hyper rate that is T.2.6. Vol 31
"			He works at DOIGHIES & BEETROOT & DEMICOURT succeeding duty. Gas practices in day outs has been carried out. 154 by Bgde O.O. 829 issued.	
"	6/3/18		Relief of Majors Rose situated by Major J/3 Hope 1st Ambl commenced today Capt. McConnachie relieved by Lt. M.K. Smith M.O.S. All three brigades of Infantry are now in the line. 154 & 152 HQ at in BEAUMETZ 153 HQ in Sunken Rd I.12.6.5.3.	

Army Form C. 2118.

2/1st HIGHLAND FIELD AMBULANCE

WAR DIARY
or
INTELLIGENCE SUMMARY.
(Erase heading not required.)

1 March 1915

Place	Date	Hour	Summary of Events and Information	Remarks and references to Appendices
GHQP1.	3/11/18		The Three Brigades having taken over, the R.A.P. at Chateau Hermes is not in a suitable place for Centre Brigade. Falkiner being too far to left of Brhs. and to far to the right for Left Brigade. Reported this to A.D.M.S. Visited all the R.A.Ps. and 3 parts of the Rgtl "party" centre Sector. Discussed the evacuation from DEMICOURT with the O.C. 4th Argylls. So decided that in event of heavy fighting a route further south should be used. DEMICOURT (HERMIES) should be adopted in addition. A good road from HERMIES and a light railway [Trench] runs between DEMICOURT & HERMIES & the road by VELU & LEBUCQUIERES. The work of preparing a principal A.D.S. at I.29 c.3.5. is proceeding. Material has been unloaded for & preliminary work in laying stone.	
do.	5/11/18		Instructions having been received from A.D.M.S. that an enemy attack was likely on 5th inst. of a nature as to resume all arrangements for firing ground to be made. I visited the advanced Dressing Stations and then proceeded to R.O.M.S. office to discuss arrangements. The O.C. Main Dressing Station was present. Efforts in hand made to complete all engineers work & S.B. work	

WAR DIARY
or
INTELLIGENCE SUMMARY.
(Erase heading not required.)

Army Form C. 2118.

2/1st Highland Field Ambulance
Méharicourt Sheet 62c. Contay 51
Sheet 3.

2/1st HIGHLAND FIELD AMBULANCE

Place	Date	Hour	Summary of Events and Information	Remarks and references to Appendices
GROVE	6/11/15		Completion of Roof of new armoured Shelter at DOINGIES accelerated by night & day shifts. The new dug out at BEETROOT FACTORY A.D.S. complete. Stretcher racks etc are now required to complete augmentation of accommodation for Stretcher Cases to 36.	
do	7/11/15		Medical Arrangements for active operations received from A.D.M.S. (No 4304 C/pr 15) with instructions as to action in the event of Retiral. Exact orders by O.C. 2/1 Hyd F.A sent to O.C's A.D.S. Copies attached.	
do	8/11/15		No attack occurred. I visited A.D.S. particularly inspected a new aid post formed by the M.O. 1/6 Gordon Highlanders on the Cambrai road T.I.P.b.O.S. and found it in satisfactory manner of brancards, look of protection against Sun or Shell fire. Found a dug out and access by which accommodates 10 Stretcher Cases & recommended it.	
do	9/11/15		154 Bgd. O. 11-C/pr 13 received refers to disposition of Ambulants attack by the many daily skirmishes today under HEENIE's running station Sr. 1712 Div. and mentioned that Carnoulis from DEMICOURT might overflow to Co	

2/1st HIGHLAND FIELD AMBULANCE

Army Form C. 2118.

WAR DIARY or INTELLIGENCE SUMMARY.

(Erase heading not required.)

March 1918

Place	Date	Hour	Summary of Events and Information	Remarks and references to Appendices
GROPI Camp	9/11/18		Also explored routes of evacuation from 1st Scottish working points of BEAUMETZ to VELU & BEUGNY. The light railway is complete and continues for running Ambulance trains from DEMICOURT to BEUGNY. The Relay point at BEAUMETZ has been augmented & improved and stocked with 100 Shelters. Two Mounted also Divis: Medical Comforts, a store for Ambulance Cars forming near by is for the M.T. Servants. Made arrangements with the Horse Ambulance Con: Commd'y routes from DOIGNIES — BEAUMETZ. Stores to BEUGNY M.D.S. The two A.D.S.s at BEETROOT & DOIGNIES have been stocked 100 Shelters Two Mounted blank. Also to forward R.A.P.s have has their Shelters increased to 28. All heavy roads have been T.R.O. off and instruct as to which R.A.D.S to go to. Portions for medical work on the Cambrai Road and light Railway immediately in rear of J.J (PROVILLE SPUR) have been wired and numbered lim marked for the event of active Operations. (I. 7. b. 8. 4.) & (I. 17. d. 5. 9.) Information received that a train running from from to BEUGNY. Commencing 9 p.m. 10th inst. This will carry all Chipotle Cases and urgent Cases — wire to transport by Car	Sheet 57C

WAR DIARY or INTELLIGENCE SUMMARY

Army Form C. 2118.

2/1st HIGHLAND FIELD AMBULANCE

March 1918

Place	Date	Hour	Summary of Events and Information	Remarks and references to Appendices
GROPI CAMP	10/3/18		Under authority from A.D.M.S. 100 bearers have been detailed for work with R.E. 3 Infantry to proceed to various rendezvous daily for work in BEAVMETZ (MDOUE 4309) in hauling cables and stretcher dug-outs. It was generally assumed that an attack by the enemy was to take place the morning. The Brigadier put two battalions into the line ready. A new R.A.P. was formed and another one at J.18.a.9.9. H Nairn bearer was detailed for the front both with W Cunard to DOIGNIES.	
do.	18/3/18		Padilion L/C. GEVERIDGE was relieved at BEETROOT A.D.S. by Capt. TORRANCE. All instructions for action in event of enemy attack given to Capt. TORRANCE. Lent the H.Q.M.S. of 1/4 H.B. Div Yesterday to 1 round of 153 62. R.A.P.s. He was making plans for an offensive against the enemy presuming he had occupied LOUVERVAL and DOIGNIES.	
		11 P.M.	This evening I received information that an attack by the enemy was expected in the morning of 13th and that their massive artillery rumble preparation would commence at 12 midnight and that all troops in front of BEAVMETZ had "Stand to" from 4.30 until receipt of the code word "KILLIEKRANKIE"	

2/1st HIGHLAND FIELD AMBULANCE

Army Form C. 2118.

WAR DIARY
or
INTELLIGENCE SUMMARY.
(Erase heading not required.)

2/1 Highland Field Ambulance
Lillers N.E. France
March 1915

Place	Date	Hour	Summary of Events and Information	Remarks and references to Appendices
GORRE CAMP	12/3/15	11 pm	I commenced inspection for the O.C. 2/1 S.C. Meanwhile arrangements and all leaves were intimated. Stores, funds, kits beside them & I stood to at 5 am. on 13th. All dispositions were arranged for immediate action.	
"	13/3/15	9 am	The Col and I visited Killefrontie who were having a commander to all units under my command.	
"	14/3/15		Decided on a relay bearer & dressing station for the left sector at J.T.G.9.0. and asked for authority from the Brown to occupy the same. Made a deep dug-out at a broken road known as the GLEN, and is now forward between BEUGNY and BEETROOT hut & Commence both for Combra Road and the light Railway running from BEUGNY to Avigne in hand of the R/F R.A.P. (100 House) and will be able to evacuate with ROUTES of evacuation.	
"	15/3/15		Permission for rebuild. A dug out at GLEN received. And 3 men sent into it to prepare & shoring out to. Also visited R.A.P. at J.10.6.3.5. and inspected the broken down 2.I.T.c.5? for a finish new R.A.P. hut in connection with O.C. 1/6 Gazette 4th VTRWH. Regrets the day in

Army Form C. 2118.

WAR DIARY
or
INTELLIGENCE SUMMARY.

(Erase heading not required.)

SHEET T.
March 1918

2/1st HIGHLAND FIELD AMBULANCE

Army J. Garie Capt R.amc QF

Place	Date	Hour	Summary of Events and Information	Remarks and references to Appendices
GROFI CAMP LEBUCQUIERE (13 D C 2 4 Sheet 51C)	17.3.18		Major J.S. McConnachie relieved Lieut (M.K. SMITH. M.O.R.C at DOIGNIES. Advd Dress Stn. Acting A.D.M.S. 51(H) Div	MAP REF V.16 a 3 2 Sheet 51C
-do-	18.3.18		Capt J G ELDER R.A.M.C T.C reported for duty from England	
-do-	19.3.18		Lieut M.K SMITH. M.O.R.C proceeded to PARIS to join American Army + struck off strength	
-do-	20.3.18		General Routine	
-do-	21.3.18	5.5AM	Our Barrage opened at 5.5AM. Telephone communication broken down got was of RE's Capt BROWN 1/2 H.Fd.Amb reported for duty + was despatched to (BEETROOT Advd Dress Stn. Capt ELDER was ordered to proceed to DOIGNIES Advd Dress Stn to assist Major McCONNACHIE. Reserve Bearers from all ambulances sent to forward posts.	MAP REF J.19 & 4.1 Sheet51 telephones
		At 11AM GROFI Camp H.Q was heavily shelled + Col ROBERTSON ordered Camp to be cleared.	
		11.15AM	Lt.Colonel Jas. ROBERTSON. R.A.M.C T.F. O.C 2/1 Highland Field Amb. was killed in action at H.Q of Unit at GROFI CAMP near LEBUCQUIERE Map Ref I 30.c.2.4. at 11-15AM CAPTAIN. BERNARD. GORDON, BEVERIDGE. R.A.M.C T.F. was mortally wounded by same shell which killed Col Robertson and DIED FROM WOUNDS at 1.15PM at the Main Dressing Station (1/3 H.F.Amb) BEUGNY-Map Ref (SReet 51C) I 21.6.2.7.	
		1 PM	Major J MARTIN SMITH, 1/3 H.F.Amb arrived to take over command of Unit at 1PM as trouble	M.S
		2.30PM	After securing as much material + documents of the Unit, in small batches departed to take up position at LOCH CAMP near FREMICOURT	

Army Form C. 2118.

WAR DIARY
or
INTELLIGENCE SUMMARY.
(Erase heading not required.)

2/1st HIGHLAND FIELD AMBULANCE

Instructions regarding War Diaries and Intelligence Summaries are contained in F.S. Regs., Part II. and the Staff Manual respectively. Title pages will be prepared in manuscript.

SHEET 8
Month March 1918

Place	Date	Hour	Summary of Events and Information	Remarks and references to Appendices
LOCH CAMP near FREMICOURT	21·3·18		All communications with BEETROOT & DOIGNIES Adv Dres Stns having ceased, a cyclist was despatched to find out the position, he was unable to reach either ADS and returned to HQ reporting same. Captain BROWN who had been despatched to assist at BEETROOT ADS earlier in the day was unable to reach BEETROOT ADS & reported same. It is presumed that Capt GUY TORRANCE RAMC TF at BEETROOT A.D.S. with personnel are prisoners of war. Also Major J.S. M°CONNACHIE RAMC TF & CAPTAIN J.G.ELDER RAMC TC and personnel at DOIGNIES A.D.S. are also prisoners. LIEUT J.E. QUIGLEY MORC.USA of this Unit who was temp°y attached to 1/7 BLACKWATCH as M.O. is believed also a prisoner and Lt Col° P. SINCLAIR SCF Senior Chaplain 51(H) DIV. The following are the casualties among personnel of the Unit during the tenure of the Advanced Dressing Stations:- 1 OFFICER (RAMC) KILLED IN ACTION 1 OFFICER R.(RAMC) DIED OF WOUNDS 5 OFFICERS(RAMC) MISSING - BELIEVED PRISONERS OF WAR - these include 1 American Medical Officer Lt. QUIGLEY 7 OTHER RANKS (RAMC) WOUNDED - (BATTLE CASUALTIES) and 1 Chaplain, Lt. Col. P. SINCLAIR. SCF. 51(H) DIV. 56 (8/3/5m) do - (RAMC) MISSING - BELIEVED PRISONER OF WAR 1 —do— (A.S.C. MT) —do— Two Riding Horses killed + 3 draught Horses wounded at GROPI CAMP HQ, one of which had to be shot.	MAP. REF. SHEET 57C J.9.b.41 MAP. REF. J.16.a.5.2 SHEET 57C

Army Form C. 2118.

WAR DIARY
or
INTELLIGENCE SUMMARY.
(Erase heading not required.)

2/1st HIGHLAND FIELD AMBULANCE

Sheet 9
March 1918

Army J. Gorrie Capt RAMCTF

Place	Date	Hour	Summary of Events and Information	Remarks and references to Appendices
LOCH CAMP near FREMICOURT	22.3.18		Lt. Col. J. ROBERTSON RAMC TF and Capt. B.G. BEVERIDGE M.C. RAMC TF were buried at FREMICOURT CHURCH CEMETERY (SHEET 57c) MAP REF. I 26.a.3.7. on 22.3.18 Officiating Chaplain Rev W WALLACE BROWN	H.J.G.
			C.F. 1/8 ROYAL SCOTS.	
			Q.M.S. L.G. TOUGH & party remained at DUG.OUT adjoining GROP.I.CAMP. LEBUCQUERE and carried on dressing wounded till afternoon of 22" when they were withdrawn to LOCH CAMP.	H.J.G
		12 Noon	Occupied LOCH CAMP near FREMICOURT as Advanced Dressing Stn which was vacated by Main Dressing Stn, who proceeded to GREVILLERS at noon	H.J.G.
-do-	23.3.18	12 Noon	Were ordered to proceed to GREVILLERS near BAPAUME and join 1/3 H.F. Amb at C.C.S. here. GREVILLERS was very heavily shelled all afternoon + evening	H.J.G. H.J.G.
GREVILLERS	24.3.18	11-30 AM	Ordered to proceed to BEAUCOURT-SUR-ANCRE along with Main Dressg Stn where we arrived at midnight.	H.J.G.
		9 PM	Ordered to move to AUCHONVILLERS where we arrived at midnight. Major J. MARTIN SMITH proceeded with car to A.D.S.m. ACHIET LE PETIT, + owing to car accident some hours later did not return + was admitted to No. 6 STATIONARY HOSP. FREVENT.	H.J.G H.J.G.
AUCHONVILLERS	25.3.18	5 PM	Moved from AUCHONVILLERS via MAILLY-MAILLET to BEAUSART when we then got orders	H.J.G.

2353 Wt. W3441/1454 700,000 5/15 D.D.&L. A.D.S.S./Forms/C. 2118.

Army Form C. 2118.

WAR DIARY
or
INTELLIGENCE SUMMARY.

2/1st HIGHLAND FIELD AMBULANCE

Army 1 Corps Capt. 1 aur of

Sheet 10   March 1918

Place	Date	Hour	Summary of Events and Information	Remarks and references to Appendices
BEAUSART	25.3.18	7 PM	Unit moved to HÉNU via BERTRANCOURT, (BUS) & COUIN reached HÉNU at 12.30 AM-26"	A.F.G.
HÉNU	26.3.18	11 AM	Marched to SAULTY (LES-ARTOIS) where we rested till 5 PM moving then to SOMBRIN, and billets Rue	A.F.G.
BARLY	27.3.18	10.30 AM	Moved to BARLY via S⁺ LÉGER, IVERGNY, BOUQUEMAISON, NEUVILLETTE, arriving at 4 PM	14.F.G. A.F.G.
-do-	28.3.18		Looking after Brigade Sick, readjusting wagon loads	
	29.3.18	7.30 AM	Transport moves with Brigade for new area near LILLERS & LT⁺QM BATTERY in charge. Convoy BARLY at 7.30 AM. Personnel march by road to FRÉVENT to entrain for LAPUGNOY, leaving BARLY at 7.30 p.m. & reaching FRÉVENT at 9.30 PM	A.F.G.
FRÉVENT	30.3.18	5 AM	Train leaves FRÉVENT at 5 AM arriving at LAPUGNOY at 10 AM. Unit marched to Billeting area, CENSE-LA-VALLÉE arriving 2 PM	A.F.G.
CENSE-LA-VALLÉE	31.3.18		Day spent in attaching of Stores & looking after Brigade sick	
-do-		7 PM	Major G.F WHYTE, RAMC.TF rejoined Unit from 29 CCS & assumed command of 2/1 3⁶ 3ᴸᵃ J.M. Amb at 7 PM	A.F.G.

G.F.Whyte
Major R.a.m.c T.F
O.C. 2/1 Highland Field Ambulance

2/1st HIGHLAND FIELD AMBULANCE
No.
Date 31.3.18

140/2900

2/1st Highland F.A.

JO 1918

SHEET 1
APRIL 1918

Army Form C. 2118.

WAR DIARY
or
INTELLIGENCE SUMMARY.

2/1st HIGHLAND FIELD AMBULANCE

G ? Wright MAJOR RAMC. TF

WO 95 32

Places	Date	Hour	Summary of Events and Information	Remarks and references to Appendices
Cense La Vallee	2.4.18		Captain G.D. Yates posted to 2/1 High. Fd Amb for temporary duty on 2-4-18	G.P.W
-do-	3.4.18		Captain G.D. Yates posted to 1/3 High. Fd Amb for duty	
-do-	"		Lieut North C.O. MORC who had been previously attached for temporary duty from 22-3-18 was taken on strength from that date by orders of ADMS 51 Div.	G.P.W
-do-	"		154. Inf Bde O O 96.16 received with instructions for move of Brigade to the AUCHEL, LOZINGHEM, RAIMBERT area on 4 Apl. 2/1 H F Amb to be billeted in AUCHEL.	G.P.W
-do-	4.4.18		Unit marched off at 11 AM leaving a rear party for cleaning billets. March accomplished without incident. Unit arriving at AUCHEL about 1.30 PM. Capt Gorrie Road billets taken in town, men being all accommodated in HOTEL DE VILLE.	G.P.W
AUCHEL	6.4.18		Warning orders received to move next day, but the order was cancelled later. During Units stay in AUCHEL the Brigade sick were collected & transferred to 1/2 High 3d Amb. Personnel were all bathed at the AUCHEL MINES BATHS	G.P.W
-do-	7.4.18		154 Inf Bde OO 90.17 received containing information that the Div would be transferred on 8 Apl from 1st Corps to XI Corps & also giving details of move of 154 Bde to GONNEHEM area on 8 Apl.	G.P.W
-do-	8.4.18		Unit moved today at 9 AM under Bde orders to CENSE-LA-VALLEE which was reached at 12.30 PM	
Cense La Vallee	"		A reinforcing draft of 6 Australian Officers arrived today & were taken on strength. Their	

Army Form C. 2118.

WAR DIARY
or
INTELLIGENCE SUMMARY.

(Erase heading not required.)

2/1st HIGHLAND FIELD AMBULANCE

G. Pulugh – MAJOR RAMC TF

SHEET 11
APRIL 1918.

Place	Date	Hour	Summary of Events and Information	Remarks and references to Appendices
CENSE LA VALLEE	8.4.18		Captain HUDSON. A.P. – AAMC. Capt. JAMIESON. H.H. – AAMC do BARROW. I.M. – do Capt. UREN C. – do do DUHIG. J.V.J. – do Capt. McLEAN. J.M. – do names being as follows :–	G.P.W.
	9.4.18		A new Enemy Attack started this morning. Wires were received from 154 Inf Bde intimating the fact that Bde was moving up in support. Capt. GORRIE was detailed to proceed to Bde HQ to receive orders. Bearer Squads were told off and Unit ordered to stand by in Billets. Wire from ADMS 51 Div received at 2.15 PM to send all available Motor Ambs to report to 1/3 H.F. Amb. At 5.20 PM a wire was received from Bde ordering all available Bearers & Motor & Horse Ambulance to report to Brigade Transport Officer at N.17.a.3.7 near AVELETTE. 4 NCOs & 40 Bearers were immediately despatched with all available Motor & Horse Ambulances under the charge of CAPTAIN JAMIESON & LIEUT NORTH. Unit warned by ADMS to be ready to move in ½ hours notice.	G.P.W. G.P.W.
	10.4.18		Wire received from ADMS at 11 AM ordering HQ to move to LA-MIQUELLERIE. Unit left at 11.30 AM & reached destination at 1 PM. Unit billeted in Barn with Transport in Field adjoining. Kept in touch with Capt. JAMIESON by Motor Cyclist & forwarded Pro reports to ADMS. 1 NCO & 1 man were reported wounded. Staff under orders to move at ½ hours notice.	G.P.W.
	11.4.18		At 12.9 noon wire received from 154 Bde to move with Brigade Transport to HAM-EN-ARTOIS. March delayed considerably en route by congested traffic and Unit arrived at 2 PM	
	12.4.18			

Army Form C. 2118.

WAR DIARY
or
INTELLIGENCE SUMMARY.
(Erase heading not required)

2/1st HIGHLAND FIELD AMBULANCE

G. McHugh - MAJOR RAMC. TF

SHEET III April 1918

Place	Date	Hour	Summary of Events and Information	Remarks and references to Appendices
HAMEN-ARTOIS	12.4.18		Billets for personnel taken in the Village & Transport accommodated in fields outside village Captain JAMIESON H.H. AAMC & Lieut NORTH MORC & Bearer Party rejoined HQ this morning, 154 INF Bde having been relieved. At 2PM a wire was received from ADMS 51 Div to send a MO to report to O.C. 1/2 H.F Amb & Cap.t DUHIG was sent. Report on work done by 2/1 Highland Field Amb Stretcher Bearer Party from 9 to 13.4.18	G. P.W.
	13.4.18		"On 9th inst 9 Left CENSE LA VALLEE at 5.30PM, HINGES was under shell fire as we passed through. Reported to A.D.M.S 55 Div at 7.30PM and at 8PM to 154 INF 13 Bde Transport Officer. Both at HINGETTE. Men & Ambulances were then quartered at a farm near by with orders from ADMS to stand to & await instructions. Booked one Runner to Brigade TO & another went out to Bde HQ with ration limber. That night sent two stretcher squads (1 N.CO & 8 men) to MO 1/7 A&SHdrs & also 5 Stretcher Squads with 1 N.CO to Bde HQ. Early next morning (10th inst) 2 Squads 1 N.CO + 7 men were sent down to A.S.C lines, first went to PONT D'AVELETTE BRIDGE to clear some men wounded by a shell. These returned, and later were sent out to MESPLAUX FARM near LOCON BRIDGE to clear wounded there. Later on 1 N.CO + 7 Bearers were sent out to R.M.O 1/4 GORDONS. The same morning Lieut NORTH	

WAR DIARY or INTELLIGENCE SUMMARY

Army Form C. 2118.

2/1st HIGHLAND FIELD AMBULANCE

SHEET 4
APRIL 1918

G. Whyte Major R.A.M.C. T.F

Place	Date	Hour	Summary of Events and Information	Remarks and references to Appendices
			went out & reported to Bde HQ & located the 1/7 A&SHdrs R.A.P. which was near by. The 1/4 Gordons had moved just about that time and the position of their R.A.P. was not known. The first Relay Post at V/100 Billet was also located by Lieut North at that time two runners were then sent out to try & locate the 1/4 Seaforths R.A.P. One of the runners Pte A.F. Thompson was wounded while returning. At that time the 154 Inf Bde was getting practically no casualties. About 11 AM acting on a message sent by RMO of 1/4 Gordons I took 2 Motor Amos & 8 Bearers to 1/7 A&SHdrs R.A.P. to remove wounded from there. The wounded from the 1/4 Gordons were being carried to the 1/7 A&SHdrs R.A.P. & removed by Ambulances from there whilst the 2 R.A.P's were in the same positions (1/7 A&SH W6.D.35 & 1/4 Gordons at W.6.a.3.3) Two Motor Ambulances were running continually from there to the A.D.S. Hinges. Cpl Pheasant was wounded in the Road slightly this morning. The same forenoon Capt. Gorrie & I went out & visited Bde HQ. 1/7 A&SH R.A.P. & 1/4 Gordon R.A.P. later on in the day, the latter R.A.P. was removed to W.6 Central. Acting on instructions from Major Whyte the Horse Ambulances were stationed about 2 miles further back at Lannoy (W.13.D.24.)	

Army Form C. 2118.

WAR DIARY
or
INTELLIGENCE SUMMARY.
(Erase heading not required.)

2/1st HIGHLAND FIELD AMBULANCE

G.F.W.Rugh - MAJOR. R.A.M.C. T.F.

SHEET 5
APRIL 1918.

All this time they were carrying walking cases to the M.D.S. During that day a large number of casualties were coming in from the 154 INF BDE. That night we were shelled out of HINGETTE & moved up to HINGES W15 & S 9 Friday 12" At dawn the 1/7 A & S Hdrs & the 1/4 GORDONS were relieved & moved back to the south side of the LA BASSÉE CANAL. During the morning there were no casualties from the Brigade. At 12-30 P.M. we were shelled out of HINGES & MAJOR YATES O.C. 2/1 WEST LANCASHIRE F Amb to which we were attached, ordered all cars & men back to CHOCQUES CHATEAU, on arriving there he informed me he was relieved & thinking this too far back I moved the horse Ambulances & the men further forward & established a RELAY POST at W14 B36 where Bde HQ were at that time. From here the Horse Ambulances carried walking wounded down to CHOCQUES CHATEAU & then took a motor ambulance down to near the LA BASSÉE CANAL & located the two R.A.P.s & arranged a point with the R.M.O.s to which the bearers were to carry & from which the Motor Ambulances would carry to CHOCQUES CHATEAU where there were several Main Dressing Stations. As the 2/1 West Lancashire F Amb was supposed to be relieved

WAR DIARY or INTELLIGENCE SUMMARY

Army Form C. 2118.

2/1st HIGHLAND FIELD AMBULANCE

G P W Lyle   MAJOR RAMC TF

SHEET 6
April 1918

Place	Date	Hour	Summary of Events and Information	Remarks and references to Appendices
			but apparently no one had yet taken their place, + as the 3rd was supposed to be relieving them, I went to the CHOCQUES CHATEAU + inquired of the DADMS. 3rd Div if we were attached to them. He informed me they were only in reserve and had not yet taken over, however he took me along to the OC 2/1 Wessex F Amb who promised me as many Motor Ambulances as I wanted at a moments notice to clear any wounded from the 1/4 Gordons + 1/7 A+S Hdrs. That night under Capt Corrie's instructions two Horse Ambulances were sent back to 2/1 HF Amb H.Q HAM-EN-ARTOIS. At about 3.30 AM Saturday 13th the 154 Inf Bde was relieved + marched back. I collected all the stretcher Bearers from the two Battalions + after picking up two 1/4 Gordon accidentally wounded cases we moved off. At BUSNETTES I transferred the two wounded men to a Motor Ambulance which was to take them to the M.D.S LOZINGHAM. Reported back at H.Q 2/1 H.F.Amb HAM-EN-ARTOIS at 6 A.M. (Signed) K H Jamieson	G PW
HAM-EN-ARTOIS	13.4.18		A large RAMC draft for the three Ambulances reported to ADMS 51 Div to day and 59 - O.Ranks were taken on strength of this Unit, one of these men became a battle casualty before reaching the Unit.	G PW

Army Form C. 2118.

WAR DIARY
or
INTELLIGENCE SUMMARY.
(Erase heading not required.)

SHEET 7
APRIL 1918

2/1st HIGHLAND FIELD AMBULANCE

E. F. Wyly — MAJOR.

Place	Date	Hour	Summary of Events and Information	Remarks and references to Appendices
HAM-EN-ARTOIS	15.4.18		Arrangements were made for this Unit to collect the sick of the 152 & 153 Infantry Brigades and convey them to 1/3 Highland Fd Amb. MAIN DRESSING STN. Refitting of personnel of Unit & of Equipment. Clothing & proceeded with. Captain DUNG rejoined HQ from 1/2 2nd Highland Fd Amb today.	4 pm
do	16.4.18		Captain GORRIE. H.A ordered by ADMS 51 Div to rejoin his Unit (1/3 H F Amb) to-day	4 pm
do	17.4.18		Captain UREN C - appointed Transport Officer to-day. Captain McLEAN. J.J. - (AAMC) Under order of ADMS 51 Div proceeded to take over duties as M.O. of 1/6 SEAFORTH HDRS, in relief of Lt HOGUE J.D (MORC USA) for duty with 2/1 S. Midland Fd Amb. Instructions intimated that Capt McLEAN was to be struck off strength of Unit & Lt HOGUE taken on the strength from 17-4-18	4 pm
do	19.4.18		A reinforcement of 2 Sgts & 2 Cpls arrived from Base for duty with this Unit.	4 pm
do	21.4.18		Captain HUDSON. A.R (AAMC) detailed to report to 1/6 ROYAL HIGHRS for duty as MO	4 pm
do	23.4.18		Lt HOGUE J.D. MORC reported from 2/1 S Midland Fd Amb to-day	4 pm
do	23.4.18		Revd Capt VALLANCE J.M - CF was posted for attachment to 2/1 H.F Amb for duty as Chaplain today. Telephone message from ADMS 51 Div received warning me that Unit would move next day to LAMBRES. Unit to be clear of HAM-EN-ARTOIS by 9-30 AM	4 pm
do	24.4.18		CAPTAIN. AMY. A.C of 1/3 H.F Amb was posted to 2/1 H.F Amb to-day. Authority ADMS 51 Div 90. 4380 & 23.4.18.	4 pm

Army Form C. 2118.

G.F. Whyte- Lt Colonel
O.C 2/1st HIGHLAND FIELD AMBULANCE

WAR DIARY
or
INTELLIGENCE SUMMARY.

SHEET 8
APRIL 1918

(Erase heading not required.)

Instructions regarding War Diaries and Intelligence Summaries are contained in F. S. Regs., Part II. and the Staff Manual respectively. Title pages will be prepared in manuscript.

Place	Date	Hour	Summary of Events and Information	Remarks and references to Appendices
HAM-EN-ARTOIS	24.4.18		Unit left HAM-EN-ARTOIS at 9AM & arrived at LAMBRES about 11AM. Some difficulty was experienced in procuring Billets & these secured were rather shattered.	G.F.W.
LAMBRES	24.4.18		By authority of G.O.C. 51st Highland Division 9C" 36/48 A d/23.4.18 and ADMS 51 B N: 4405 2/24.4.18 MAJOR G.F. WHYTE. RAMC.TF was authorised to wear the Badges of rank of LIEUT-COLONEL, whilst commanding 2/1 HIGH FD AMB	G.F.W.
do	25.4.18		This afternoon orders were received from A.D.M.S. 51 Div to send 2 Officers + 20 - O.R.s to take over the X1 Corps Reft Stn at RELY. Capt AMY & Capt BARROW with B Section sent Sub Division were detailed for this duty and left at 5.30PM. CAPTAIN AMY to be Officer I/C REST STN. Later full electronic equipment in charge of Sgt GRAY & Sgt TAYLOR with Transport + 1 Large Motor Amb were sent on to join Capt AMY.	G.F.W.
do	26.4.18		The a/m Officers of 2/1 H.F.Amb were posted to sections to-day as follows :- A. SECTION. Lt Col G.F. WHYTE. OC Capt C. UREN. T.O QMr+Hon Lt W.A BUTTERY B. SECTION. Capt A.C. AMY. I/C Capt I.M. BARROW. Lieut J.D. HOGUE C. SECTION Capt H.H. JAMIESON. I/C Capt J.V. DUTHIC.	
do	do		1/Lt NORTH C.O MORC. USA was posted to 1/1 ROYAL HSRs to-day and 1/Lt MUIR. J.M RAMC posted to 2/1 Bgh 3d Amb from 1/1 ROYAL HSRr Auth ADMS 51 B 904415 d/25.4.18	G.F.W.

Army Form C. 2118.

WAR DIARY
or
INTELLIGENCE SUMMARY.

SHEET 9
APRIL 1918

G.F. Whyte Lt Colonel
O.C. 2/1st HIGHLAND FIELD AMBULANCE

(Erase heading not required.)

Instructions regarding War Diaries and Intelligence Summaries are contained in F. S. Regs., Part II. and the Staff Manual respectively. Title pages will be prepared in manuscript.

Place	Date	Hour	Summary of Events and Information	Remarks and references to Appendices
LAMBRES	26.4.18		A party consisting of 1 Officer + 50 O.R. Under ADMS 51Div instructions reported to O.C. XI Corps Stores Officer RE at LA LACQUE to work with RE in dismantling an Ammunition Shed which on demolition is to be conveyed to Corps Rest Stn.	G.F.W.
-do-	28.4.18		Early this morning the remainder of B Section personnel was despatched to join Capt AMY under the charge of Lt. J.D. Hogue. The demolition of the Hut at LA LACQUE was completed today notification of same to ADMS 51 Div.	G.F.W.
-do-	30.4.18		A Kit inspection of the Unit was held today & deficiencies noted	G.F.W.

G.F. Whyte
Lt Colonel
Commanding 2/1st Highland Field Amb.

140/2983.

51st Div.

2/1st Highland F.A.

COMMITTEE FOR THE
MEDICAL HISTORY OF THE WAR
Date 9 JUL 1918

Army Form C. 2118.

WAR DIARY
or
INTELLIGENCE SUMMARY.
(Erase heading not required.)

Sheet 1
MAY. 1918

G. Risley. Lt Colonel RAMC TF
2/1st HIGHLAND FIELD AMBULANCE

Place	Date	Hour	Summary of Events and Information	Remarks and references to Appendices
LAMBRES (near AIRE)	1.V.18		Warning order received from ADMS 51 Div for move of Division to XVIII Corps. 1 Officer + 25 OR's proceeded to LIGNE this morning to report to O.C. Detach 15 Field Amb for constructional work at New Corps Rest Stn. Personnel of Unit was bathed to-day at RELY Rest Stn Baths and received a complete change of clean underclothing	G.R.W
	2.V.18		One WO, CO + 19 OR's with 5 horses were despatched to LA LACQUE for loading the dismantled Hut. Captain H.H. JAMIESON. A.A.M.C. was posted to 1/6 GORDONS for permanent duty and is struck off strength of Unit Captain D. McKELVEY. M.C. RAMC was posted to 2/1 26 High Fd Amb from 1/6 GORDONS to-day. Captain A.R. HUDSON. A.A.M.C. posted to 1/6 BLACK WATCH for permanent duty on 21.4.18 is struck off strength of Unit today O.O. 96/18 received late tonight for move of Transport to ECOIVRES, NEUVILLE ST.VAAST Area	G.R.W G.R.W
	3.V.18			
	4.V.18		Transport moved off at 7.30 AM under 154 Inf Bde Orders - Route via LIERES - AMES - FERFAY - CAMBLAIN CHATELAIN & DIVION. Transport at RELY REST STATION joined them on the road. CAPTAIN AMY with party from XI Corps Rest Stn RELY joined HQ 2/1 H.F Amb tonight, having been relieved by 2/2 South Midland Fd Amb. Lieut MUIR's party also rejoined Unit from LIGNE tonight	G.R.W

Army Form C. 2118.

WAR DIARY
or
INTELLIGENCE SUMMARY.

SHEET II
MAY 1918

(Erase heading not required.)

J.F.W.Pleyle Lt Colonel R.A.M.C. T
2/1st HIGHLAND FIELD AMBULANCE

Place	Date	Hour	Summary of Events and Information	Remarks and references to Appendices
LAMBRES (near AIRE)	5.V.18		Unit proceeded to carry out move to XVIII Corps Area, starting off from LAMBRES at 2 P.M. LILLERS being reached three hours later. March accomplished under very disagreeable conditions, rain falling very heavily. While entraining at the Station, several shells fell in town and around station. Train left about 7 P.M. without incident and arrived at MAROEUIL at 10.30 P.M. Marched to MONT ST ELOI where Unit was accomodated in Nuts Sea was served out to the men at once. Having been prepared by Advanced Party.	J.F.W.
MONT ST ELOI	6.V.18		Unit engaged in receiving Sick of 154 Inf Bde and dispatching same to 1/3 86 yg 3d Amb. Sanitation of Camp was also improved. 154 Bde OO 95.20 received intimating move of Bde to receive lines.	J.F.W.
	7.V.18		Received wire from ADMS 51 Div to move to ECOIVRES, as Unit was in wrong area. Proceeded to new billets & expected same & arranged for the cleaning up, before Unit moved in. Unit left MONT ST ELOI at 4 P.M. and occupied new quarters at ECOIVRES at 4.30 P.M. Captain I.M. BARROW appointed Sanitary Officer of Unit.	J.F.W.
ECOIVRES	8.V.18		Opened Hospital for Sick of Bde. Unit engaged in Sanitary Work at New Billets & various improvements were carried out. Captain J.V. DUHIG & Lt MUIR with 2 NCO & 32 OR detailed for duty as Bearer Party with 1/3 Hyd 3d Amb. to-day	J.F.W.

Army Form C. 2118.

WAR DIARY
or
INTELLIGENCE SUMMARY.
(Erase heading not required.)

G McVeigh Lt Colonel RAMC T

2/1st HIGHLAND FIELD AMBULANCE

SHEET III   MAY 1918

Place	Date	Hour	Summary of Events and Information	Remarks and references to Appendices
ECOIVRES (near MONT ST ELOI)	9.V.18		51 Div Medical Arrangements received 2/1 H.F.Amb being made responsible for collection and disposal of sick of Reating Bde also for Eye, Ear, Nose & Throat cases and for Treatment and detention, and for observation of cases slightly gassed & doubtful cases of gas poisoning. Opened Hospital for Gased cases at the School ECOIVRES with accomodation for 50 Patients. C Section Tent Sub Div Being detailed to run this Hospital. Additional 21- OR Bearer Party sent to 1/3 H.F. Amb today	G McV
-do-	10.V.18		B. Section Tent Sub Div under Lt Hogue were detailed for duty with 95/7 CCS at LICNY - ST FOCHEL, under instructions of ADMS 51.Div.	G McV
-do-	16.V.18		Unit engaged in Sanitary Duties about the Billets. Built Barbers & Drying sheds Hut & Meat Safe. Billets Whitewashed outside & inside. Collecting of sick from Reating Bde & Units in Billeting Area carried on. Gas Hospital receiving & treating Patients.	G McV
-do-	20.V.18		Party of 25. OR detailed for duty with 1/3 as working party in front area. Confirmation received of the appointment of MAJOR G F WHYTE. RAMC.T to be acting Lt Colonel from 15.4.18 and Captain A C AMY to be acting Major from 24.5.18	G McV
-do-	21.V.18		Large Booking Range in Bookhouse completed	G McV
-do-	23.V.18		Captain BARROW AAMC relieved Lt MUIR. RAMC.TC in forward area this morning Lt Muir returned to HQ tonight.	G McV

SHEET 4

WAR DIARY
or
INTELLIGENCE SUMMARY.
(Erase heading not required.)

Army Form C. 2118.

C Kelly Lt Colonel
2/1st HIGHLAND FIELD AMBULANCE

MAY 1918

Place	Date	Hour	Summary of Events and Information	Remarks and references to Appendices
ECOIVRES (near MONT S:ELOI)	24.V.18		12 - O.R. to report to O.C 1/3 H.F.Amb. for duty as a working party on new Advanced Dressing Station ECURIE	G.Pu
-do-	-do-		MAJOR A.C. AMY RAMC Granted Special Leave to U.K from 25.5.18 to 8.6.18	G.Pu
-do-	25.V.18		Lt MUIR RAMC relieved Lt HOGUE MORC at N°.7 CCS today the latter rejoining HQ today	G.Pu
-do-	26.V.18		A competition among Transport of the three Ambulances of the Division was held today. 1/800ac Ambulance, 1 G.S Wagon & 1 Water Cart competed from each Field Ambulance. The Turn-Out was excellent and the marks very close. The result was 1st -do- 2nd 1/3 x 3rd 2/1.	G.Pu
-do-			Captain UREN AAMC and 1 NCO proceeded today to attend a Course of Instruction at 2nd Army School at N°.1 CCS ELNES from 28 May to 18 June 1918	G.Pu
-do-	19.V.18		N°. 301288 Sgt P.B. ELMSLIE. MM RAMC was awarded the D.C.M for gallantry displayed in the field between 21-26-3-18. Authority 2nd Army N° HR/1360/425 of 11.6.13 V.18.	G.Pu
-do-	27 V.18		Captain J. M°W. VALLANCE C.F. proceeded to England on completion of duty on 27.V.18 in accordance with 51.Div wire N° A.B. 831 d/20.V.18	G.Pu
-do-			Captain D. M°KELVEY. M.C. Appointed A/Major whilst commanding C SECTION from 2.V.18. Authority List N° 188 Appointment Commissions approved by FM. C.I.C d/19.V.18	G.Pu
-do-	28.V.18		Captain D M°KELVEY. M.C. Awarded Bar to M.C for gallantry displayed in the field between 9.15.4.18 Authority X1 Corps R.O N° 267 d/24.V.18	G.Pu

Army Form C. 2118.

WAR DIARY
or
INTELLIGENCE SUMMARY.

SHEET V
MAY 1918

G.F.Wyly- Lt Colonel
OC 2/1st HIGHLAND FIELD AMBULANCE

Place	Date	Hour	Summary of Events and Information	Remarks and references to Appendices
ECOIVRES (MONT-ST ELOI)	28.v.18		Captain J.V. Duhic A.A.M.C. was relieved by Lt J.D Hogue M.O.R.C. USA today and rejoined HQ this evening	G.F.W
-do-	29.v.18		S/Sgt McGillivray W.H.J was detailed to attend a course at XVII Corps Gas School and left today	G.F.W
			All available Bearers of this Unit today for constructional work at new Advanced Dressing Station.	G.F.W
-do-	30.v.18		Personnel of Unit were bathed today & received a clean change of underclothing. Hospitals, billets and Lines inspected today by D.D.M.S. XVII Corps.	G.F.W
-do-	31.v.18		Captain UREN. A.A.M.C. & 2.O.R. returned from 1st Army School of Instruction today. The School having disbanded on account of changing its location.	G.F.W

G.F.Wyly- Lt Colonel
OC 2/1st HIGHLAND FIELD AMBULANCE
Dated 31.V.18

160/3016

COMMITTEE FOR THE
MEDICAL HISTORY OF THE WAR
Date 7 AUG 1918

Army Form C. 2118.

G. Paleyh Lt Colonel RAMC
2/1st HIGHLAND FIELD AMBULANCE T.F.

WAR DIARY
or
INTELLIGENCE SUMMARY.
(Erase heading not required.)

Sheet I JUNE 1918

Place	Date	Hour	Summary of Events and Information	Remarks and references to Appendices
ECOIVRES (MONT ST ELOI)	4.6.18		Various improvements put in hand at Gas Hospital. Erection of Bathing Range. Ablution Bench, Racks for Pack Store and Latrine. Construction of Beds for 40 Patients proceeded with	G.P.W
	5.6.18		Captain J.V. Duhig A.A.M.C detailed for temporary duty with 1/8 Royal Scots today. Lieut J.M. Muir R.A.M.C rejoined H.Q from 57 C.C.S today. No 303 254 Pte A. Smith awarded Military Medal for gallantry displayed on 22 May 1918. Intimation received that No 301345 S/Sgt W. McGillivray R.ad successfully passed the Anti-Gas course held at XVII Corps Gas School	G.P.W
	6.6.18		Captain C. Uren A.A.M.C relieved Captain Barrow in front area today	G.P.W
	7.6.18		Captain I.M. Barrow detailed for temporary duty with 57 C.C.S	G.P.W
	9.6.18		Major A.C. Amy rejoined Unit from leave to United Kingdom today. Erection of Beds for Sick Hospital proceeded with and for patients	G.P.W
	10.6.18		The Village and surrounding country has been heavily shelled during the last fortnight with high velocity shells. Only one casualty has occurred in the Unit, one Private being struck by ricochet of the base of a shrapnel shell. There has been no shelling today	G.P.W

Army Form C. 2118.

G. Tulloch Lt Colonel RAMC TF
2/1st HIGHLAND FIELD AMBULANCE

WAR DIARY
or
INTELLIGENCE SUMMARY.
(Erase heading not required.)

Sheet II
JUNE 1918

Place	Date	Hour	Summary of Events and Information	Remarks and references to Appendices
ECOIVRES (MONT ST ELOI)	9.6.18		Lt J.M MUIR R.A.M.C. detailed for temporary duty with 1/7 Gordon Highrs today	G.T.W
-do-	11.6.18		Unit was bathed today and received change of underclothing	G.T.W
-do-	12.6.18		QM v Lt BUTTERY R.A.M.C. appointed Inemaster of Unit	G.T.W
	14.6.18		Intimation received that 96.301.337 7/Sgt G SNAPP Rao successfully passed Anti Gas Course held at XVII Corps Gas School.	G.T.W
	15.6.18		Lt J D HOGUE M.O.R.C rejoined Unit from duty with 1/3 H.F. Amb	G.T.W
	16.6.18		Unit engaged in erecting protective embankments in Horse Stables. Plot of ground taken over from Town Mayor + prepared for planting Vegetables	G.T.W
	17.6.18		Four Other Ranks Divisional Artillery reported tonight for a weeks course in cooking instructions under my Sergeant Cook. Fire Orders drawn up by Inemaster of Unit and after approval by O.C. became Standing Fire Orders of this Unit.	G.T.W
	18.6.18		Lt J.M MUIR. R.A.M.C. handed over by 1/7 Gordon Highlanders today under "close arrest" awaiting F.G.C.M on charge of DRUNKENNESS	G.T.W
	19.6.18		Lt J.D HOGUE M.O.R.C detailed for temporary duty with 1/4 Gordon Highrs	G.T.W

Army Form C. 2118.

WAR DIARY
or
INTELLIGENCE SUMMARY.
(Erase heading not required.)

2/1st HIGHLAND FIELD AMBULANCE

G M Ryle
Lt Colonel

Place	Date	Hour	Summary of Events and Information	Remarks and references to Appendices
ECOIVRES (MONT ST ELOI)	19.6.18		Rules for administration of Unit Canteen drawn up and Committee appointed to carry out same.	G.McW
	20.6.18		No 301241 S/Sgt. (A/Q.M.S.) L.G. TOUGH of 1/1 Highfield Amb awarded Meritorious Service Medal (London Gaz. 17.5.18)	G.McW
	21.6.18		An epidemic of P.U.O (Influenzal type) has arisen, causing large numbers of sick in Division and other Units. Hospital Staff kept very busy admitting cases. 13 men of this Unit are at present in Hospital through this cause.	G.McW
	24.6.18		P.U.O (Influenzal type) still very prevalent, 40 men of this Unit having been admitted, while the admissions from surrounding Units are still very high. Hospital full and new Hut obtained from Town Major opposite H.Q. This Hut is being used for the accommodation of Convalescent P.U.O Patients. Extension of accommodation to the extent of 17 Beds also obtained at school.	G.McW
	25.6.18		Inter area area (Group) Hospital and Isolation with our potatoes. Over 60 men of unit in Hospital with Influenzal P.U.O.	G.McW
	26.6.18		Fatigues went on Bricks and transfer tins used temporarily by cars reminders of personnel being sick in hospital.	G.McW
			Allowable Lining - 3 Nursing tent, 9.6 Bivouac Pitches or vacant from our other sect of Camp. North H.Q. to be used as a Convalescent Camp for P.U.O.	G.McW
	27.6.18		Capt Duff acting returned from 1/8 Royal Scots	G.McW
	29.6.18		Capt Duff acting Capt Barrow at 6-9 C.C.S.	G.McW
	30.6.18		Capt Barrow relieved Capt Ure at Advanced Collecting Post.	G.McW

140/3131.

2/I.- Highland 1 F.A.

July 1918

Army Form C. 2118.

WAR DIARY
or
INTELLIGENCE SUMMARY.
(Erase heading not required.)

G Sheet I
1918 JULY

G.W.Leigh — Lt Colonel
O.C. 2/1st HIGHLAND FIELD AMBULANCE

Vol 35

Place	Date	Hour	Summary of Events and Information	Remarks and references to Appendices
ECOIVRES (MONT ST.ELOI)	3.7.18		Captain DUHIG. J.V. relieved Captain BARROW at 57 CCS on 29.6.18	G.W.
			A Kit inspection of the Unit was held today and all deficiencies were made good.	G.W.
	4.7.18		Drifting Return by the Three Field Ambulances of Div for the period 15-30 JUNE/18 was 2/1 H.F. Amb 27 PB; 1/2 H.F.Amb 26 PB; 1/3 H.F. Amb 18 PB.	G.W.
	6.7.18		Captain UREN. C - A.A.M.C. detailed for temporary duty at 51 H.M. Gun Corps today	G.W.
	8.7.18		LIEUT HOGUE J.D - M.O.R.C. posted for permanent duty with 1/4 GORDON H.DRS from 30/6/18 and struck off strength same date	G.W.
	10.7.18		Capt. BARROW. J.M. A.A.M.C. and all Bearers att 1/3 H.F.Amb have now returned to H.Q. the last batch arriving today	G.W.
	11.7.18		Unit was bathed today and received a clean change of underclothing	G.W.
	12.7.18		Received A.D.M.S. 51 Div. instructions to move under orders of 152 INF BDE on 13.7.18 to PERNES AREA, also received 152 INF BDE to move by march route on 13 inst to HOUVELIN	G.W.
	13.7.18		Captn BARROW. J.M. A.A.M.C. Detailed for permanent duty as M.D.I/c 1/6 BLACK WATCH from todays date & struck off strength.	G.W.

Army Form C. 2118.

WAR DIARY
or
INTELLIGENCE SUMMARY.
(Erase heading not required.)

Army Form C. 2118.

SHEET II
JULY - 1918

G.P.Walsh - Lt Colonel RAMC
O.C. 2/1st HIGHLAND FIELD AMBULANCE

Place	Date	Hour	Summary of Events and Information	Remarks and references to Appendices
ECOIVRES (Mont St Eloi)	13/7/18	6.30am	Unit moved from ECOIVRES at 6.30AM after 9 weeks stay, in Rainy rain, & after a quick march reached HOUVELIN about 11.30AM. Major A.C. AMY proceeded in advance to procure Billets. Billets in Village very scattered and village itself found to be in very insanitary condition. Capt DUHIG J.V. - AAMC + 18 - OR rejoined HQ from 57.C.C.S. AUBIGNY.	G.P.W.
HOUVELIN	14/7/8		Opened up Hospital to receive sick of 152 Inf Bde. Proceeded to clean up village and generally improve sanitation. Received Warning Order from 154 Inf Bde for move by train to new area. Later instructions were received from 51 Div for the entraining of the Unit at PERNES on 15/8 at 9AM. (A1 %. 55) All surplus baggage to be stored at AUBIGNY. Journey expected to take 40 hours. Capt DUHIG detailed as detraining Medical Officer for 152 Inf Bde at PERNES, while Major MCKELVEY proceeded with 2nd Car on first train to act as detraining Officer at destination station.	G.P.W.
-do-	15/7/18		Transport left this morning at 3AM under charge of Lieut BUTTERY for Entraining Stn PERNES. The remainder of Unit left at 4AM. Train left PERNES at 10.15AM. Tea being served prior to departure. The route following was via St POL; ETAPLES; ABBEVILLE; and the outskirts of PARIS was reached the following morning about 6.30AM	G.P.W.
HERME (SEINE & MARNE)	16/7/18		Unit detrained at HERME about 2.30PM and were joined by Capt ROY - RAMC - and Lieut PHILLIPS. RAMC of the 1/2 High Fd Amb	G.P.W.

WAR DIARY or INTELLIGENCE SUMMARY

Army Form C. 2118.

SHEET III

2/1st HIGHLAND FIELD AMBULANCE

JULY - 1918

E.W.Wyly - Lt Colonel R.A.M.C.

Place	Date	Hour	Summary of Events and Information	Remarks and references to Appendices
HERME (SEINE & MARNE)	16/7/18	3-30 PM	After tea had been prepared Transport left by road under Major Amy's charge. Motor Buses had been arranged for by French Authorities, but as these had not arrived by 9 AM the Unit was marched to a corner of a wood and laid down to obtain some sleep	E.W.W
-do-	17/7/18	12-30 AM	Word was received that Buses had arrived, Unit was awaked and marched to Embussing Point, it was found that there had been some misunderstanding and that the Buses which had arrived were not for this Unit. Men lay down beside the road until morning.	E.W.W
-do-	"	9 AM	Breakfast was served by the roadside + Buses arrived at midday. Unit moved off about 2-45 P.M. After a long journey the Unit debussed on a hillside above LE-MESNIL after dark. The latter part of the journey being performed in a severe Thunderstorm. No Billets being available Unit had to seek what shelter they could among the trees on the hillside.	
LE-MESNIL SUR-OGER	18/7/18	1-30 AM	The Thunderstorm of last night continued until 1-30 AM, rain falling very heavily all the time, and the men and their equipment being thoroughly soaked. Sleep was next to impossible and most of the men spent the early hours of the morning walking about in an effort to get their clothes dry. Fortunately the weather improved and during the day it was found possible to get everything thoroughly dried. Men proceeded to erect BIVOUACS and in the afternoon the men bathed in an open pond	E.W.W

WAR DIARY or INTELLIGENCE SUMMARY

Army Form C. 2118.

SHEET IV JULY 1918

G.W.Wylie Lt Colonel RAMC O.C 2/1st HIGHLAND FIELD AMBULANCE

Place	Date	Hour	Summary of Events and Information	Remarks and references to Appendices
LE MESNIL-SUR-OGER	18 7/8		51 Div Med¹ Arrangements were received intimating that Field Amb on arrival at their locations would open out to accomodate casualties in wounded. Billets were alloted to Unit at night in town of LE MESNIL by 152 Staff Rde.	G.W.
-do-	19 7/8	1 AM	Transport arrived this morning at 1 AM and camped on top of hill	G.W.
		5 AM	Were received in the early morning from 152 INF Bde intimating move of Units to new area. Unit left LE MESNIL at 9 AM by road via EPERNAY and arrived at CHAMPILLON at 5 PM	
CHAMPILLON	-do-	5 PM	Prepared to open up Adv Dressing Stn cut later RAMC Operation Order No 70 was received under para 4 of which, the Unit was ordered to move on to ST IMOGES to form an Adv Dressing Stn there. Under para 5 instructions were also given to open up a W.C. Post at LA BRIQUETERIE. 3. Bearer Squads, altogether will one Tent Sub Div at LA BRIQUETERIE = 72 Bearers 24 men were sent to each INF BDE. 152, 153 & 154 BDEs. 9 was detached to form & command a Temporary CCS at AVISAN-MOËT. EPERNAY for severely wounded of XXII Corps. Staffed by 3 Medical Officers of the Division and 2 Tent Sub Div of the 1/3 H.F. Amb¹	G.W.
-do-	-do-	MID. 12 NIGHT	Unit moved at midnight. C Sec. Tent Sub Div under Major McKELVEY proceeding to BELLEVUE to open up W.W.C Post and the rest of the Unit under Major AMY to ST IMOGES which was reached 1½ Hours later	

SHEET N
JULY 1918

Army Form C. 2118.

WAR DIARY or INTELLIGENCE SUMMARY.
(Erase heading not required.)

G.F.Wyly Lt Col
2/1st HIGHLAND FIELD AMBULANCE
O.C

Place	Date	Hour	Summary of Events and Information	Remarks and references to Appendices
ST IMOGES (RHEIMS)	20.7.18	2AM	Arrived at 2 AM and immediately preparations were made for Advanced Dressing Station for the whole Division with the cooperation of the French ADMS. All arrangements completed by noon on the 21st. Major McKelvey replaced by a Junior Medical Officer at BELLEVUE. The former took over the forward Area Disposition in the morning. Heavy fighting took place during the day and about 500 wounded passed through our hands. Great difficulty was necessarily experienced in the matter of transport, and as regards stretchers, blankets, the only supplies at first available being war establishment. Every assistance, especially as regards transport was given to us by the French Authorities – A.D.M.S. 120 French Div Transport Groupe de Houbent. Three men of this Unit were wounded today – one severely.	G.F.W.
-do-	21.7.18		Difficulties in great measure overcome. Casualties this day considerably less. Other two men of this Unit wounded in forward area, also Capt BARRON. I.M.-A.A.M.C. (M.O. 1/6 BLACK WATCH) late of this Unit was wounded today and passed through my A.D. Stn.	G.F.W.
-do-	22.7.18		Quiet day – 2 more men of 2/1 H.F.Amb were wounded today in forward area	G.F.W.
-do-	23.7.18		Operations recommenced. Over 500 casualties passed through. Everything including forward zone A.D.S. + W.W.C. Post worked very satisfactorily although continuous heavy rain storm prevailed.	G.F.W.

Army Form C. 2118.

WAR DIARY
or
INTELLIGENCE SUMMARY.
(Erase heading not required.)

SHEET VI
JULY 1918

2/1st HIGHLAND FIELD AMBULANCE

Place	Date	Hour	Summary of Events and Information	Remarks and references to Appendices
ST IMOGES (RHEIMS)	23/24 7.18	Night	Heavy Bombing and several casualties. 3 more men of this Unit were wounded in Forward Area	GPW
-do-	24/25 7.18	-do-	Quiet day. Nothing of special importance to report. Supplies of Medical Comforts is the main difficulty. Much of the work was harmoniously carried out in conjunction with the Authorities of the 62 Div. which evacuations was carried out was largely due to the excellent arrangements that were made by Major McKELVEY M.C in the Forward Zone. Lt Col. G.F WHYTE returned to H.Q at St IMOGES this afternoon. The Temporary C.C.S taken over at 12 NOON by Advanced Operating Party of 48 C.C.S. 4 Officers & 36 O.R. all dangerously wounded were handed over.	GPW
-do-	25/7/18			
-do-	-do-		Extract from Part II Daily Orders 2/1 HIGHLAND FIELD AMBULANCE. R.A.M.C 25/7/18 No 2840 FIELD GENERAL COURT MARTIAL. The court sentenced the accused Temporary Lieut JOHN MONCRIEFF MUIR - M.M attd 1/7 Batt. GORDON HIGHLANDERS to be dismissed from His Majesty's Service Signed in the field at ECOIVRES, this 19 day of July 1918. KA Buchanan, Brig-Gen C.E MORAN Capt PRESIDENT Judge Advocate Confirmed - D HAIG F.M 17 July 1918 Promulgated - 25 July 1918	GPW

WAR DIARY
or
INTELLIGENCE SUMMARY.
(Erase heading not required.)

Army Form C. 2118.

C Pulryl Lt Colonel
OC 2/1st HIGHLAND FIELD AMBULANCE

SHEET VII
JULY 1918

Place	Date	Hour	Summary of Events and Information	Remarks and references to Appendices
ST IMOGES (RHEIMS)	25/7/18		Visited Forward Posts with Major McKELVEY. Post in NANTEUIL (Cpl Game) and in ST DENIS (Sgt SNAPP). Relay Post established in evening in BOIS DE COURTON clearing to ST DENIS W.W.C. Post. The Advanced Post was formed in wood near NANTEUIL	GPW
-do-	26/7/18		Relay Post in Left sector in BOIS DE COURTON withdrawn as no cases passing through and it was more in the French Area	GPW
-do-	27/7/18		Our attack this morning took place at 6AM. Advance. Clearing through ST DENIS. Night J 27 a Post was formed at MARFAUX consisting of 1 NCO + 4 men	GPW
NANTEUIL LA FOSSE	28/7/18		Unit left ST IMOGES and opened up Ads Dressing Stn + HQ at NANTEUIL at 8AM also W.W.C Post - Advanced NWCP established at foot of Rill on MARFAUX Rd. Collecting Post established in CHAUMUZY of 1 NCO + 4 men + 1 Ambulance Car. 2 Cars stationed in front of MARFAUX. Four Cars + Reserve Bearers at ST DENIS. In the evening numbers at CHAUMUZY in cellars increased by 4 more squads	GPW
d	29/7/18		Evacuation working well. More cellar accommodation received in CHAUMUZY and more Bearers moved up. Long carry to CHAUMUZY of 2 Kilometres. I visited CHAUMUZY. Advanced WWC Post pushed forward to MARFAUX. 1 man was killed in Action + 3 others wounded with a shell today	GPW

Sheet VIII
July 1916

WAR DIARY
or
INTELLIGENCE SUMMARY.
(Erase heading not required.)

Army Form C. 2118.

C. Welsh Lt Colonel
OC 2/1st HIGHLAND FIELD AMBULANCE

Place	Date	Hour	Summary of Events and Information	Remarks and references to Appendices
NANTEUIL LA FOSSE	30/7/18		Gassing in CHAUMUZY. Eye cases & some Bearer Gassed at 1/4 GORDON Adv Post. Many Gassed cases coming down. Capt DUHIG (M.O. 1/6 GORDONS) badly gassed this evening. Thro unit came through A.D.S. slightly gassed. About 60 gassed cases last night passed through A.D.S. Division to be relieved tonight	6 PM
-do-	31/7/18		Lt J.D. HOGUE MORC USA having been posted to 2/1 High Fd Amb from 1/4 GORDONS on 26/7/18 is taken on strength from that date Capt J.V. DUHIG AAMC having been detailed for duty with 1/4 GORDON on 26/7/18 is struck off strength from that date 2 more Battle Casualties of men of this Unit today	6 PM

SHEET 5
JULY 1918

G.F.W. Leigh LtCol
2/1st HIGHLAND FIELD AMBULANCE

Army Form C. 2118.

WAR DIARY
INTELLIGENCE SUMMARY

Place	Date	Hour	Summary of Events and Information	Remarks and references to Appendices
AUSAN-MOËT EPERNAY	20.7.18 to 25.7.18		Short account of work done in Temporary CCS for 22nd Corps, established in Military Pavillon Militaire Hôpital AUSAN-MOËT EPERNAY from 20th to 25 July. Staff:- Lt Col. G.F. WHYTE 2/1 H.F.Amb; Capt H GORRIE 1/3; Capt THOMSON AAMC 1/2; Capt DUHIG. AAMC. 2/1; Two Sent Sub Div 1/3 H.F.Amb with equipment. Rationed 1/3 H.F.A. Italians evacuated Hospital at 8AM on 20th inst. Available accommodation in Hospital, Ward on ground floor of 18 beds, same number in Ward immediately above. Officers Ward of 5 Beds on ground floor. Three Operating Rooms, Large Pavillon off side of which 9 had use of the ground floor able to accommodate 100 lying cases. Only severe cases were brought into Hospital for dressing and operation. Many less severe were kept over in large pavillon awaiting evacuation. All were fed. Operations performed.— All cases requiring amputation. All tourniquet cases. wounds excised + vessels ligated. Many bad wounds excised F.G. removed + drainage established. Several head cases treated by removal of broken + depressed fragments. Abdomens + Chests could only be treated conservatively. All patients undressed put in pyjamas in bed in comfortable position. M.O.i/R. to Abdomens + Chests. A considerable number of Abdominal cases were doing well after 4 days in Hospital notably 4 cases of penetrating wounds over the Liver. One case of penetrating wound of the Bladder two cases of wounds penetrating	

WAR DIARY or INTELLIGENCE SUMMARY

Army Form C. 2118.

SHEET X
JULY 1918

G. Pullyn LtCol.
2/1st HIGHLAND FIELD AMBULANCE

Place	Date	Hour	Summary of Events and Information	Remarks and references to Appendices
AVISAN-MOËT EPERNAY	20/25.7.18		descending colon extra-peritoneally with faecal fistula. Also a penetrating wound of the stomach and one case from side to side of the abdomen. None of these showed signs of General Peritonitis. Several sucking wounds of the chest were stitched up or plugged with gauze causing great relief to the distressing symptoms. Many of abdominal cases & poorer others were moribund on admission. A moribund ward was established upstairs. Altogether about 50 deaths occurred during period 20-25". About 700 cases passed through the A+D Books and about 1000 others who had already been through the Books of 1/2 H.F. Amb & 2/1 West Riding F. Amb. M.D. Stn. Evacuation was carried on by M.A.C. assisted by the French "Station Section Sanitaire" The Staffs worked continuously with only an hour or two off after the first 24 hours and the operating work never ceased till relieved at 12 noon on 25" by Advanced Operating Party with two surgical teams of 48 CCS. Considering the equipment was only that of a Field Ambulance the small staff & the large & continuous rush of severely wounded, I think the work done & results achieved were remarkably good. G.P.W.	

SHEET XI
JULY 1, 1918.

G.P.Ely/G LTCOLONEL
O/1st HIGHLAND FIELD AMBULANCE

WAR DIARY
or
INTELLIGENCE SUMMARY. OC

Army Form C. 2118.

Summary of Medical Arrangements in Forward Area during active operations from 20th to 31st July 1918.

From 20 to 25th Major Amy was in charge of Forward Evacuation. From 25 to 31st P. Col G.F.L.Ryfe. During the whole period Major McKelvey had charge of forward collecting posts and relay posts and acted as Liaison Officer with the Brigades. The disposition of the bearers was left entirely in his hands.

DISPOSITION ON 20th:—
(10 A.M.)

153 BDE R.A.P. (BOIS DE COURTON)

Collecting Post Courton Ruine (1 NCO + 4 men later increased) (CARS)

154 BDE R.A.P. (BOIS DE COURTON)

Collecting Post Hill outside NANTEUIL (CARS)

A.D.S. ST IMOGES

M.D.S. CHAMPILLON

4 P.M.

Army Form C. 2118.

WAR DIARY
or
INTELLIGENCE SUMMARY.
(Erase heading not required.)

SHEET XII
JULY 1918

A Pulyh Lt Col
2/1st HIGHLAND FIELD AMBULANCE

Place	Date	Hour	Summary of Events and Information	Remarks and references to Appendices
			DISPOSITION ON 20th (5 PM)	E.2u

153 BDE RAP.
(BOIS DE COURTON)
Collecting Post
COURTON RUINS
1 NCO + 12 men
(CARS)

154 BDE RAP.
(BOIS DE COURTON)

ST DENIS
Coll Post
(CARS)

NANTEUIL Coll Post

ST IMOGES
A.D.S

M.D.S CHAMPILLON

A.D. Stn. ST IMOGES Reception Room formed by a large tarpaulin shelter at back of house. Cases carried from there through back room where particulars were taken and tallies affixed to Dressing Room with two

WAR DIARY or INTELLIGENCE SUMMARY.

Army Form C. 2118.

SHEET XIII JULY, 1918.

G.W.Pugh Lt Colonel
OC 2/1st HIGHLAND FIELD AMBULANCE

Place	Date	Hour	Summary of Events and Information	Remarks and references to Appendices
			tables. From there to Evacuation department consisting of a large room in another house and a large open barn at the back	G.W.
			DISPOSITION ON 25":–	
			New Relay Post 1 NCO + 12 men established in BOIS DE COURTON in site of 4th GORDON HIGHdn + 4th SEAFORTH HDRS R.A.P's. Evacuation of 152 Bde + 7th GORDON HDRS through this post to ST DENIS	G.W.
			DISPOSITION ON 26":–	
			Courton Ruine Post withdrawn as Brigade had been relieved by French on previous night	G.W.
			DISPOSITION ON 27":–	
			Three new Relay Posts formed	
			(1). 1 NCO + 8 men at site of 7 Gordon's RAP in BOIS DE COURTON.	
			(2) 1 NCO + 12 men at site of 152 Bde RAP to right of BOIS DE COURTON	
			(3) 1 NCO + 4 men in MARFAUX (with cars)	
			(1) + (2) evacuated through the Relay Post in BOIS DE COURTON formed on 25"	G.W.

Instructions regarding War Diaries and Intelligence Summaries are contained in F. S. Regs., Part II. and the Staff Manual respectively. Title pages will be prepared in manuscript.

SHEET XIV
JULY, 1918

WAR DIARY
or
INTELLIGENCE SUMMARY.
(Erase heading not required.)

Army Form C. 2118.

G F Wright LT COLONEL
O.C 2/1st HIGHLAND FIELD AMBULANCE

Place	Date	Hour	Summary of Events and Information	Remarks and references to Appendices
			DISPOSITION ON 28th. A.D Stn evacuated (St IMOGES) which was taken over by 1/2 High Fd Amb as M.D Stn. A.D.S established in NANTEUIL in an old Estaminet	G F W

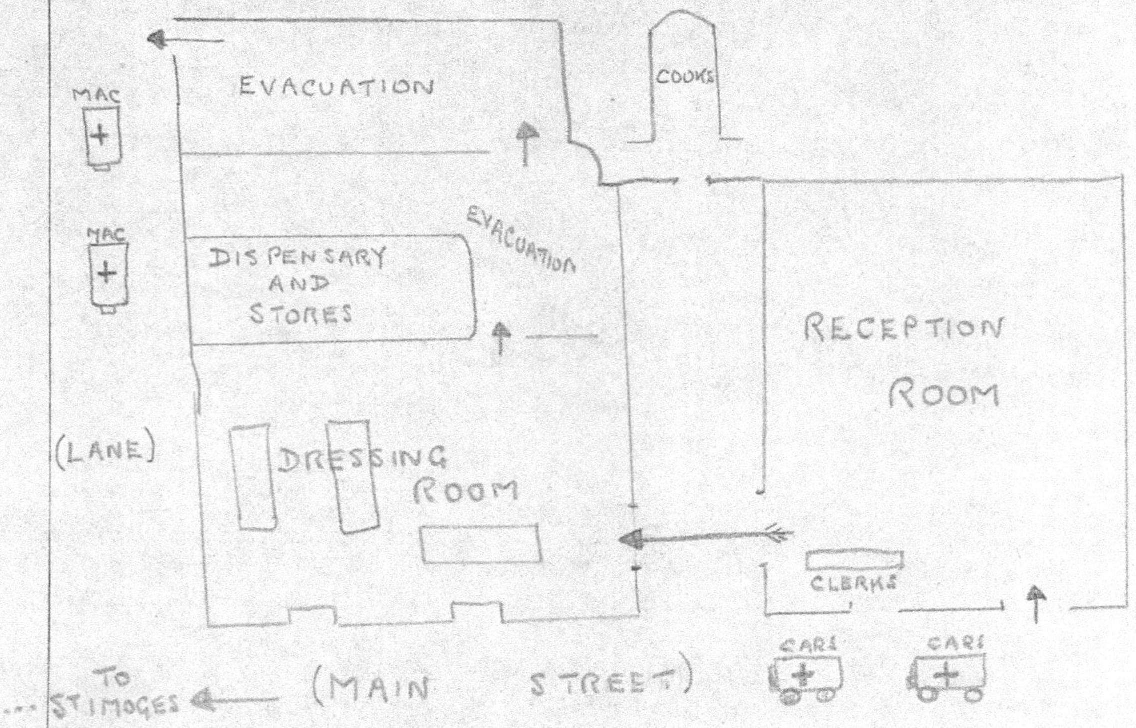

EVACUATION
COOKS
MAC
MAC
DISPENSARY AND STORES
EVACUATION
RECEPTION ROOM
(LANE)
DRESSING ROOM
CLERKS
CARS
CARS
TO St IMOGES
(MAIN STREET)

D. D. & L., London, E.C.
(A8004) Wt. W1771/M2031 750,000 5/17 Sch. 52 Forms/C2118/14

Army Form C. 2118.

WAR DIARY
or
INTELLIGENCE SUMMARY.
(Erase heading not required.)

SHEET XV
JULY, 1918

OC 2/1st HIGHLAND FIELD AMBULANCE   Lt Colonel

Place	Date	Hour	Summary of Events and Information	Remarks and references to Appendices
			Early in day a Collecting Post of 1 NCO & 4 men with Car was formed in CHAUMUZY. This was gradually increased to 7 Squads. Accomodation in 2 large Cellars. All other Relay Posts withdrawn. Evacuation by cars from CHAUMUZY. Relay car posts being formed 2 Cars at MARFAUX, 4 at ST DENIS remainder at NANTEUIL. As cars came down from CHAUMUZY another moved up & so on all along the line. Evacuation from CHAUMUZY always difficult on account of heavy shelling with H.E. & especially with Gas. Scheme of Evacuation from CHAUMUZY :— ○ Collecting Post CHAUMUZY (1 Car) ○ MARFAUX (2 Cars) ○ ST DENIS (4 Cars) + Reserve Bearer Post ○ A.D.S. - NANTEUIL (Rest of Cars) ○ M.D.S - ST MOCES	

Army Form C. 2118.

G. Pullyh Lt Colonel
2/1st HIGHLAND FIELD AMBULANCE
OC

WAR DIARY or INTELLIGENCE SUMMARY.

(Erase heading not required.)

SHEET XVI
JULY, 1918.

Place	Date	Hour	Summary of Events and Information	Remarks and references to Appendices
	29th		Stretcher Trolley being used along CHAUMUZY – SARCY ROAD from R.A.Pt about 1 mile in front of CHAUMUZY. Roads impassible for Cars in front of CHAUMUZY on account of debris.	G.P.W
	31st		All Bearers + Cars relieved by 11-30PM on Division coming out.	G.P.W
	Aug 1st		Personnel of Field Amb left ADS for CHAMPILLON.	G.P.W

140/3200.

2/Lt Nish. L.O.

Aug 1918

Army Form C. 2118.

WAR DIARY
or
INTELLIGENCE SUMMARY.
(Erase heading not required.)

SHEET 1.
AUG 1918

L. Hulph Lt Colonel
OC 2/1st HIGHLAND FIELD AMBULANCE

WH 36

Place	Date	Hour	Summary of Events and Information	Remarks and references to Appendices
NANTEUIL-LA-FOSSE (MARNE)	1.8.18		51.Div A.I 96.50 received w/R entraining table for new Area Unit left NANTEUIL LA FOSSE under 154 INF Bde orders to CHAMPILLON and took over Billets occupied by 1/3 H.F.Amb Enemy aircraft bombed the village & close vicinity of the Camp but fortunately no casualties occurred. Received instructions from ADMS 51.Div that we would move under 153 Bde orders instead of 154 Bde. 153 INF Bde OO 96.318 received, giving new Time Table of trains to new area, showing 2/1 H.F.Amb entraining w/R 153 Bde at AVIZE.	G.Th
CHAMPILLON (MARNE) near EPERNAY	2.8.18		Major McKelvey left at 11AM for Entraing Stn as Train Medical Officer at OIRY. QMS Tough + 3 OR's left at 3AM as Billeting N.C.O for new area. Unit left CHAMPILLON at 8AM & arrived at MOSLINS at 3.15PM and took over Billets adjoining 153 INF Bde HQ in Huts. Received ADMS instructions that Unit would move by train from VERTUS under 153 INF Bde Orders	G.Th
MOSLINS (MARNE)	3.8.18		Left MOSLINS at 3AM by march route to VERTUS - entrained at 10AM going via outskirts of PARIS and arrived at PERNES at 4.30PM. After detraining Unit marched at 5.15PM to AUBIGNY and arrived at 10PM which was a record march for the Unit. Rainy done 24 Kilometres in 4 hours 45 minutes. Billeted in Village. Men + HQ all in own Billet	G.Th

Army Form C. 2118.

WAR DIARY
or
INTELLIGENCE SUMMARY.
(Erase heading not required.)

Sheet II
AUGUST 1918

G. M. Leys. Lt Colonel
OC 2/1st HIGHLAND FIELD AMBULANCE

Place	Date	Hour	Summary of Events and Information	Remarks and references to Appendices
AUBIGNY (PAS DE CALAIS)	4.8.18		Received message from DDMS XXII Corps through ADMS 51 Div of Appreciation of Medical Services - Congratulating on their excellent work done during the recent (Marne) Operations; continuing he says "The work, in spite of numerous difficulties was splendidly performed. Both from the point of view of rapidity of evacuation & the conditions in which the patients reached the CCS." The GOC 51 Div also read his report with great satisfaction.	G.M.
	7.8.18		Lieut J W Robinson & Lieut C Ashby both MORC USA joined 2/1 H.F.Amb today. The former was posted to C Section & the latter to B. Section	G.M.
	8.8.18		Lt J.D.Hogue. MORC. USA having been detailed to proceed to 66 Base Hospital at AEF for duty is struck off strength	G.M.
	10.8.18		Unit started Intensive Field Training:- Physical Drill Lectures & Demonstrations on Sanitation; Squad Drill Water Duties; Personal Hygiene; Gas. Stretcher Drill First Aid in Collecting Posts & ADS Gas Drill with Formation of Adv Dressing Station & Collecting Posts Box Respirator Lessons from Recent Operations Route Marches Wagon Drill Four hours /work/day between 6.45 a.m. and 12.30 p.m. Recreational training in afternoon.	G.M.

Army Form C. 2118.

WAR DIARY
or
INTELLIGENCE SUMMARY
(Erase heading not required.)

Sheet III
AUGUST 1918

G. P. Wyllie Lt Colonel
O.C. 2/1st HIGHLAND FIELD AMBULANCE

Place	Date	Hour	Summary of Events and Information	Remarks and references to Appendices
AUBIGNY (PAS DE CALAIS)	11.8.18		Lt ASHBY & Lt ROBINSON & 20 – OR' RAMC were detailed for duty at No. 15 CCS today in accordance with ADMS instructions. Capt UREN. C. AAMC also detailed to attend 1st Army RAMC School of Instruction & 1 – OR' USMC	G 2W
	"		Lt B MALTBY joined 2/1 H F Amb today from England and so posted to A Sec. Lt Col G F WHYTE granted special leave to U.K. from 14/8/18 to 28/8/18	G 2W
	12.8.18		Major A.C. Army took over charge of Unit from 14/8/18	G 2W
	14.8.18		51 Div O.O. 90074 received intimating the taking over of the line of the 156 Bde 52 Div & 171 & 172 Bde 57 Div – 2/1 H F Amb to relieve 2/2 Wessex F.A. Amb at D.R.S. – AGNEZ-LES-DUISANS on night of 18–19th	G 2W
	15.8.18		After arrangements were completed for taking over D.R.S. a letter was received from 2/2 Wessex F.A. Amb intimating that move of their Unit would not take place till afternoon of 19th inst. Arrangements made for a small advance party to proceed to D.R.S. on afternoon of 18th & for the movement of the Unit on morning of the 19th.	G 2W
	17.8.18			
	19.8.18		Unit moved at 9 A.M. this morning & opened at DUISANS as a D.R.S. on site of CCS Handing over took place at 12 noon & duties were at once detailed for the carrying on of D.R.S.	G 2W

Army Form C. 2118.

G ZWright Lt Colonel
O.C. 2/1st HIGHLAND FIELD AMBULANCE

WAR DIARY or INTELLIGENCE SUMMARY.
SHEET IV
AUGUST 1918
(Erase heading not required.)

Place	Date	Hour	Summary of Events and Information	Remarks and references to Appendices
AGNEZ-LES DUISANS	21.8.18		Ordered to open as a Corps Rest Station	G.W.
	22.8.18		51. D.R.O. of this date contained information that 9 Military Medals had been awarded to men of this Unit for gallantry displayed between 20 & 30 July 1918.	
		3.00 noon	Inspected by D.D.M.S. Canadian Corps & ordered to form a M.D.S. for 51 (H) Div and Gas Centre for the Corps.	
		Afternoon	Opened as a M.D.S. Site inspected by D.M.S. & Consulting Surgeon 1st Army with a view to C.C.S. reoccupying the place.	G.W.
	23.8.18		Lt. Malloy. B. U.S.M.C. detailed for temporary duty with 1/6 Gordon Hdrs	G.W.
			Lt. C. Ashby. U.S.M.C. detailed for temporary duty with 255 Bde R.F.A. Passed out of XVII Corps to Canadian Corps.	
	24.8.18		Very few wounded arriving ; A fair number of Gas Cases. Capt. C. Uren. A.A.M.C. rejoined Unit from 1st Army School of Instruction today Some difficulty in getting rid of the residue of Rest Stn Patients including Scabies cases left by the XVII Corps	G.W.
	25.8.18		Party of 40 Bearers detailed for duty with 1/2 H.F.Amb making 64 Bearers in all in the Line Horse Ambulance & Cars were also sent to join 1/2 HFA	G.W.

Army Form C. 2118.

WAR DIARY
or
INTELLIGENCE SUMMARY.
(Erase heading not required.)

Sheet V

AUGUST 1918

G.P.Whyte - Lt Col
O.C. 2/1st HIGHLAND FIELD AMBULANCE

Place	Date	Hour	Summary of Events and Information	Remarks and references to Appendices
AGNEZ-LES-DUISANS	26.8.18	(Afternoon)	Ordered to pack up & be ready to move.	G.P.W.
		(Night)	Received orders to open as a D.R.S. but to remain as mobile as possible	G.P.W.
	27.8.18		Still a D.R. Stn.	
	28.8.18	(Morning)	A.D.M.S. 51 Div & Colonel Commanding 23 C.C.S. arrived, latter to take over the site	
		(Afternoon)	Ordered to move to ECOIVRES & there open a D.R.S.	G.P.W.
	29.8.18	6 P.M.	Unit moved to ECOIVRES & took over old site of School & Chateau previously occupied by this Unit. D.R.S. opened at ECOIVRES. Accommodation for 400 Patients. Officers & Scabies Patients to be treated at 1/3 H.F.Amb - MAROEUIL, others including Gas to be treated here. Lt. Colonel G F WHYTE rejoined Unit from leave to U.K. today. Under authority granted by His Majesty the King the Field Marshall C-in-C has awarded the decorations stated to the u/m for gallantry displayed between 20-30 July 1918. The XXII Corps & Divisional Commander congratulate the recipients.	

SECOND BAR TO MILITARY CROSS
/CAPT (a/MAJOR) D McKELVEY MC M.B. (RAMC att)

MILITARY CROSS
1/6 BLACK WATCH (late 2/1 H.F.Amb)
CAPT J M BARROW AAMC att

DISTINGUISHED CONDUCT MEDAL
2/1' HIGHLAND FIELD AMBULANCE RAMC T.F.
301337 L/CPL (A/SGT) G SWAPP MM
301286 PRIVATE W S FORREST.

G.P.W.

[signature] 2/1st HIGHLAND FIELD AMBULANCE 31.8.18

116/3259.

9/1st Mgl. 7.O.

Oct. 1918.

Army Form C. 2118.

O.C., 2/1st HIGHLAND FIELD AMBULANCE

WAR DIARY
or
INTELLIGENCE SUMMARY.
(Erase heading not required.)

Sheet I
September, 1918.

Place	Date	Hour	Summary of Events and Information	Remarks and references to Appendices
ECOIVRES	2/9/18	7 P.M.	Under instructions of A.D.M.S., this Ambulance ceased today to function as a Divisional Rest Station, but continued to receive N.Y.D. Gas Cases. 51st (H) Div. Medical Arrangements received tonight confirmed these instructions, and contained arrangements for disposal of Eye, Ear, Nose, & Throat cases, and also Dental Cases through 2/1st H.F.A. Arrangements were made accordingly, & the bulk of the patients in Hospital transferred to Corps Rest Station.	6 P.M.
	3/9/18	7 P.M.	Test fire Alarm carried out, & several points noted for improvement.	6 P.M.
	4/9/18	8.30 P.M.	Amendments to Medical Arrangements of the 2nd inst. received. 2/1st H.F.A. being instructed to receive all Gas Cases from 51st (H) D.V.	6 P.M.
	5/9/18	9 P.M.	Further amendments to Medical Arrangements received today. Opened at 12 noon as a Corps Gas Centre to receive Gas Cases from all the Divisions of the Corps. Large numbers of Cases started to arrive in the afternoon, & by 5 p.m. about 80 cases had been received, principally from Artillery Units. Lt. B. Maltby rejoined from duty with 1/6th Gordons tonight.	6 P.M.
	6/9/18	8 P.M.	Gassed Cases continued to arrive in a steady flow, & there were again close on 80 admissions, mostly from the same Units as yesterday. Arrangements made for the accommodation of N.Y.D. Gas cases in one building; the more serious cases being distributed between the Schoolhouse and various huts. Gas cases seem to have been mostly caused by Yellow Cross (Mustard) Shell, with a few exhibiting symptoms of the Blue Cross variety. Bot. Bicarb. sol. and by paraffin for eyes, washing of skin c̄ Bicarb. change into substitute clothing [Birmingham], and continuous mask inhalation with Inhalation mixture [Birmingham], are the principal lines of treatment. Clothing sent to ECURIE for de-gassing.	6 P.M.
	7/9/18	6 P.M.	Flow of cases slackened somewhat today, the majority appearing to be less severe than on the previous days.	6 P.M.
	9/9/18	6.30 P.M.	Admissions of Gas Cases considerably decreased, and normal conditions prevailing. Cases have been received from six different divisions as well as numerous Corps Units, some of which have been transferred from Field Ambs. of 11th & 56th Div. [Over.	6 P.M.

Sheet II.
SEPTEMBER, 1918

WAR DIARY
or
INTELLIGENCE SUMMARY.
(Erase heading not required.)

Army Form C. 2118.

E Raleigh Lt Col.
O.C., 2/1st HIGHLAND FIELD AMBULANCE

Place	Date	Hour	Summary of Events and Information	Remarks and references to Appendices
ECOIVRES	9/9/18 (cont)		Test fire Alarm carried out today. Some improvement shown as regards the turning out of the Piquet, but more practice needed in reminder of Unit forming a chain for constant supply of water.	G.R.W.
	10/9/18	6 P.M.	Q.M. & Hon. Lt. W.A. Battery left today on Special Leave to United Kingdom from 11/9/18 to 25/9/18.	G.R.W.
	11/9/18	8:30 P.M.	Lt. C. Ashley, U.S.M.C., posted to 255 Bde, R.F.A., from 11/9/18, and struck off strength. Lieut. N.A. Young, M.O.R.C., U.S.A., (who is at present on leave) has been posted to 2/1st H.F.A. from 11/9/18, & taken on strength from that date. [Auth: -A.D.M.S., 51 (H.) Div. No. 4562, d/11-9-18]. The 51st (H) Div. R.A.M.C. O.O. No. 75, with Administrative Instructions, received today, intimating the relief of the Division by the 49th Division on 11, 12, & 13 September. 2/1st H.F.A. ordered to proceed to Brant Camp, MONT ST ELOI, on relief by 1/1st (W.R.) F.A. Ambulance. Handing over to be arranged by O.C's concerned.	G.R.W.
	13/9/18	8:30 A.M.	All bearers attached to 1/2nd H.F.A. have now rejoined Unit. Advance party at Brant Camp have been engaged in cleaning up new billets and general sanitary work around same.	G.R.W.
BRANT CAMP (MONT ST ELOI).	14/9/18	6 P.M.	Handed over Corps Gas Centre at 9 a.m. this morning. Obtained receipts for stores handed over, & certificates as to cleanliness of Billets and grounds. Unit moved at 9:15 a.m. to Brant Camp, and arrangements were at once made for the reception and treatment of the Sick of 154 Inf. Bde., C Section (under Major McKelvey) opening up Hospital. Arrangements also made for the reception of Dental Cases, and the provision of a Surgery for accommodation of Dental Surgeon from 59 C.C.S., who is to treat cases here on Mondays, Wednesdays & Fridays. Intimation that Major D. McKelvey has been awarded the Croix de Guerre, with Palms, for services rendered between 21st & 31st July, while the Division was with the Fifth French Army	G.R.W.

Army Form C. 2118.

Sheet III
SEPTEMBER, 1918.

WAR DIARY
or
INTELLIGENCE SUMMARY.
(Erase heading not required.)

O.C., 2/1st HIGHLAND FIELD AMBULANCE
Lt Col...

Place	Date	Hour	Summary of Events and Information	Remarks and references to Appendices
BRANT CAMP. (MONT ST ELOI)	15/9/18	6.30 p.m.	Instructions received from A.D.M.S., 51(H) Div., that arrangements should at once be made to receive and treat the Scabies patients of the Division. Arrangements made accordingly.	G McH
	16/9/18	8.30 a.m.	Training of Unit continued — Physical Drill, Route Marches, Company and Wagon Drill. Recreational training encouraged in afternoon.	G McH
	18/9/18	8 p.m.	Lt. J.W. ROBINSON, U.S.M.C, has today been detailed to report for duty to A.D.M.S., 51st Div. and is struck off strength of this Unit. [Auth.—A.D.M.S., 51(H) Div. No. 4569, d/17-9-18] Lt. B. MALTBY, M.B.R.C., U.S.A., detailed for temporary duty with No. 2 C.C.S., in relief of Lt. Robinson. Capt. C. UREN, A.A.M.C., rejoined Headquarters from duty with No. 2 C.C.S. today.	G McH
	19/9/18	6 P.M.	Improvements made in Brant Camp during our stay consisted of building brick cooking range in Officers' Cook House, repairing and distempering huts, digging two soakage pits, mining pit, and two latrines. Similar improvements carried out at hospital staff on Main Road. Unit Sports on Saturday, 21st inst., at Lancaster Camp, Mont St Eloi. Capt. C. UREN is in charge of arrangements.	G McH
	21/9/18	8.30 p.m.	Unit Sports held today. Ground very wet through the heavy showers in forenoon but recovered wonderfully. Sports proved quite a success, there being keen competition in all the events. C. Section carried off most points, with A Section second. 154 Inf. Bde. O.O. No. 29 received, intimating the relief by them in the line of 148th Inf. Bde., on 22nd inst. 51st Div. R.A.M.C. O.O. No. 76 received, with 51st Div. Administrative Instructions and Medical Arrangements. 2/1st H.F.A. ordered to relieve the 1/1st W.R. Field Ambulance at Corps Gas Centre, ECOIVRES, on 24th. O.C., 2/1st H.F.A. also to detail an Officer and Party to take over W.C.P., St. NICHOLAS. Four bearers of 2/1st to be attached to each battalion in 154 Inf. Bde., the remainder — as well as Units' Motor Ambulances, &c one — to be at the call of O.C. 1/3rd H.F.A.	G McH
	22/9/18	8 P.M.	154 Inf. Bde. move cancelled. Continued to collect their Sick. Amendment to R.A.M.C. O.O. received tonight. Date of handing over altered, and this Unit ordered to take over Corps Gas Centre at 8.30 a.m. 23rd inst. Small holding party to be detailed to W.C.P., T 17 ORS to be detailed to relieve Unit Sub Division of 1/3rd H.F.A. at No. 2 C.C.S. on 23rd inst	G McH

Sheet IV.
SEPTEMBER, 1918.

Army Form C. 2118.
G. ZeDugh LT-COL.,
O.C. 2/1st HIGHLAND FIELD AMBULANCE

WAR DIARY or INTELLIGENCE SUMMARY.
(Erase heading not required.)

Place	Date	Hour	Summary of Events and Information	Remarks and references to Appendices
BRANT CAMP, MONT ST ELOI. (cont)	22/9/18		Permission to hand over certain mobilization Equipment considered unnecessary in Field Ambulance having been obtained from A.D.M.S., this was carried out today and receipts obtained for articles handed in.	6 p.m.
ECOIVRES.	23/9/18	8.30 p.m.	Capt. C. UREN and 3 O.R's left this morning to take over Walking Wounded site at ST NICHOLAS. Major M°KELVEY and a party proceeded to Ecoivres to take over Corps Gas Centre. Packing completed at 10.30, & Unit left for Ecoivres at 11 a.m., the usual certificates of handing over being obtained from 49th Div. Reception Camp. On arrival, C Section Sub. took over main part of Hospital, B. Section taking over the remainder. At 2 p.m. Sgt. Taylor and 16 O.Rs proceeded to No. 2 C.C.S. to relieve Sub-Division of 1/3rd H.F.A. Circ. memo. from A.D.M.S. received with proposed scheme of Medical Operations in the event of an advance. Intimation having been received that all Australian medical officers arriving with the Division had to proceed to join Australian Base Hospitals, Lt. N.A. YOUNG relieved Capt. C. UREN at W.W.D.P. this afternoon, the latter returning to Headquarters.	
	24/9/18	6 p.m.	Very few Gas cases arriving, + these mostly transfers from other field Ambulances. Recalled Lt. N.A. YOUNG today, + sent Q.M.S. TOUGH up in his place.	6 p.m.
	25/9/18	6 p.m.	Capt. C. UREN left this morning for No. 2 Australian Gen. Hosp., + is struck off strength. New Medical Arrangements received today.	6 p.m.
	26/9/18	8 p.m.	Lieut. B. MALTBY, U.S.M.C., posted to 1/6th Gordon Hdqtrs. from today, he having returned to Headquarters last night. He is struck off strength from today's date. Admission of Gas cases still keeps low, there being 44 cases remaining in Hospital tonight. Most of these are slight cases. Lieut. W.A. BUTTERY returned from leave to U.K. today.	6 p.m.
	28/9/18	9 p.m.	Capts. J.M. FALKINER (T.C.) and J.V. COPE, M.C. (T.C.) were posted to this Unit today and are taken on strength. They are temporarily attached to 1/3rd H.F.A. Received orders from A.D.M.S. 51 D. to hold Ambulance in readiness to move at shortest notice in the event of an advance. Made arrangements accordingly.	9 p.m.

2/1st Highland Fd A.

Sheet V
SEPTEMBER, 1918.

WAR DIARY
or
INTELLIGENCE SUMMARY.
(Erase heading not required.)

Army Form C. 2118.

E. J. Wylie Lt. Col.,
O.C., 2/1st HIGHLAND FIELD AMBULANCE

Place	Date	Hour	Summary of Events and Information	Remarks and references to Appendices
ECOIVRES	29/9/18	8.30am	Personnel were bathed today and received clean change of underclothing. Large number of Gas Cases admitted today, mostly transfers from F.A. Ambces. of 56th Div., and there are 125 cases remaining in hospital tonight	G.740
	30/9/18	6.30am	Big evacuation of Gas patients today, 72 going to CCS, & 20 to duty. Admissions fell considerably, only 35 cases being brought in. 20 Reinfs. under a Sergeant, went out today to 1/3rd H.F.A. for work in the line. Under the orders of A.D.M.S., 51(H) Div., Lt. B.T. BAGGOTT, U.S.M.C., left today for No. 12 Stationary Hosp., & is struck off strength.	G.740

E. J. Wylie Lt. Col.,
O.C., 2/1st HIGHLAND FIELD AMBULANCE

WAR DIARY
INTELLIGENCE SUMMARY

Army Form C. 2118.

G.F. Wyatt Lt Colonel
O.C. 2/1st HIGHLAND FIELD AMBULANCE

Sheet 1
OCTOBER 1918

91038

Place	Date	Hour	Summary of Events and Information	Remarks and references to Appendices
ECOIVRES	1.X.18		Capt. J.V. COPE M.C. 2/1 H.F.Amb. at present attached to 1/3 H.F.Amb. was today detailed to take over temporary Medical Charge of 256 Bde R.F.A. Received 51.Div. A.I regarding relief of 51 Div in the line by 8 Div. 2/1 H.F.Amb to remain in present location	G.F.W.
do	2.X.18		Capt. J.M. FALKINER has been posted to B. Section & Capt. J.V. COPE to C	G.F.W.
do	3.X.18		Major A.C. AMY rejoined Unit from Hospital at PARIS today	G.F.W.
do	5.X.18		Received 152 Inf Bde Order No. 273 intimating that 51 Div would relieve 3rd Canadian Div in the Sector East of CAMBRAI. 2/1 H.F.Amb to be attached to 152 Inf Bde. Transport of Units of 152 Bde ordered to proceed by road. Personnel to embus on the evening of 6th inst.	G.F.W.
do	6.X.18		A.I from 152 Bde received this morning with march table for Transport. Transport left early this morning under charge of Lieut. Young. Advanced party for Billeting, consisting of Major McKelvey + 5 O.R. left by Motor Amb. at 09.00. Unit Embussing table received at midday. 152 Bde Group to embus at 16.30. Unit moved at 15.30 after being relieved by Canadian Fd.Amb. to HAUTE AVESNES (Embussing Point) Busses left at 18.30 + proceeded via ARRAS to a point near	

WAR DIARY
INTELLIGENCE SUMMARY

Army Form C. 2118.

SHEET 2
October 1918

E. Pugh - Lt Colonel
O.C. 2/1st HIGHLAND FIELD AMBULANCE

Place	Date	Hour	Summary of Events and Information	Remarks and references to Appendices
QUEANT RIENCOURT	8.X.18		QUEANT, which was reached about 22.30. Some enemy bombs dropped in the vicinity shortly after arrival last night at Debrucourt Point but no casualties to men of this Unit, some difficulty experienced in getting personnel to camping ground about 4 kilometres away, but all eventually got under canvas by 00.30 on morning of 9 inst. Unit remaining in this area at present.	E Pugh
RIENCOURT	9.X.18		Unit still at RIENCOURT.	E Pugh
do			152 Bde OO N° 274 with A.I received today providing for move to BOURLON area tomorrow. This Unit to have starting point at 12.00.	E Pugh
do	10.X.18		Left RIENCOURT at 10.30 & proceeded to PRONVILLE, MOEUVRES, BAPAUME-CAMBRAI Road to FONTAINE NOTRE DAME where Major McKelvey had arranged for Billets	E Pugh
FONTAINE NOTRE DAME	11.X.18		152 Inf Bde N° 275 received, providing for relief of 2° Canadian Div tonight. Zero hour to be notified later. Unit moved at 14.00 but shortly after starting we were held up for nearly two hours by pressure of traffic. Outskirts of CAMBRAI reached about 18.00 & Unit & Transport eventually turned into a field at POINT DE TOUR about 19.00. Here we waited for 4 hours. Jean Cerny	

Army Form C. 2118.

WAR DIARY
or
INTELLIGENCE SUMMARY.
(Erase heading not required.)

SHEET 3
October 1918

E. Gulph Lt Colonel
O.C. 2/1st HIGHLAND FIELD AMBULANCE

Place	Date	Hour	Summary of Events and Information	Remarks and references to Appendices
POINT DE TOUR	11.x.18		ceased to personnel in the interim. Unit resumed march at 23.00 and reached ESCAUDOEUVRES at 23.59. Accommodation found in the CONVENT. R.A.M.C. O.O. No. 79 received today. 2/1 H.F.Amb to relieve 5th Canadian Fd Amb tonight + take over A.D.S + Car Collecting Post	E.M.
ESCAUDOEUVRES	12.x.18		Owing to late arrival last night A.D.Stn was not taken over until 12.00 today. 1/2 H.F.Amb arrived this morning. Under instructions of A.D.M.S the A.D.S moved forward to THUN. ST MARTIN at 15.30. 1/2 H.F.Amb taking over site at CONVENT as a M.D.Stn	SHEET 51A. T10 c.1-8 E.M.
THUN-ST MARTIN (T10 c.1-8)	12.x.18		Forward Collecting Posts under charge of Major McKelvey were established in IWUY. Major McKelvey slightly wounded, one man KILLED + another seriously wounded today. Major McKelvey remaining on duty. Capt Falkner detailed for duty at 152 Bde H.Q. as LIAISON OFFICER	E.M.
do	13.x.18		2 Bearers of the Unit were wounded today, one seriously. Called on Bearers of 1/2 H.F.Amb and a party of 1 Officer + 33 O.R. now attached with Horse + Motor Ambulances. Visited Advanced Posts this morning + found evacuation proceeding satisfactorily.	E.M.

Army Form C. 2118.

WAR DIARY
or
INTELLIGENCE SUMMARY.
(Erase heading not required.)

Sheet 4
October 1918

E. Pulugh Lt Colonel
O.C. 2/1st HIGHLAND FIELD AMBULANCE

Place	Date	Hour	Summary of Events and Information	Remarks and references to Appendices
THUN-ST MARTIN '18	13.x.'18		Endeavoured to open at AVESNES-LE-SEC but 152 INF Bde states that this is not possible	E.P.W.
do	14.x.18		51 (H) Div Medical Arrangements received today. I visited Advanced Posts again this morning. 1/4 GORDON HIGHD" were shelled out of their Reg" Aid Post. Some Gas Shelling on Divisional front, 2 men of this Unit having to be evacuated to CCS in consequence. Called on party of 28 Bearers of 1/3 H.F.A. whose Horse & Motor Ambulances are also attached here.	E.P.W.
do	15.x.18		Capt J.M. Falkiner rejoined Unit today. Car Collecting Post moved forward to O.27.c.7.9 this afternoon, with small party. IWUY very heavily shelled this evening with H.E. & Blue Cross Gas. Many gas casualties coming in + 8 of my Bearers were evacuated from this cause.	E.P.W.
do	16.x.18		Went round advanced Posts this morning & found all going well	E.P.W.
do	17.x.18		Made my usual morning round of Posts, everything was found in order	E.P.W.
do	18.x.18		51 Div Med Arrangements received. Advanced Collecting Post at N.36.c.15.15 + Car Collecting Post still at O.27.c.7.9.	(Sheet 51A) E.P.W.
do	19.x.18		Locations of Reg" Aid Posts of 153 INF Bde unknown at present as they have not yet moved forward.	E.P.W.

WAR DIARY
INTELLIGENCE SUMMARY

Sheet 5
October 1918

O.C. 2/1st HIGHLAND FIELD AMBULANCE

Place	Date	Hour	Summary of Events and Information	Remarks and references to Appendices
THUN ST MARTIN	19.x.18		Car Collecting Post moved forward this morning to O 27.8.1.6 & later was established with 1. N.C.O. & 8 men at NC 8.7.2. Additional Medical Arrangements received. Preparations made under the DADMS for feeding recovered civilians and giving Medical assistance where necessary.	MAP REF (SHEET 51A) G.R.
do.	20.x.18		Yesterday afternoon enemy were discovered to be evacuating, and Division proceeded to follow up. Large number of Civilians were reported to have been released and to be on their way to THUN-ST MARTIN. Accommodation for these, not being available at THUN-ST MARTIN. Refugees were collected at INUY and attended to under the arrangements of French Mission 7.51 D.A.D.M.S. This morning I made a tour of inspection of the Advanced Posts accompanied by the A.D.M.S. 51 Div. & Lt Col Miller 1/2 Bligh Fd Amb. Collecting Post is now established at I 27.8.8.3 with Cars at Cross Roads in I 27.6.4.0. This Post will collect from I 34 & 7.5 in the meantime until NOYELLES - AVESNES LE SEC road has been repaired. Then cases from the right Brigade will be brought to Post situated near Church in AVESNES LE SEC O 22.6.4.0	G.R. 4 pm

WAR DIARY or INTELLIGENCE SUMMARY

Army Form C. 2118.

O.C. 2/1st HIGHLAND FIELD AMBULANCE — Lt Colonel [signature: E. W. Hugh]

SHEET 6, October 1918

Place	Date	Hour	Summary of Events and Information	Remarks and references to Appendices
THUN-ST MARTIN	20.X.18	14.50	At this hour the line ran 1000 yards in front of DOUCHY and only just in front of NOYELLES which is still under Machine Gun fire. Car Relay Post at W.W.C.P. in PAVE-DE-VALENCIENNES at N6a9.0 (SHEET 51A). Another W.W.C. Post has been established on this side of AVESNES at 0.27.C.26 each of these posts has the same staff namely 1. S/Sgt + 6 men (including 1 cook) + has supplies of dressings, food + cooking utensils. These posts will evacuate by Horse Ambulance to H.Q at THUN-ST MARTIN + thence cases will be sent to W.C.C.S at CAMBRAI by Horse Amb. or Motor Lorries when available. 1/2 H.F. Amb. moved up to IWUY + opened M.D.S. in at CHATEAU N.29.a.6.4 at 17.00	[initials]
PAVE DE VALENCIENNES	21.X.18	17.00	Under A.D.M.S Instructions. H.Q moved to PAVE DE VALENCIENNES at N.6a9.0. Forward Collecting Post with Major McIlroy with 3 3ord Amb. established at I.18.a.6.2. Large Car Relay Post on west side of River Selle at DOUCHY Map Ref. I.22.a.2.6. (Red 51A) Two Large cars here w/R loading + unloading parties. Bearer relay Posts under Capt. Falkiner at I.27.C.8.3. Main Car Post w/R. H.Q at PAVE DE VALENCIENNES. It is not yet possible to get Large Cars across River Selle owing to bad condition of road near PONTOON BRIDGE and Trestle Bridge.	[initials]
do	22.X.18		A.D.S. in still at PAVE DE VALENCIENNES. W.W.C Posts were established this Morning at FRETE-AU-POIRIER (I.27.C.8.3.) and at NOYELLE (I.34.a.8.5)	

Army Form C. 2118.

WAR DIARY
or
INTELLIGENCE SUMMARY. /Hulyh/ Lt Colonel
2/1st HIGHLAND FIELD AMBULANCE
(Erase heading not required.)

SHEET 7 October 1918

Instructions regarding War Diaries and Intelligence Summaries are contained in F.S. Regs., Part II. and the Staff Manual respectively. Title pages will be prepared in manuscript.

Place	Date	Hour	Summary of Events and Information	Remarks and references to Appendices
PAVE de VALENCIENNES	22.x.18		POSTE DE SECOURS CIVILS established in DOUCHY under Lieut YOUNG where the finding and treatment of rescued civilianers carried on. Captain Falkner and loading Party moved forward last night on East side of River Selle in DOUCHY at I 22 d 3 y. New post under Cpl Benzie with one squad of Bearers formed at J 14 d 8.6. Advanced Collecting Post still at I 18 a 6.2. The collection from R.A.P's is by Ford Cars. Bridge at DOUCHY over river SELLE completed and	MAP REF SHEET 51A G Hu
-do-	23.x.18 15.00		New A.D. Stn formed today under Major Amy in DOUCHY at I 22.G.S.I. (SALLE DU PATRONAGE) Advanced Collecting Post CROIX ST MARIE, Collecting Post J 14 d 8.6. W.W.C Posts at NOYELLES and FRETE-AU-POIRIER with relay Post PAVE DE VALENCIENNES. Soup Kitchen is now in the hands of the French Mission. Casualties about 100, evacuations go on steadily.	G Hu
-do-	24.x.18		Many cases evacuated from THIANT by Hand Carriage to post on West Side of Railway Bridge. Locations same as yesterday.	G Hu
-do-	25.x.18		Relay Posts established at J.15.c.54 (Bolt Factory THIANT) and J 22.a.3.7, and in the evening a further Post at J 23.a.1.6 on THIANT-MAING Road. The bridge across river ECAILLON which was blown down by the enemy in their retreat has been reconstructed and is expected to be open tomorrow by 12.00 hours. Casualties not numerous.	G Hu
LA PYRAMIDE DE DENAIN.			A.D.S moved forward to LA PYRAMIDE DE DENAIN under Major AMY. There is excellent	G Hu

WAR DIARY

Army Form C. 2118.

SHEET 8 INTELLIGENCE SUMMARY. E. McHugh Lt Colonel
October 1918. OC 2/1st HIGHLAND FIELD AMBULANCE

Place	Date	Hour	Summary of Events and Information	Remarks and references to Appendices
				(SHEET 51A)
LA PYRAMIDE DE DENAIN	26 X 18		W.W.C. Post at NOYELLE & FRETE AV POIRIER closed, and new W.W.C.P. established at CROIX ST MARIE evacuating to IWUY. HQ moved to A.D.S at LA PYRAMID this afternoon. Collecting & Large Car Post is in BOLT FACTORY - THIANT with "Ads" Collecting FORD CAR Post at J 22 & 87. Ford Cars run from the front forward to R.A.P. in MAING. In spite of the forward movements of ADS & MDS the evacuation has gone on uninterruptedly and satisfactorily. Locations are as yesterday but W.C.P. is now evacuating to HASPRES where Corps W.W.C. Stn has been established.	J 15 c 55 E 7ul
do.	27 X 18		RAMC. OO 70.80 received today intimating the relief of the Division on 28/29 inst by the 49 Div, details of relief of ADS to be arranged by OC concerned	E 7ul
do	28 X 18		ADS forward Posts were relieved by 1/1 West Riding Amb 49 Div relief being completed by 16.30 hours. This Amb has established its ADS at BOLT FACTORY - THIANT.	E 7ul
		29.15	Tonight three Heavy High Velocity Shells landed on the road close to ADS. One only one casualty resulted, an Amb driver being hit and Car badly damaged Captain LAING + 34 OR 1/2 HFAmb were returned to their Unit tonight	E 7ul

WAR DIARY
or
INTELLIGENCE SUMMARY

Army Form C. 2118.

SHEET 9 October 1918

G. Pullugh - Lt Colonel
OC 2/1st HIGHLAND [F.A.?] AMBULANCE

Place	Date	Hour	Summary of Events and Information	Remarks and references to Appendices

LA PYRAMIDE DE DENAIN.	28.X.18		Total Casualties passed through A.D.Stn & W.C. Post during my period in charge of forward evacuation were as under:-
			
			 51st (HIGHLAND) DIVISION
			               WOUNDED SICK
			 OFFICERS 46 9
			 OTHER RANKS... 1196 345
			    TOTAL 1242 354
			
			 OTHER FORMATIONS
			              WOUNDED SICK
			 OFFICERS. 6 2
			 OTHER RANKS 151 101
			    TOTAL 157 103
			
			 GRAND TOTAL SICK & WOUNDED 1856 Officers + O.R'
			 GERMAN PRISONERS OFFICERS 1 OTHER RANKS 53
			 CIVILIANS passed through 32 SICK + WOUNDED
			 CIVILIANS treated 30.
				G.P.W

-do- DOUCHY	29.X.18		Move to DOUCHY today at 10.00 hours. Unit billeted in same quarters as before. Proceeded to collect sick of 154 Inf Bde. Remainder of attached Bearer + Amb Cars returned to their Units this morning	G.P.W
-do-	30.X.18		Carried on extensive sanitary work today and mapped out scheme of sanitation for the village with the Town Mayor.	G.P.W
-do-	31.X.18 09.30		154 Inf Bde O.O No 71 received intimating move of Brigade to Fbg ST ROCH on 31st. Unit moved this morning under Brigade arrangements to Fbg ST ROCH where billets	G.P.W

Army Form C. 2118.

WAR DIARY
or
INTELLIGENCE SUMMARY.

(Erase heading not required.)

Sheet 10
October 1918

G. F. Wright Lt Colonel
O.C. 2/1st HIGHLAND FIELD AMBULANCE

Place	Date	Hour	Summary of Events and Information	Remarks and references to Appendices
Fbg St ROCH near CAMBRAI	31 x 18		Had been arranged by Major Amy. All Bearers are now returned from Battalions. Opened up for reception of Bad Sick. Lt Young M.O.R.C. detailed to report to M O in charge of 1/17 A.S.H. dus on 30 inst and is struck off strength. Capt J M Faulkner r 20 O.R' detailed on 30 x 18 for duty with 77 CCS under ADMS instructions.	G.F.W.

G. F. Wright Lt Colonel
O.C. 2/1st HIGHLAND FIELD AMBULANCE

140/3401

COMMITTEE FOR THE
HISTORY OF THE WAR
10 JAN 1919

1/5 High Star
8/

Nov 1918

Army Form C. 2118.

WAR DIARY or INTELLIGENCE SUMMARY.

(Erase heading not required.)

Sheet 1
Nov 1918

OC 2/1st HIGHLAND FIELD AMBULANCE
51(H) DIV

Place	Date	Hour	Summary of Events and Information	Remarks and references to Appendices
ST ROCH CAMBRAI	3.XI.18		CAPTAIN J. CATHCART. RAMC. TC posted for duty with 2/1 H.F.Amb 3d Amb today and is taken on strength.	GM
			Unit engaged in collecting and breaking up of the 154 Inf Bde	GM
	7.XI.18		Under the Educational Scheme a lecture was given to Officers & Men of this Unit on "CITIZENSHIP" by the REV W M GILLIESON. S.C.F. Capt. J CATHCART detailed for temporary duty with 1/2 High 3d Amb today	GM
	8.XI.18		A Debating Society was formed in the Unit, under the Educational Scheme and the first meeting took place tonight.	GM
	9.XI.18		Lecture by Captain MOIR — R.E. on "WONDERS" of Wireless Telegraphy was given tonight Div. Sch M.	GM
	11.XI.18		Armistice with Germany was signed at 05:00 hours this morning and Hostilities ceased at 11:00 hours. Wire from Div received that hostilities ceased at 11:00 hours A general Holiday was granted throughout the Division. A special parade was held at 11:00 hours of this Unit which in announcement of the conclusion of the armistice to the personnel	GM
	12.XI.18		Lieut J.R.T SNYDER. MORC posted to 2/1 H.F.Amb and taken on strength Major D M°KELVEY MC was granted leave to U.K. from 11-25.XI.18	GM

Army Form C. 2118.

WAR DIARY
or
INTELLIGENCE SUMMARY

Sheet 2
Nov 1918

OC 2/1st Highland Field Ambulance 51 (H) Div

O.C. E. Walsh Lieut Col

(Erase heading not required.)

Place	Date	Hour	Summary of Events and Information	Remarks and references to Appendices
ST ROCH CAMBRAI	13.XI.18		Second Anniversary of BEAUMONT HAMEL VICTORY was celebrated in a suitable way by a Special Dinner and Supper to personnel of Unit and a Concert was held in the evening.	E.W.
	14.XI.18		Capt J. CATHCART was granted leave to U.K. from 14-28.XI.18. Lieut J. CRAIG. RAMC detailed for duty with 2/1.H.F.Amb. is taken on strength. A lecture was given tonight by L'Col D. RORIE. DSO. ADMS 51 Div on "Rings of Interest round about us".	E.W.
	16.XI.18		Lieut Craig having been detailed for temp'y duty with 1/8 ROYAL SCOTS from 14.XI.18 is struck off ration strength.	E.W.
			Capt J.M. Falkiner T/1 other ranks rejoined Unit from 22 CCS on 15.XI.18 A reinforcing draft of 11- Other ranks joined Unit today from Base Depot.	E.W.
	17.XI.18		Men of Unit were bathed today & received clean change of underclothing.	E.W.
	18.XI.18		An inspection of the equipment of men of the Unit was held today by myself Haversacks & Valises were found to be sulphed and Belts & Buckles cleaned. An afternoon Transport Inspection was also held by the IOM. All available vehicles being present.	E.W.
	21.XI.18		Capt. J.M. Falkiner took over Medical Charge of 1/6 A.S.H. today & is struck off strength of Unit.	E.W.
	22.XI.18		L'Col G.F. WHYTE was granted leave to PARIS from 22-29.XI.18 Major Ony took over charge in my absence.	E.W.

Army Form C. 2118.

WAR DIARY
or
INTELLIGENCE SUMMARY.
(Erase heading not required.)

G. Pulleyn Lt Colonel.
OC 2/1st HIGHLAND FIELD AMBULANCE

Instructions regarding War Diaries and Intelligence Summaries are contained in F. S. Regs., Part II. and the Staff Manual respectively. Title pages will be prepared in manuscript.

Sheet III NOV 1918

Place	Date	Hour	Summary of Events and Information	Remarks and references to Appendices
ST ROCH (CAMBRAI)	23.XI.18		**HONOURS & AWARDS**	
			Under authority granted by His Majesty the King, the F.M. C.I.C. has awarded the decorations stated to the undermentioned for gallantry displayed. The Divisional Commander congratulates the recipients.	
			BAR TO MILITARY MEDAL	
			2/1 H.F.Amb 96/301052 Pte (9Cpl) P.M. MORRISON M.M. RAMC T	
			MILITARY MEDAL	
			2/1 H.F.Amb 96/305118 Cpl R.K. REEKIE RAMC T	
			301268 Cpl A. BENZIE do	
			301533 Pte C. FARQUHAR do	
			301401 " J.G. SMITH do	
			93847 " T.D. McKENZIE RAMC att	
			301500 " W. SMITH RAMC T	
			M/ 055191 " C. BORLACE ASC MT att	
			M/ 098018 " M.R. CLARK do	
			M/ 076963 " WAC ISLAND do	
	18.XI.18	1730	A lecture on INDIA was given by Major Amy today	G.Pu
	23.XI.18	do	Lecture on INDIA was continued this evening, and proved to be a very interesting one	G.Pu
			Special	
	24.XI.18		Major A.C. AMY was granted ^Leave to UK from 28/11/18 to 28/12/18 (1 month)	G.Pu
			Major D. McKELVEY returned from UK leave. Bokore George of Unit.	
			A Lecture was delivered tonight by Rev. W. JARDINE 1/7 A & S Hdrs on "BOOKS THAT HAVE BORED ME".	G.Pu

Army Form C. 2118.

WAR DIARY
or
INTELLIGENCE SUMMARY.

(Erase heading not required.)

Sheet A

G. Tulloch Lt Colonel
OC 2/1st HIGHLAND FIELD AMBULANCE

Place	Date	Hour	Summary of Events and Information	Remarks and references to Appendices
ST ROCH (CAMBRAI)	29.XI.18		A Lecture on VENEREAL DISEASE & TREATMENT was given to men of this Unit today by Lieut SNYDER USMC	G.T.W
	30.XI.18		51 DIVISION Sports were held today & one man of the Unit received 3rd prize (BRONZE MEDAL) in 220 yards race	G.T.W
	30.XI.18		Lieut- B. MALTBY USMC att GORDON HDRS & Late of 2/1 H.F.Amb was awarded the MILITARY CROSS for gallantry in the field under authority delegated by His Majesty the King the Field Marshall C in C	G.T.W

WORK ON EDUCATION.

On Nov 14th copies of G.H.Q letter T 2176 of Nov 2 (revised Nov 14th) and First Army 9/1704 (G) of Nov 7 were received from the Educational Officer 51 (H) Div, with instructions to start classes as soon as possible. Unit E.O's were also to compile Registers of (a) Occupation & Demand for instruction (b) Unit facilities.
G.H.Q letter explains the Army Education Scheme which would be largely extended on the cessation of hostilities.
The Armistice came into force on Nov 11th
On Nov 23 a meeting of the E.O' of the Division was held at D.H.Q to consider the formation of further classes and to arrange for the supply of instructors.
The following Classes have been started by the Unit:—

	STUDENTS
ENGLISH GRAMMAR & COMPOSITION	L/QM Buttery 11
ENGLISH LANGUAGE & LITERATURE	MAJOR AMY 15
ARITHMETIC	S/Sgt McGILLIVRAY 20
FRENCH	MAJOR AMY & Sgt SWAFF 24
BOOKKEEPING	PTE WILSON 10

Army Form C. 2118.

WAR DIARY
or
INTELLIGENCE SUMMARY.
(Erase heading not required.)

Sheet 5
Nov 1918.

Place	Date	Hour	Summary of Events and Information	Remarks and references to Appendices
ST ROCH (CAMBRAI)			EDUCATIONAL SCHEME CONTINUED	
			LECTURES have been given as under:	
			1. DEMOBILIZATION — Rev Major G Ellison on 7.11.18	
			2. WIRELESS TELEGRAPHY — Captain Moir — 9.11.18	
			3. THINGS OF INTEREST } Col. Rorie DSO 14.11.18	
			ROUND ABOUT US } ADMS 51st Div	
			4. INDIA I — Major Amy — 18.11.18	
			5. INDIA II — -do- — 23.11.18	
			6. BOOKS THAT HAVE } Rev Capt JARDINE 27.11.18	
			BORED ME	
			Further lectures are being arranged.	
			RECREATION	
			Training + Trials for Divisional Sports	
			Inter-section Football League.	
			154 Inf Bde Football League.	
			Recreation + reading room with Piano	
			Numerous Concerts by Concert Troupe and Impromptus.	

G.F.Wylie Lt Colonel
OC 2/1st HIGHLAND FIELD AMBULANCE

2/1st Highland F.A.

Army Form C. 2118.

WAR DIARY
or
INTELLIGENCE SUMMARY.

(Erase heading not required.)

Sheet I.
December 1918.

G.F.K.Hyte Lt Colonel
O.C. 2/1st HIGHLAND FIELD AMBULANCE

Instructions regarding War Diaries and Intelligence Summaries are contained in F.S. Regs., Part II. and the Staff Manual respectively. Title pages will be prepared in manuscript.

Place	Date	Hour	Summary of Events and Information	Remarks and references to Appendices
(F⁰ S⁺ ROCH) (CAMBRAI)	1.12.18		Capt J. Cathcart RAMC rejoined unit today from U.K. leave.	5pm
	4.12.18		A lecture was given this evening by Major Watt 1/4 Gordons on the Daily Newspaper	5pm
	6.12.18		Capt Cathcart was detailed to take over Medical Charge of 1/6 R⁹ Highrs today and is struck off strength of Unit. Lieut J. Craig rejoined Unit from temp⁰ duty with 1/8 Royal Scots. 9 Nursing Orderlies was despatched for temp⁰ duty with 96/1 CCS Mons	5pm 5pm
	7.12.18		Lieut J Craig is appointed Transport Officer of Unit	5pm
	8.12.18		Immediate Awards Lieut C.Q. North M.R.C. USA att Royal H⁰ld. Cate 2/Lt H Fownles was awarded the Military Cross for gallantry in the field	5pm
	9.12.18		Capt Rev P. Higham CF (C+E) was posted to this Unit today	5pm
	10.12.18			
	13.12.18		Demobilizing of Coal Miners started today and three men of this Unit were despatched to Concentration Camp for Evacuation to England. A Kit inspection was held today, and deficiencies were made good	5pm
	15.12.18		Lieut J Craig proceeded today to U.K. to report at the War Office under authority of DDMS XXII Corps & is struck off Strength of Unit	4pm

Army Form C.2118.

WAR DIARY
or
INTELLIGENCE SUMMARY.

(Erase heading not required.)

Army Form Sheet II
December 1918

2/1st HIGHLAND FIELD AMBULANCE
O.C. A.F.Wylie Lt Colonel

Instructions regarding War Diaries and Intelligence Summaries are contained in F.S. Regs., Part II. and the Staff Manual respectively. Title pages will be prepared in manuscript.

Place	Date	Hour	Summary of Events and Information	Remarks and references to Appendices
Fd STROCH) CAMBRAI	17.12.18		**IMMEDIATE AWARD** Under authority delegated by His Majesty the King, the Field Marshal C in C has awarded the D.S.O. to Major A.C. Amy M.D. R.A.M.C. 2/1st Highland Field Amb for gallantry in the field. Authy 21/2075/118/AMS dated 6-12-18.	GFW
			4. Pipers of 6/7th Gordon Hdrs were attached to this Unit today	GFW
	19.12.18		A lecture was given today by Captain Christie "Burns. The Man & Poet"	GFW
	23.12.18		No parades today. Xmas dinner 13-30 hours. Concert at night	GFW
	26.12.18		During the month the health of the 154 Inf Bde has been very good. The average daily number of patients in Bde Hospital being only 7. The Educational Classes have been successfully carried on & well attended.	
	31.12.18		A new class in Latin has been started and also one in Political Economy. The latter having an attendance of 15 Students	GFW

A.F.Wylie
Lt Colonel

O.C. 2/1st HIGHLAND FIELD AMBULANCE

51 DIV
Box 2706

2/1st Highland + A

COMMITTEE FOR THE
MEDICAL HISTORY OF THE WAR
10 MAR 1919

Army Form C. 2118.

WAR DIARY
or
INTELLIGENCE SUMMARY.
(Erase heading not required.)

2/1st HIGHLAND FIELD AMBULANCE

January 1919 Sheet I

Place	Date	Hour	Summary of Events and Information	Remarks and references to Appendices
St ROCH (CAMBRAI)	1.1.19		Lt Col G.F. Whyte was granted leave to U.K from 2-1-19 to 1-2-19. Major O.O Amy DSO took over command on 1.1.19	(1)
HOUDIENG-GOEGNIES (BELGIUM)	11.1.19		Unit moved today from St ROCH (CAMBRAI) by buses to HOUDIENG-GOEGNIES (BELGIUM) and arrived during the afternoon. The Billets had all been engaged some weeks before and all men were billeted in private billets.	(2)
"	12.1.19		Pte R. Snyder USMC was detailed to take over Medical Charge of 1/6 Seaforth on 12.1.19 and is attached for strength. An early treatment room has been established at the hospital for all ranks.	(3)
"	13.1.19		Weekly Health Inspection of men of the Unit was held today. The health of the men was very satisfactory. Billets and clean under clothing being issued weekly. On inspection of Billets was made by OC and all were found to be clean and tidy. The men are all comfortably billeted in private billets and most men have beds & one Boyd under good conditions. No. 301320 Sgt Major DAVIS WTG, RAMC T.F. Sgt Major 2/1" Bbigh Fd Amb was transferred to No. 50 CCS suffering from Aortic V.D.H and died shortly after admission.	(4)
"	14.1.19		Lt & QM Buttery was granted leave to PARIS for 7 days 14-21.1.19	

Army
Major
Rausl

Army Form C. 2118.

WAR DIARY
OF
INTELLIGENCE SUMMARY.
(Erase heading not required.)

2/1st HIGHLAND FIELD AMBULANCE

Sheet II
January 1919

Instructions regarding War Diaries and Intelligence Summaries are contained in F.S. Regs., Part II. and the Staff Manual respectively. Title pages will be prepared in manuscript.

Place	Date	Hour	Summary of Events and Information	Remarks and references to Appendices
HOUDENG-GOEGNIES (BELGIUM)	14.1.19		Leave to BRUSSELS granted to all Officers & men of this Unit and has been steadily taken advantage of. Arrangements also made for parties of N.C.O.s & men to visit the Battlefield of Waterloo every Saturday. Conveyances being provided, and a short description of the Battle will be given on the evening before the party proceed to Waterloo.	(iv)
	15.1.19		Educational Classes are still being well attended. Funeral of the late Sgt Major DAVIS took place today from 96.30 CCS to La Louvière Military Section of the Curlcan Cemetery.	
	"		Honours & Awards. CROIX DE GUERRE. Gold Star. Lt. Col. G. F. WHYTE 2/1st H.F.Amb. was awarded the CROIX DE GUERRE GOLD STAR Authority XXII Corps A 2383/30 dated 11.1.19. Extract from R.T. French 5th Army (Translation) "Lt. Col. G. F. WHYTE M.B. RAMC (T.F. attd. 1/4 Batt The Black Watch. Ry Hdrs. now O.C. 2/1 Highland Fd Amb.	(x)
	17.1.19		In recognition of distinguished services during the last operations, South West of Rheims, from 20-26 July 1918 when he took charge of a temporary CCS in EPERNAY formed by the three Ambulances of the Division. It was mainly due to his great ability and untiring efforts that over 1700 cases were attended to under very trying circumstances. When relieved by a regular CCS he took charge of an Adv Dressing Stn at NANTEUIL where he again attended a large number of cases. Throughout he showed the greatest energy & initiative.	Acting Major Rawle

Army Form C. 2118.

WAR DIARY
or
INTELLIGENCE SUMMARY.

2/1st HIGHLAND FIELD AMBULANCE

Sheet IV
January 1919

(Erase heading not required.)

Instructions regarding War Diaries and Intelligence Summaries are contained in F. S. Regs., Part II. and the Staff Manual respectively. Title pages will be prepared in manuscript.

Place	Date	Hour	Summary of Events and Information	Remarks and references to Appendices
HOUDENG- GOEGNIES (BELGIUM)			Ration supplies satisfactory. Ordnance supplies (Clothing etc) very limited indeed. Health of the men is excellent, no venereal disease so far. Horses are in good condition, exercising difficult as all roads & byroads are pavé. A Concert was held on 29 ult in aid of the Widows & Orphans Fund. Total receipts amounted to 100 Francs & was despatched to the above Fund.	(See)
	31/1/19		Clothing & Equipment Inspection of men of the Unit was held today. Satisfactory. Sanitation of the Area is satisfactory, but Latrine pails are not sufficient very difficult to procure.	

H.C. Hunt
Major
O.C. 2/1st HIGHLAND FIELD AMBULANCE

2/1st Highland F.A.

Army Form C. 2118.

WAR DIARY
or
INTELLIGENCE SUMMARY.
(Erase heading not required.)

E. M. Pugh Lt. Colonel O.C. 2/1st HIGHLAND FIELD AMBULANCE

February 1919
Sheet 1

Place	Date	Hour	Summary of Events and Information	Remarks and references to Appendices
HOUDENG-GOEGNIES. BELGIUM	1/28		EDUCATIONAL CLASSES. These classes were continued until Feb 22nd, when, owing to lack of Instructors, caused by Demobilisation, it was found necessary to discontinue same. Men desirous of continuing individual Studies were informed that class books were available on application to the Education Officer.	4 pm
			REORGANIZATION OF UNIT. Letter 13/1/France/3194 (S.D.2) dated 19.12.18. The equipment of 1 Tent Sub-Division was returned to No.19 Advanced Depot Medical Stores. In accordance with above instructions of reorganisation Captain McKelvey M.C. commanding "C" Section ceases to hold acting rank of Major from 15.2.19. Auty DGMS 94-18/53.	4 pm
			LECTURE. A Lantern lecture entitled "A Talk about Japan, and Japanese Soldiers" was delivered by 97th Divisy G.H.Q. on the 26th Feb. and was attended by men of the Unit.	4 pm
			RACE MEETING XXII Corps held a race meeting at MONS on the 26th Feb. Facilities were given to all men desirous of attending, and transport from h.u. Division put at their disposal for the day	4 pm

Army Form C. 2118.

WAR DIARY
or
INTELLIGENCE SUMMARY.

(Erase heading not required.)

Instructions regarding War Diaries and Intelligence Summaries are contained in F.S. Regs., Part II. and the Staff Manual respectively. Title pages will be prepared in manuscript.

Army Form C. 2118. SEct II February 1919

G.F.Wligh Lt Colonel
OC 2/1st HIGHLAND FIELD AMBULANCE

Place	Date	Hour	Summary of Events and Information	Remarks and references to Appendices
HOUDENG - GOEGNIES (BELGIUM)	1/28		**DANCES.** During the month of February, a Unit dance was arranged once every week. These functions were well attended by Officers + men, and Civilian friends invited by them and gave great pleasure to all participating.	GFW
			ENTERTAINMENT + SPORTS COMMITTEES A meeting of above Committees was held for the purpose of winding up affairs, and disposing of property acquired for the use of the Unit. It was agreed, to dispose of all property by private sale for best offers; proceeds to be handed over to Canteen fund.	GFW
			Hockey and Rugby took month has been put. Low order of receipts were received, bills had meaning of Early Testament Room	GFW

G.F.Wligh Lt Colonel
OC 2/1st HIGHLAND FIELD AMBULANCE

Mob 3551

2/12 Nogl. 9.0.

Nov. 1919

17 JUL 1919

Army Form C. 2118.

WAR DIARY
or
INTELLIGENCE SUMMARY.
(Erase heading not required.)

Mulvey Capt.
2/1st HIGHLAND FIELD AMBULANCE

MARCH 1919
Speet I

Place	Date	Hour	Summary of Events and Information	Remarks and references to Appendices
HOUDENG-GOEGNIES	1-3-19		Acting that Mulvey M.C. Commanding "E" Section, ceases to hold the Acting Rank from 15-2-19 - also of reorganization of Field Ambulance	App K
	9-3-19		Hon. Capt. R. Highton C.F. returned on granted Special Leave to U.K. from 9-3-19 to 23-3-19	App K
	16-3-19		Lt. Col. G.J. Whyte Rouse proceeded to take over command of the 90 C.C.S. during the absence of Lt. Col. White Kelly Raine, on leave	App K
	17-3-19		Maj. O.C. Camp Ramsd. took over Command of Unit	App K
	19-3-19		Lt. Col. W. Buxton Raine was granted Special Leave to U.K. from 19-3-19 to 2-4-19	
	21-3-19		A copy of the following was handed to each N.C.O. + man of the Unit in warning against venereal disease.	App K

"The opportunity now for venereal disease to work higher than is chased to N.C. Officers and to rankfile during the time we are in two been found that over 75% have NOT said as fairly treating Raine. Knowingly every man knows something of venereal disease, and are exposed your exposure have Given you Gentian or at endipris, Demoralization and retention to Camp proves strong, do not coax your Medical Lenies, as we carry no disease home. —

THEREFORE —

Permits to the visit to Ypres due to Yprostier and is given by moving the "Early" Question Russia. L. Col. commander after, you have been exposed to infection."

Army Form C. 2118.

WAR DIARY
or
INTELLIGENCE SUMMARY.
(Erase heading not required.)

MARCH 1919 Sheet 2

Au Rainey Capt.
2/1st HIGHLAND FIELD AMBULANCE
O/C.

Instructions regarding War Diaries and Intelligence Summaries are contained in F. S. Regs., Part II. and the Staff Manual respectively. Title pages will be prepared in manuscript.

Place	Date	Hour	Summary of Events and Information	Remarks and references to Appendices
HOUDENG-GOEGNIES	22-3-19		A famous zoure was given to civilian friends at Houdeng-Goegnies which was very much appreciated	JMcR
BELLECOURT	25-3-19		Unit moved to new area – BELLECOURT	JMcR
	23-3-19		Demobilization has been proceeding smoothly up till this date. By order of the Army Command it is now stopped, until further orders owing to strikes in England	JMcR
	24-3-19		That O.C. Army D.S.O. proceed to Advanced HQrs, London and to ascertain Off strengths. Capt Priestly M.C. took over command of unit this aft.	JMcR
	25-3-19		Demobilization has to be commenced this day. Per Capt A Highness Cf ord received from above. All ranks have now been disposed of.	JMcR
	27-3-19		Ration supplies during the month satisfactory. Health of unit has been very good during month.	JMcR

Au Rainey
Capt. R.A.M.C.
2/1st HIGHLAND FIELD AMBULANCE
O/C.

21st Nov. 40.

WAR DIARY
INTELLIGENCE SUMMARY

Army Form C. 2118

2/1st HIGHLAND FIELD AMBULANCE

APRIL 1919 Sheet 1

Place	Date	Hour	Summary of Events and Information	Remarks and references to Appendices
Bellecourt Belgium	1-4-19		Lt Col G L Hope, O/C 2/1 H.F.A. arrives to take over command and 2nd I/C on 31-3-19 and is struck off strength of this unit from that date. Capt. McKelvin takes over command of unit.	Dr McK
	2-4-19		Special orders of the War by Gen Sir H G Horne K.C.B, N.C.M.G received here & forwarded to the troops of the First Army - hailed with great enthusiasm.	Dr McK
	4-4-19		Orders received from A.D.M.S. for unit to be prepared to entrain on 6-4-19 en route for Sluis.	Dr McK
	6-4-19		No transport arrived to send from this unit.	D. McK
	7-4-19		Orders received for Unit to entrain as heavy as possible at 11pm. 13 Renne personnel & officers transferred to 1/2 H.F.A.	Dr McK
	8-4-19		Came arrival of moving units. A.C.C. M.T. transport to 510 M.T. Coy came complain.- Capt Stenhouse M.C. R.A.M.C to 1/2 H.F.A. Lt Young M.R.C transferred to 1/3 H.F.A. 15 R.A.M.C O.R.	Dr McK
	9-4-19		Camp arrived Dieppe/some seen never cause trouble to conveyed in a written manner.	Dr McK
	10-4-19		Capt (Rev) P. Higham C.F in doing of arrived here transport leaves came arrived here on board S/S Hourisa Sailed from Dunkirk for Southampton at 19.30 hrs.	D. McK

McK OC Capt 2/1st HIGHLAND FIELD AMBULANCE